Jesus in the
Hispanic Community

Jesus in the Hispanic Community

Images of Christ from Theology to Popular Religion

EDITORS

Harold J. Recinos

Hugo Magallanes

WESTMINSTER
JOHN KNOX PRESS
LOUISVILLE · KENTUCKY

© 2009 Westminster John Knox Press

First edition
Published by Westminster John Knox Press
Louisville, Kentucky

10 11 12 13 14 15 16 17 18 19—10 9 8 7 6 5 4 3 2 1

Scripture quotations from the New Revised Standard Version of the Bible are copyright © 1989 by the Division of Christian Education of the National Council of the Churches of Christ in the U.S.A. and are used by permission. Scripture quotations from the Revised Standard Version of the Bible are copyright © 1946, 1952, 1971, and 1973 by the Division of Christian Education of the National Council of the Churches of Christ in the U.S.A. and are used by permission.

Chapter 2, "The Galilean Jesus as Faithful Dissenter: Latino/a Christology and the Dynamics of Exclusion" by Michael E. Lee was originally published as "Galilean Journey Revisited: Mestizaje, Anti-Judaism, and the Dynamics of Exclusion" in *Theological Studies,* vol. 70, no. 2 (2009): 377–400. Used by permission. Excerpt from *Thinking of Christ: Proclamation, Explanation, Meaning,* edited by Tatha Wiley, copyright © 2003. Reprinted by kind permission of The Continuum International Publishing Group. The photographs in chapter 11, "Three Visual Images of Jesus the Christ from the Latino/a Community," were taken by Eduardo C. Fernández and used with the permission of Eduardo C. Fernández. The photographs in chapter 12, "La Capilla de Nuestro Señor de los Milagros," are used with the permission of the University of Texas Institute of Texan Cultures. The San Antonio Light Collection, UTSA's Institute of Texan Cultures, #L-2956-A; Courtesy of the Hearst Corporation. The San Antonio Light Collection, UTSA's Institute of Texan Cultures, #L-2956-B; Courtesy of the Hearst Corporation. UTSA's Institute of Texan Cultures, #103-0037. UTSA's Institute of Texan Cultures, #068-0533; Courtesy of the American Folklore Society, 1907. The poems "The Water," "The Kiss," and "Speak" are written by Harold J. Recinos and used with the permission of Harold J. Recinos. The lyrics to the hymn "El amor de Dios" by Rafael Cuna are copyright © 1955 Abingdon Press (Administered By The Copyright Company Nashville, TN). All Rights Reserved. International Copyright Secured. Used by Permission. The lyrics to the hymn "Al Abrigo del Altísimo" by Rafael Cuna are used with the permission of Chalice Press. The lyrics to the hymns "Acaríciame" and "Mi Testimonio" by Abigail Ortega are used with the permission of Abigail Ortega.

Book design by Sharon Adams
Cover design by Night & Day Design
Cover art: Mural in Highland Park, Los Angeles, California,
Photographer: © Steve Crise/Corbis Corporation

Library of Congress Cataloging-in-Publication Data

Jesus in the Hispanic community : images of Christ from theology to popular religion / editors, Harold J. Recinos, Hugo Magallanes.
    p. cm.
    Proceedings of a conference held in Oct. 2008 at Southern Methodist University.
    Includes bibliographical references (p.   ) and index.
    ISBN 978-0-664-23428-7 (alk. paper)
    1. Jesus Christ—Hispanic American interpretations—Congresses.   I. Recinos, Harold J. (Harold Joseph), 1955–   II. Magallanes, Hugo.
    BT304.918.J47 2010
    232.089'68073—dc22

                                                                                      2009028355

PRINTED IN THE UNITED STATES OF AMERICA

∞ The paper used in this publication meets the minimum requirements
of the American National Standard for Information Sciences—Permanence
of Paper for Printed Library Materials, ANSI Z39.48-1992.

Westminster John Knox Press advocates the responsible use of our natural resources.
The text paper of this book is made from 30% post-consumer waste.

Contents

Acknowledgments

This book was made possible by support from Perkins School of Theology's Center for the Study of Latino/a Christianity and Religions, and funds provided by the Henry Luce Foundation. There are also many people to thank along the way. First, thank you to David Maldonado Jr., William Lawrence, and the board of the Center for the Study of Latino/a Christianity and Religions at Southern Methodist University's Perkins School of Theology for supporting this project. Second, thank you to Cristina Uranga, who helped coordinate logistical matters for the authors symposium that took place on the SMU campus in October 2008. Third, a very special word of thanks to Carolyn Douglas, who coordinated meeting space, copied and distributed early drafts of the work for review at the symposium, and patiently supported every stage of the project.

The Water
Harold J. Recinos

when the city was
new to us faces

smiled on all the
corners, fire

hydrants in summer
opened, kids made

holes at each end of
thrown away cans to

spray water, skinny old
men jumped puddles, bag

carrying abuelas laughed
in colorful mists, wet

children ran to the
bodegas with nickels

enough for five cookies,
music loudly played, the

Sabado domino games never
ended, girls jumped rope

to church bells keeping
time, nights were never

wounded by fear, and we
believed there were no

strangers.

Introduction

HAROLD J. RECINOS

Latinos/as are the nation's largest community of color, and in about two decades the United States will be the second-largest Spanish-speaking nation in the world. Latino/a history in North America dates back before the founding of what is now called the United States of America, yet we are most typically viewed by both African American and white Americans as the troublesome outsiders who take jobs away from them, Latin America's social problems on U.S. soil, or simply aliens unwilling to adapt to U.S. society.[1] In fact, Latinos/as prefer to be seen in terms of their religious, racial, ethnic, political, economic, social, linguistic, and cultural diversity.[2] Latinos/as who are new arrivals, aliens on their own land, and poorly understood are changing and will continue to change the American church and wider society.

Latinos/as are made up of many different groups in the United States. Their national and cultural heritage is Mexican, Honduran, Salvadoran, Guatemalan, Puerto Rican, Cuban, Chilean, Argentinian, Dominican, Colombian, Venezuelan, Ecuadorian, Bolivian, Peruvian, Panamanian, Costa Rican, Nicaraguan, among others. The full color spectrum of humanity is among them, while they represent various ethnic backgrounds and personally decided racial preferences. Latino/a religious affiliation is more complex than the stereotypical thinking that describes them as essentially Roman Catholic. Latinos/as are Catholic, Protestant, Jewish, Muslim, Buddhist, Santeros, and Curanderos, but agnostic and atheist, too. For the most part, the Latinos/as who arrive in the United States from twenty-two different countries do self-identify as Christian, however.[3]

Black and white citizens have noted the growth of the Latino/a population fueled by new immigration and high birth rates. Many believe the country is being invaded by Spanish-speaking migrants who increase the ranks of the poor and threaten the linguistic and cultural unity of the nation. The fear projected on the new generation of Latin American immigrants and the dismissive ways of talking about them justifies relational systems of exclusion, ethnic hate, social hostility, and tragic immigration policies. Meanwhile, the long-standing Latino/a presence in the United States whose roots can be traced back five hundred years is a reminder that not all Latinos/as are newcomers. Nevertheless, for subdivisions of American society Latinos/as continue to be treated as permanent outsiders despite the ability of some Latinos/as to trace their family line back many generations on North American soil.

For the most part, Latino/a newcomers are not viewed as immigrants who exemplify prized American virtues of family and hard work; instead, they are called illegal aliens, criminals, and a social burden driving up crime and public expenditures. Latino/a immigrant identity is constructed by what anthropologist Leo Chavez calls a Latino Threat discourse, which is a formation of ideas, images, and practices that produces "knowledge of, ways of talking about, and forms of conduct associated with a particular topic, social activities, or institutional site in society."[4] The anti-Latino/a speech pervading popular culture, mainstream intellectual production, and political speech making has been termed by Chavez as "the Latino threat narrative," which he explains as follows:

> Latinos are unable or unwilling to integrate into the social and cultural life of the United States . . . They do not learn English. . . . They seal themselves off from the larger society, reproducing cultural beliefs and behaviors antithetical to a modern life, such as pathologically high fertility rates that reduce the demographic presence of white Americans. [Latinos] are . . . an unchanging people, standing outside the currents of history, merely waiting for the opportunity to revolt and to reconquer land that was once theirs. They live to destroy social institutions such as medical·care and education. They dilute the privileges and rights of citizenship for legitimate members of society.[5]

The Latino threat narrative is not only divisive but it helps slow the process of recognizing Latino/a social, religious, and cultural contributions to American society. In response to the Latinophobia overtaking the country, Latino/a immigrants and citizens marched on April 10, 2006, in cities all around the country in defense of immigrants' rights. Chanting African American civil rights songs in the company of their allies, Latinos/as took their struggle for equality and inclusion to the streets in over one hundred cities. I remember that the sanctuary movement of the 1980s was conceived by religious communities to protect undocumented Latino/a newcomers from the abuses of power and a growing anti-immigrant movement in the United States; however, the current immigrants' rights movement looks a lot like the African American civil rights movement of the 1950s and 1960s, especially when it crosses cultural and ethnic lines and invites all members of society to reformulate their ethic of belonging. Latinos/as and their citizen allies have claimed their legitimate voice to enter the public realm to work for the social good.

Religion plays a role in the project of Latino/a self-identity and inclusion in American society; thus, the way Latinos/as construct their theological identity and negotiate power in light of their understanding of the life and ministry of Jesus requires serious consideration. Not only is the supposed difference of Latino/a immigrants not a threat to U.S. society, but the fresh theological insight that is issuing forth from their diverse communities offers to renew the theological thinking of mainstream culture and its mainline churches. Latino/a newcomers and those rejected generations that have always called America home offer American Christians an opportunity to discover the presence of the crucified Christ who came to break down the walls of dividing hostility in order to create a new humanity (Eph. 2:14–16). The emergent varieties of Latino/a Christology examined in this work will be regenerative for the church, while representing those considered permanent suspects and outsiders in U.S. society.

We approach the study of U.S. Latino/a Christology concerned to claim our place in the discussion of the meaning of ethnically conscious Christology and its contribution to the formation of North American theological identity. The writing of U.S. Latino/a theologians has only recently won attention in the U.S. theological academy, but the rich and creative expression of U.S. Latino/a Christology that has existed alongside other contextual theologies of racial, ethnic, class, and gender construction has been largely unacknowledged. The best antidote to exclusionary readings of North American Christology is to have a cast of Latino/a theologians engage in foundational and innovative christological reflection that extends the interpretive range of North American Christology by delving into the experiences, insights, identities, and agency of Latinos/as in the United States.

We live and work in a multiracial America, but the christological reading of racial inequality, power, and national identity mirrors the concerns of mostly black and white humanity. For example, in "Theology's Great Sin: Silence in the Face of White Supremacy," James Cone—who writes extensively on racism in American theology—notes that white male theologians have not engaged the ideology of white supremacy as a "moral evil and as a radical contradiction of our humanity and religious identities."[6] Cone explains that white male theologians have engaged Latin American theologies on class issues, feminist theology on gender issues, and the Jewish intellectuals on the question of Christian anti-Semitism, but they have failed to tackle white supremacy as America's central theological problem. Cone is correct that the antiracist struggle is a necessary calling for religious communities, but his vision for that struggle cannot today be limited to black and white concerns.

African American and white theologians must admit in their writing and lectures that America was not shaped by black and white humanity alone; instead, various communities of color contributed to the formation of national identity and nourished the political struggle that made democratic and religious institutions possible. American national and religious life was conceived in the contradiction between the idea of equal and inalienable rights for all people, while Native Americans were being exterminated, blacks enslaved, Latinos/as disinherited on their homelands, and Asians exploited and killed. Cone suggests that white theologians' feelings of guilt prevent them from talking about white supremacy, but why do most established black and white public theologians ignore and avoid engaging Latinos/as on the subject of white supremacy, the antiracist struggle, social change, and matters concerning how to understand Jesus?

The growth of the Latino/a population by way of documented and undocumented immigration and high birth rates requires thinking about interethnic conflicts among different peoples of color, racism, xenophobia, and anti-immigrant attitudes from the citizenry. Religious leaders should challenge the hostile treatment given to new Latino/a immigrants due to their complexion, limited English-speaking abilities, or cultural traditions. Moreover, black and white theologians who see the struggle against racism in biracial terms must discontinue to marginalize as permanent foreigners the U.S. Latino/a community. These theologians need to open themselves up to the challenges presented by the growing Latino/a community, engage in new thinking about society, and unfold the dialogue that leads to a deeper reflection on the meaning of religion in our multiethnic social context of unequal power.

As active agents in U.S. society and religious communities, the work of Latino/a theologians needs to be deliberately examined by both white and black theologians who position themselves at the privileged center of the theological community. In the early 1970s, when the first publications in U.S. Latino/a theology appeared, Latino/a theologians developed their perspectives from marginalized social contexts in order to understand God from within the Latino/a experience of social invisibility, cultural marginality, economic inequality, discrimination,[7] and everyday struggles for a better life. Latino/a theology's articulation of religious experience included naming one's culture and context in light of the concern to empower rejected people with a prophetic agenda for addressing the racism, sexism, and classism embedded in dominant theologies and society.[8]

While intellectuals in the theological academy and leaders of mainstream religious denominations were overlooking barrios and colonias, U.S. Latino/a theologians looked to them to discuss in their work the various and creative ways that novel approaches to God-talk were produced in local communities. Latino/a theologians' work also offered ethnographically detailed stories of various Latino/a groups that helped to expand how Americans talk of life together in society. In the twenty-first century, black and white theologians may no longer ignore how Latino/a theological scholarship is a vital terrain of study that provides ways to refocus the theological thinking that informs practical efforts for overcoming the failures of society and sharpened approaches to expand the understanding of the varieties of religious experience in the United States.

Latino/a theology has been steadily building a distinctive contextual liberation theology in the United States that encompasses the varieties of religious experiences found within Latino/a communities. The early stages of Latino/a theological production were more closely tied to grassroots communities and practical pastoral concerns, while more recent work is more intentionally seeking to find a voice in the academy and in public theology.[9] Our aim in this study is to offer contemporary essays that give evidence to the promise of a culturally contextualized U.S. Latino/a Christology. Those communities that have been treated as irrelevant by progressive theologians in the United States offer fresh answers to the following questions: Who is Jesus? How does Jesus address the concerns of humanity? How is Jesus relevant to the suffering of the oppressed? Does Jesus know the struggle of abused Latinas? What does the ministry of Jesus tell us about multiethnic relationships?

RETHINKING CHRISTOLOGY

From the creedal formulations of Nicaea (325 CE) and Chalcedon (451 CE) through today's barrios and colonias in the United States, Christians attempt to express a definitive word regarding the person and purpose of the Christ event. In this endeavor, Latino/a Christology has been faulted for not deepening its dialogue with New Testament scholarship, mostly avoiding the classical christological themes that have historically shaped Christian discourse, and neglecting christological reflection from the perspective of women.[10] Even so, Latino/a Christians have confessed Christ in terms of their freedom and commitment to understand the biblical witness and their longing for personal and social transformation in specific contexts of the suffering of the oppressed. Perhaps the people of the barrios and colonias are correct to question creedal formulas that "jump from affirmation of an ahistorical birth to falsification of a real death."[11]

In earlier years, Latinos/as mostly centered attention on the image of a suffering Christ, underscoring his identification with people in need of comfort (Matt. 11:28–30). But the image of a suffering Christ amounted to an inwardly focused Christology of suffering, which dismissed the idea that the existential plight of abused and oppressed Latinos/as could be overcome. This variety of U.S. Latino/a Christology offered Latinos/as an ahistorical image of Jesus not supported by the gospel's challenge to social institutions, structures, and relations at the root of their experience of social injustice and the oppressed's suffering. Another contextual christological formulation that had wide currency was to view Jesus as the glorified Christ who conquers sin in the world (John 17:4–5). This image of a glorified Christ promised a better life in heaven by the experience of personal salvation, which meant not taking up God's project of social, economic, political, and institutional redemption.

Although the Christology of suffering and glorification provided a strong point of identification for Latinos/as living at the edges of society, more and more Latinos/as now admit that following Christ requires individuals to develop a more critical understanding of the structures of sin in determining their conditions of marginality and daily unjust suffering. They have become more aware that the Gospel narratives speak of a Jesus who sees injustice in the world, teaches followers to risk transforming it, and discloses the God who promises deliverance by standing with the oppressed against the unjust systems of the powerful. Today, Latinos/as acknowledge that Jesus lived and identified with the marginalized, and his suffering and exaltation cast a light on God's plan to end crucifixion as a model for society.

Latino/a Christology now holds that the brutally tortured and murdered Jesus cannot be understood by ahistorical readings of suffering and escapist theologies of personal salvation won by the ransom paid by a glorified Christ. Traditional Latino/a Christology played an ideological role in the social control and exploitation of people with limited resources; however, the new contextual interpretations emerging in the barrio and from postcolonial migrants are destabilizing the older system of understanding. Latino/a contextual Christology speaks with greater urgency now of the importance of rethinking Christ from the standpoint of Latino/a histories of marginality, economic exploitation, political disempowerment, and existential subjugation. Those who never surrendered their memories of struggle, voice, and place are more insistently articulating christological reflections that make sense of self-identity, society, and the church, especially in light of God's liberating concerns for the marginalized and society's outsiders.

The reformulation of Christology in the U.S. Latino/a community not only reflects the concern to think independently of mainstream Christology, but it questions earlier escapist and subjectivist images of Jesus. The newer image of the carpenter from Nazareth determined by subdivisions of the U.S. Latino/a community sees Jesus standing with the poor, denouncing the accumulation of wealth, rejecting social systems that abuse strangers, and demanding that discipleship start in the world of crucified people. Because christological thinking is evolving in U.S. Latino/a communities by taking seriously the world of those not counted, a clearer image of Jesus as the One who confronts the problems of everyday life and the social forces dealing injustices to the poor is emerging with the specificity of the North American Latino/a reality. Today, Latino/a Christology issues forth from the concrete lives of communities which know that God's love and justice become flesh in the Son who experienced the world as a rejected and marginalized human being.

Interestingly, only a couple of books deal substantially with Christology from a Latin American perspective: Jose Miguez Bonino, ed., *Face of Jesus: Latin American Christologies* (Maryknoll, N.Y.: Orbis Books, 1984), and Jon Sobrino, *Jesus in Latin America* (Maryknoll, N.Y.: Orbis Books, 1987). Although they are valuable for an understanding of Christology in Latin America, these volumes offer limited insight for understanding Christology in the U.S. Hispanic context. We propose to document for the first time in a single volume Latino/a Christologies and show how Christology is rethought and experienced in the specific world of U.S. Latino/a communities.

OVERVIEW OF BOOK

The Jesus of the forgotten people is the center of U.S. Latino/a rethinking of Christology. The crucified Christ accompanies Latinos/as in their daily struggle for a better life. In this collection, Latino/a theologians seek to interpret the meaning of the Galilean Jew who was a victim of organized religion and oppressive political power. Their work reflects from the standpoint of the lived experience of Latino/a men, women, and children on the Jew from Galilee who affirmed the reality of the reign of God facing suffering and death on the cross. The U.S. Latino/a theologians contributing to this collection seek to understand the meaning and purpose of Christ revealed to, and through, the poor, powerless, and unlettered people of Latino/a contexts who need liberation from suffering, economic systems of exploitation, political marginalization, and gender subjugation. Perhaps you will discover in these essays how the God of Jesus continues to look upon and hear the cry of suffering and exploited people, delivering to them the promises of a new life.

Within the larger scope of Latin American Christology, we focus on the emerging Christology of the U.S. Latino/a communities. This approach permits the collection of scholars in this work to produce various contextually grounded essays that capture the richness of thinking about Jesus in the U.S. Latino/a context. We do not try to provide an exhaustive view of the reformulation of Christology in light of the U.S. Latino/a agenda; rather, we have selected from among the most active scholars of the U.S. Latino/a community to write on this topic and to show the complex interplay between Christ and culture. These essays expand the knowledge base for thinking about Jesus in the North American context, especially suggesting the need to reflect on the formation of North American theological identity by way of ethnic diversity.

The first part of the book explores from a variety of perspectives constructive theological reflection on U.S. Latino/a Christology, whereas part 2 consists of three exemplary essays on U.S. Latino/a popular religious representations of Jesus. In chapter 1, Virgilio Elizondo explains that foundational for Christology is the ongoing conversation between the human experience of the Latino/a community and the experience of liberated existence witnessed in the New Testament and Christian tradition. He reflects on the meaning of Jesus from the existential situation of Mexican American marginality, demonstrating how God is ultimately self-disclosed through persons living in rejected contexts. Elizondo engages in a cultural rereading of Jesus' Galilean identity in first-century Palestine and connects it with Latino/a *mestizo* identity. The human experience of biological-cultural admixture (*mestizaje*) is treated in the essay as a fundamental theological category for thinking about the person, presence, and purpose of Jesus. Elizondo's work suggests that theological discourses need to seriously consider questions of cultural self-identity, power, marginalization, rejection, and the meaning of the plural character of social reality.

In chapter 2, Michael Lee provides a detailed reflection on Virgilio Elizondo's important work *Galilean Journey: The Mexican-American Promise*. Although Elizondo is considered the "father of Hispanic American theology," Lee notes that his landmark work has been criticized by some for reflecting anti-Jewish rhetoric in its portrayal of Galilee, and Jesus' conflict with Jewish authorities in Jerusalem; anti-intellectual romanticism and unexamined anti-Judaism stemming from a naïve use of source material; and anachronism relative to reading back into first-century Galilee a contemporary cultural theory of *mestizaje*.

Lee appreciates that critics raise significant questions about *Galilean Journey* and theologians' use of biblical-historical scholarship for purposes of interpreting sacred texts. By examining more recent historical research on Galilee, Lee responds to Elizondo's critics and argues that more recent historical research on Jesus and Galilee provides a corrective lens to aspects of Elizondo's theological message; moreover, the more recent work that shifts the interpretive focus from the *historical* Jesus to the *historic* Jesus—the person remembered in the scriptural narrative by followers—offers a better standard for judging Elizondo's work, given that it seeks not so much to describe a historical Jesus than the theological value of the Gospels' description of him for marginal U.S. Latino/a readers. Lee responds to the criticism that *Galilean Journey* romantically portrays first-century Galilee and evidences an anti-intellectual viewpoint.[12]

Lee agrees that *Galilean Journey*'s rural romanticism, which includes sweeping generalizations that contrast Galilean faith with negative readings of Jerusalemite religious rulers, requires correction, especially given the history of anti-Semitic scholarship. Lee disagrees with the charge that *Galilean Journey* is an anti-intellectual work that places Jesus outside the circle of Judaism. Lee finally addresses the criticism that Elizondo superimposes *mestizaje* on Galilee, arguing that the critics fail to appreciate that Elizondo does not superimpose a contempory cultural theory on Galilee; rather he rereads the gospel from the perspective of the Mexican American experience of *mestizaje* to offer insight on issues of power, marginality, and exclusion. The genius of Lee's essay is found in a rigorous analysis of scholarship and the suggestion that not only does recent biblical scholarship offer helpful corrections for Elizondo's work, but the insights of *Galilean Journey* help the theological community more deeply understand religious legitimations of the logic of exclusion.

In chapter 3, Ada María Isasi-Díaz develops a constructive Christology from a *mujerista* theological perspective by centering attention on Latinas' insistence that what is believed about Christ must follow from the ethical understanding of struggle and liberation initiated by U.S. Latinas–enacted Christology. This chapter grounds Christology in the religious beliefs of Latinas and looks at a Christ who has a deep personal relationship with women, a Christ who helps women care for the most vulnerable in Latino/a communities, and a Christ who is an older brother in the kin-dom of God, *la familia de Dios*. Isasi-Díaz is not so concerned to provide a theological elaboration on christological dogmas; rather her *mujerista* Christology centers attention on the meaning of Jesus for Latinas who experience marginality and yearn for a liberated existence. *Mujerista* Christology seeks to empower critical reflection on oppressive structures and internalized ideologies, while helping Latinas and communities understand the practical commitment needed to act in ways that contribute to a more just and humanized life.

Mujerista Christology does not pretend to be able to reconstruct the historical Jesus nor define itself by way of past christological formulas that are historical and culturally laden with understandings specific to their formulation; instead, *mujerista* Christology responds to what Latinas believe about the message of Jesus, while rooting belief in the Latino/a hunger for sustaining relationships in ongoing life struggles, the need to discover God as a companion in community care, and the experience of being a part of God's family. In other words, in *mujerista* Christology the Christ figure is understood and believed by way of Latinas' social location of race, class, and gender. Although in an earlier work coauthored with Yolanda Tarango, Isasi-Díaz did not consider christological reflection an important concern for theological reflection on the experience and beliefs of Latinas,[13] Isasi-Díaz's essay in this collection reflects a clear change of mind.

Chapter 4, written by Miguel De La Torre, begins by briefly reflecting on the way Euro-American Christology has been used to justify the practices that have contributed to Latino/a marginalization, especially by way of wars of territorial expansion and the politics of empire building. The white Christ of Euro-American history, De La Torre explains, legitimated the beliefs and practices that justified colonialism, slavery, racism, and oppression. The white Christ who protects the dominant system from Latino/a inferiority must be deconstructed to create the Latino/a space needed to recognize a Christ who is ontologically Hispanic. In other words, the Latino/a Christ will not be informed by nor legitimate white power and privilege in society; rather, this Christ who points to the God who takes the side of the lowly against their oppressors is informed by the historical experiences of those who suffer.

De La Torre explains a Hispanic Christ who incarnates the gospel message in the disempowered spaces of the barrio, where people struggle to survive and hope for liberation. He argues that in the Latino/a context, one understands Christ within the sociohistorical and ecopolitical realities of Hispanic life and their responses to the biblical message of liberation. The essay particularly reflects on how Christ has been historically constructed within Cuban culture, beginning with a discussion of Christ in the colonial and neocolonial enterprise. After discussing how a conquest-and-Protestant-imperial Christ contributed to death, exploitation, and the suffering of the oppressed in Cuban society, De La Torre reviews five cultural building blocks drawn from Cuban society for the construction of a Cuban-centric liberative Christ, named the ajiaco Christ (an ethnotheological symbol representing the diverse ethnic groups that came together in the formation of the Cuban community).

In chapter 5, Loida Martell-Otero uses a contextual methodology to give expression to Christology from a Puerto Rican *evangélica* perspective that draws insight from the religious experiences of women. Informed by the work of missiologist Orlando Costas and theologian Virgilio Elizondo, Martell-Otero draws on a scriptural foundation to develop Christology from a Puerto Rican perspective that builds on a culture-specific term of marginality identified, *sato* (mutt/ mongrel). In Puerto Rican society, *sato* was first applied to mixed-breed dogs; hence, the term connotes mongrelization or a mutt identity. In time, the vernacular speech of island society related the term to persons of questionable character, or persons deserving rejection. In other words, *satos/as* are the rejected, the nonpersons, the impure, or the worthless dregs of society. When Martell-Otero speaks of a Sato Jesus, she describes how the word becomes flesh in the concrete history of marginality, rejection, abandonment, and shameful pedigree. In short, the Sato Jesus embodies the voiceless and rejected of society, while calling *satos/ as* to be the good news that overturns the unjust structures of the world.

In chapter 6, Arlene Sánchez-Walsh offers the reader a reflection on Latino/a Christology from a pentecostal perspective. First, Christology in the pentecostal experience manifests itself in many different varieties, such as Jesus the Baptizer in the Holy Spirit, Jesus the Healer (Liberator), or Jesus the King (Political Jesus). Typically, Pentecostals first encounter a doctrinal Jesus who communicates to the believer the way, the truth, and the life in a thoroughly evangelical way—personal confession of Christ as Lord and Savior. From the power of narrative in the pentecostal experience, another conventional image is that of Jesus the Healer/ Liberator typified by the view that Jesus heals believers from ill health, and the understanding of liberation in a way unrelated to systemic ills or sociopolitical transformation. Pentecostal Christian identity is also shaped by the Christology of Jesus the King (Political Jesus), which issues forth in a last-days theology for Latino/a Pentecostals that mitigates against an overpolitical agenda. Sánchez-Walsh carefully examines these christological views, noting that for Latino/a Pentecostals, influenced by a cultural context, Jesus is a pliable figure—fully human and divine—who "baptizes, heals, saves, and is coming again."

In chapter 7, Hugo Magallanes develops his constructive Hispanic Christology by seeking to understand the identity of Jesus from a point of departure of the experience of marginality known by Latinos/as in the United States and the exclusionary practices and discourses of the dominant American culture. Magallanes's essay reflects on the question Jesus poses in the Synoptic Gospels, "Who do you say that I am?" (see Mark 8:27–30; Matt. 16:13–20; Luke 9:18– 21). He argues that not only can the question not be answered self-servingly, but the identity of Jesus positions theological understanding in the subversive context of the gospel that challenges rules of exclusion, privilege, and domination. Magallanes suggests that, in the Latino/a context, Jesus is found not by associating him with the powerful whose exceptionalist ideologies and cruel practices toward those on the underside of history discredit God, but by way of conversion to the perspectives on Jesus' identity issuing forth at the margins of society.

In chapter 8, Zaida Maldonado Pérez's essay existentially explores the question of Christology by engaging aspects of Scripture and church tradition in relation to Latino/a experience in the United States. Pérez engages in a sustained discussion of the meaning of honorific titles in society and remarks on Latino/a evangelicals' understanding of some of the titles applied in Scripture to Jesus, while underscoring the subversive Christ. Pérez explains that her essay offers general existential musings concerning the person and work of Christ from a U.S. Latina evangelical/pentecostal perspective. In her writing, she meditates on pieces of art portraying Jesus on the cross that give rise to a Christology of a broken Christ, a fork Christ, the prophet, *mestizo*, and mulatto Christ. Pérez's Christology from below and mulatto Jesus suggest that God enters history to do justice and affirm difference as divinely ordained.

Chapter 9, written by Luis Rivera, explores how the experience of Latin American migration and becoming immigrants in the United States, along with the struggles for the rights of immigrants, creates the conditions for a retrieval and reinterpretation of the biblical motif of the migrant Jesus (e.g., Matt. 2:19–23; John 1:14). At a time when media metaphors depict Latino/a immigration as an invasion and U.S.-born Latinos/as as foreigners, this chapter's examination of the theological and ethical implications of a migrant Christology will help the church define its starting place in the immigration debate. Rivera observes that in the spirituality of Latino/a Christians and in some of the reflection of pastoral and professional theologians, Jesus is seen as a migrant savior. Rivera's essay systematically develops the idea of a migrant Christ drawing out the humanitarian, social, ethical, and political implications of this Christology for the Latino/a communities in struggle and the wider Christian community.

Carlos Cardoza-Orlandi, in chapter 10, explores the Latino/a world of body and soul by reflecting on grassroots Caribbean, Latin American, and Latino/a Protestant hymnody and *coritos* (short Christian songs). The musical traditions that Latino/a Christian communities enact in their gathering make Jesus a tangible companion in daily life struggles and communicate spirituality in often erotic ways. In the Latino/a religious experience, music is an important spiritual resource that reinforces the particularity of Christian identity, promotes group solidarity, and creates avenues for theological expressions unlike those specific to the traditional orthodoxies of dominant organized religious life. As a form of communicative action, Cardoza-Orlandi suggests that some Latino/a hymns and *coritos* especially overcome the body-and-soul divide, especially the spiritual songs that center attention on the erotic Jesus—songs that use body language to communicate a spiritual focus.

As religious identity formation, Cardoza-Orlandi argues that the *eros* or unifying force of Jesus expressed in Latino/a song is a way to portray Jesus Christ as one who embodies love in the form of closeness, intimacy, and caress. The aural nature of Christology examined by Cardoza-Orlandi suggests that complex and

innovative theological ideas can be communicated in ways other than the spo-
ken word. One of the implications of Cardoza-Orlandi's essay is that Latino/a
hymns and *coritos* are a powerful way to experience liberation from the artificial
split between the religion of the mind and the spirituality of the heart. In the
richness of this variety of Latino/a constructive Christology, the saving power of
Christ "is translated into a loving and palpitating heart, tender and embracing
hands, and seductive intoxicating aroma."

In the Latino/a community, popular religious discourse and ritual practices
convey cultural meaning in sites within and outside the framework of institutionalized religion. Popular religion is how Latino/a laypersons communicate
ideas and engage in practices that provide meaning for their daily lives. In chapter 11, Eduardo Fernández, S.J., asks readers to think about aspects of Latino/a
popular religious practices in the United States and the meaning of symbolic
material culture and ritual in communicating messages about Jesus. Digging
into the popular religious images found in the Santuario de Chimayo, located
outside of Santa Fe, New Mexico, Fernández discusses the meaning of three
popular symbolic representations of Jesus: (1) *El Niño Dios* or *El Santo Niño*,
(2) various representations of the crucifix, and (3) *El Sagrado Corazón de Jesús*
(images of the Sacred Heart of Jesus). Fernández concludes that visual images
of Christ articulate religious truth in nonverbal ways, suggesting that the divine
cannot be limited to words; religion is a matter of the heart, as well as a way to
contemplate the vulnerability, brokenness, and character of divine love.

In chapter 12, Timothy Matovina asks readers to consider yet another important site of Latino/a popular religiosity, located in San Antonio's Capilla de
Nuestro Señor de los Milagros (Chapel of Our Lord of Miracles). He argues that
theological reflection on this private chapel renowned among devotees on both
sides of the U.S.-Mexican border sheds light on the understanding of Christ in
Mexican and Mexican American piety, especially in relation to how these cultural actors focus by way of the visual representations in the chapel on Jesus'
most vulnerable moments, childhood, and crucifixion. The rich ethnographic
details of the essay help readers understand how christological insights and ideas
do issue forth from the practices and experience of Latino/a pious traditions.
Although the images at La Capilla de los Milagros do not explicitly image Jesus'
Galilean ministry, his struggle to transform oppressive realities, or conflict with
religious authorities, Matovina nonetheless insists on the importance of reflecting
theologically on the sacred symbols and pious practices of Latino/a communities.

SUMMARY

This work on Latino/a Christology is not to be viewed as a comprehensive
account of the various ways of thinking about Jesus that can be found in the
different ethnic communities constitutive of North American "Hispanic" reality. We prefer that it be read as challenging assumptions about what constitutes

normal, legitimate, and authentic Christology in the context of North American Christianity. We both reflect on the meaning of Jesus from a Latino/a perspective and demonstrate the richness and insight that come from the Latino/a cultural production of Christology. Some mainstream Christians think Latino/a Christology is of value only for the Latino/a community; however, we argue that the study of Latino/a Christology enables U.S. Christians to more accurately understand the different dimensions of their Christian reality.

The person and message of Jesus for our changing twenty-first-century society challenges us to learn how to live with human diversity and understand God's call for reconciled community. Mainstream theologians who remain ignorant of, or who ignore or suppress in their work, the issues and interpretations of Jesus voiced by Latinos/as will persist in imposing culturally hegemonic views like the typical biracial normative gaze that interprets social relations and memory in U.S. society in terms only of black and white, but which is inconsistent with the plural character of life in the United States. We hope that culturally established theologians, church leaders, and students of religion turn their heads in the direction of the Latino/a margin and take the opportunity to define themselves for a moment through the identity of the Latino/a other.

We ask you to consider that thinking about Christology in the academy and church today requires imagining ethnic, racial, and cultural border crossings to entertain the possibility of encountering in various and different ways the God of all nations. This collection offers readers the possibility of deepening normative christological thought, and maturing what is meant by self-identity in our multicultural, multiethnic, and multireligious society. We hope these essays encourage some readers to cross the borders of their imagined community to take a step toward shaping a multicultural, multiethnic, and multiracial reading of Christology. We also hope that various readers find in them contributions for determining a framework for constructing a vision of Jesus that connects Christians to the larger vision of life offered to them by a peacemaking, community-gathering, and life-giving God.

NOTES

1. See especially Samuel Huntington, *Who Are We? The Challenges to America's National Identity* (New York: Simon and Schuster, 2004). In part, Huntington argues that increased Hispanic immigration and growth threaten to divide the nation between two cultural and linguistic groups, hence undermining the Anglo-Protestant culture at the core of American national identity; the American dream for him only happens in English. Huntington is not only wrong about what threatens American life, but he grossly misrepresents the Latino/a contribution to American democratic traditions and national identity. Anglo-Protestant revivalism is not the path to make America strong, but settling for nothing better than our diversity. I also recommend Peter Brimelow, *Alien Nation: Common Sense about America's Immigrant Disaster* (New York: HarperPerennial, 1996), whose writing reflects racist nationalist sentiment

that also targets "surging Hispanic immigration," which Brimelow believes must be stopped in defense of the European common stock of America.

2. See Jorge J. E. Gracia and Pablo de Greif, eds., *Hispanics/Latino in the United States: Ethnicity, Race, and Rights* (New York: Routledge, 2000), 1.

3. For an excellent study on Latino/a demographics and social reality, see Havidán Rodríguez, Rogelio Saénz, and Cecilia Menivar, eds., *Latinos/as in the United States: Changing the Face of America* (New York: Springer, 2008).

4. Leo Chavez, *The Latino Threat Narrative: Constructing Immigrants, Citizen, and the Nation* (Stanford, CA: Stanford University Press, 2008), 22.

5. Ibid., 177.

6. James Cone, "Theology's Great Sin: Silence in the Face of White Supremacy," *Black Theology: An International Journal* 2, no. 2 (2004): 143.

7. Latinos/as have experienced moments of solidarity with African American political and religious leaders, but there is a documented history of discrimination experienced by Latinos/as attributable to both blacks and whites in the context of U.S. society. See especially Nicolas Vaca, *The Presumed Alliance: The Unspoken Conflict between Latinos and Blacks and What It Means for America* (New York: HarperCollins, 2004).

8. See especially Miguel De La Torre and Edwin Aponte, *Introducing Latino/a Theologies* (Maryknoll, NY: Orbis Books, 2001).

9. See the promising work of Benjamin Valentin, *Mapping Public Theology: Beyond Culture, Identity and Difference* (Harrisburg, PA: Trinity Press, 2002). Valentin argues that Latino/a theologies' sociological and cultural focus, especially on identity and difference, constrain the development of a broader liberative political project and concerns for the meaning of the common good in the national society.

10. Michelle A. Gonzalez, "Jesus," in *Handbook of Latino/a Theologies*, ed. Edwin Aponte and Miguel De La Torre (St. Louis: Chalice Press, 2006), 22–23.

11. Jack Nelson-Pallmeyer, *Jesus against Christianity: Reclaiming the Missing Jesus.* (Harrisburg, PA: Trinity Press International, 2001), 151.

12. See especially Jean-Pierre Ruiz, "Good Fences and Good Neighbors? Biblical Scholars and Theologians," *Journal of Hispanic Latino Theology* (May 2007).

13. In *Hispanic Women: Prophetic Voice in the Church* (San Francisco: Harper and Row, 1988), Isasi-Díaz and Tarango make the statement that Latinas' belief system does not give interpretive priority to Jesus; also see Gonzalez, "Jesus," 23.

PART 1
CONSTRUCTIVE THEOLOGY

The Kiss
Harold J. Recinos

In the morning
while walking toward
the corner I saw Lela

returning from church
checking her watch as
the wind pushed doves

overhead. she heard talk
of ashes, dust, and love
at work in the sadness

of this violent age; the
Lord in the world of the
humiliated who fight for daily

bread. you could still see
the truth in her eyes looking
now at those once abandoned

for dead. these forgotten ones
smiled when Lela passed by
each Sunday telling them never

leave everything to God.
I remember the darkness tumbled
in the light of her world and

settled in our hearts.

Chapter 1

Elements for a Mexican American *Mestizo* Christology

VIRGILIO ELIZONDO

The Mexican American Christian, like every Christian, has the privilege and the obligation of searching for the answer to the important question that Jesus continues to ask each one of us: "Who do you say that I am?" Out of the attempts to answer this question, Christology emerges. In the past, we have certainly learned who others say that Jesus is for them, but today we are seeking to formulate our own response. The responses of others are great and enlightening, but they are not yet our own response. Christianity will never become liberating and salvific until we succeed in answering the question ourselves. As long as we simply accept someone else's answer, we will be dominated by them and fail to mature as a church. We can certainly learn a lot by the way others have answered the question, and the rich and varied tradition of the church will certainly enlighten our efforts, but nothing can substitute for our own response.

Our response will emerge through the patient and sincere dialogue between our own specific sociohistorical experience of suffering, margination, enslavement, and struggles for liberation and the sociohistorical experience of liberation and new life brought about by the Jesus event. As we reread the New Testament

Original essay written in September 1988, revised for this collection in August 2008.

from within the context of our own experience, new, exciting, refreshing, and life-giving elements will emerge that have always been there, but others have not discovered before. At the same time, this new reading of the New Testament will reveal new, liberating aspects about the ultimate meaning of our own human situation and struggle that the best of human scientists have not even started to suspect. It is through this ongoing dialogue between our own human experience and the experience of liberation as recorded in the New Testament and Christian tradition that our own Christology will emerge. As every true Christology, it will not only be salvific for the group for which it is the answer to the question, "Who do you say that I am?" but it will be equally enlightening for the universal church.

The Christologies of others have been of tremendous value to us, but today we are struggling to make our own contribution to the Christian understanding of the human story. We are not seeking universal answers, but answers that emerge out of our own particular situation will certainly have universal value and significance. Our Christologies will not replace others, but they will contribute to the growth and development in the appreciation of the full mystery of Christ.

MEXICAN AMERICAN EXPERIENCE

In brief, we can say that Mexican Americans are people who in recent times have been twice conquered, twice mestisized, twice dominated, and twice oppressed by all the institutions of society. Yet we have not lost our inner freedom, integrity, dignity, and desire to live as a people. We were first conquered and mestisized by Spain beginning in the 1500s and then by the United States in its great western movements in the mid-1800s. Initially we did not migrate to the United States. The United States crossed our borders and took over our lands. It prohibited our language and imposed new social institutions. Because of the conquest and subsequent *mestizaje*, the Mexican American has always had to struggle with questions of identity and belonging. It has been easier to say who we are not than who we are. We are not Mexican, we are not mainstream U.S. Americans; then who are we? For Mexicans we are too Americanized, and for mainstream U.S. Americans, we are too Mexican. Hence we have been excluded and distanced from both parent groups. Not only have the customs and way of life of the people been subject to ridicule, but the children have been denied a true education and the adults have been exploited and mistreated. Schools ignore our history and deprive us of learning about our heritage, thus eroding our collective memory. Mexican Americans have in many ways been the untouchables of the United States. This is certainly beginning to change, but it has a long way to go. Our own self-image, created by the dominant group, has to be redeemed.

The experience of rejection and margination has been the common, everyday experience for the masses of the people. We have been forced to live the experience of being the permanently excluded other. Yet, because of the *mestizaje*, Mexican and U.S. cultural realities form our innermost identity. Furthermore, in us, both the Mexican and U.S. identities began to become fused and synthesized so as to form a new existence. Herein lies both the root of the suffering and the potential for new life. In our very existence we are transgressing the ultimate barrier of separation: body and blood. Furthermore, in us there is a new blood and a new body. In us there is the beginning of a new way of life, a new language, and a new humanity. The old, intransigent barriers will no longer hold. What the old Mexican philosopher Octavio Paz called the border of absolute otherness is now the very cradle of a new people. This is happening slowly, and certainly with a lot of resistance, but it is taking place.

When one studies the human story across the ages, the tendency of group inclusion/exclusion—that is, protecting our own by keeping others out—appears to be one of the most consistent and fundamental anthropological rules of society. Dominant groups struggle to keep outside influences out in a multiplicity of ways, and weaker or dominated ones likewise fear and resist any type of intrusion. The purity of the group must be maintained. Human barriers of race, class, language, family name, education, economic status, social position, and religion are regularly used as signals to distinguish "our own" from "the others."

The second tendency appears as an anthropological societal rule: Others can be used and enjoyed, but a social distance must be maintained. Deep friendships and even strong love relationships might develop, but the social barriers are so deeply interiorized and assimilated that they are very difficult to eliminate. There are not just laws that keep people apart, but the relationship of superior-inferior that is established, projected, transmitted, assimilated, and even sacrilized by religion. This divide keeps people from truly appreciating each other as fully equal and from seeing one another's true human dignity. Even the best among the dominant group tend to see and treat the others as inferior and different. We can even do good things for the lesser others, but they remain lesser. They can be exploited legitimately because the culture and the laws of the dominant sanction the superior-inferior relationship, giving the "master" the right and the obligation to use and "protect" the lesser ones.

This law of social distance is probably the hardest one to break through, because not only is it enforced by external laws and the economic-political mechanisms of the land, but the law is also interiorized in a multiplicity of ways. For example, in ordinary commercials, we see African Americans waiting on whites, but I have never seen a commercial with a white person serving an African American. Blacks appear in commercials, but rarely racially mixed families. Brown-skinned persons occasionally appear on commercials today. Social barriers of separation are drilled into people through all the media of communication and education. Even religious educational material and religious images in our churches exhibit a definite racial preference, thus indirectly telling persons of color that they cannot be reflected in the sacred.

Finally, the third constant appearing as an anthropological societal rule is that anyone who threatens to destroy or annul the barriers of separation will be an outcast—an impure untouchable who must be eliminated. As should be evident by now, *mestizaje* is feared by the established groups because it is the deepest threat to all the humanly made barriers of separation that consecrate exclusion, oppression, and exploitation. It is a threat to the security of ultimate human belonging—that is, to the inherited national/cultural identity that clearly and ultimately defines to myself and to the world who I am. It is even a deeper threat to established societies, because the *mestizo* cannot be named with clarity and precision. The real meaning and mission of the *mestizo* identity is our own messianic secret. Just who people say we are is one thing, but who we know ourselves to be in the eyes of God is quite something else.

There is so much in the mystery of a name. I am comfortable when I can name you, for, in many ways, it indicates that I am somewhat in control of the situation. I may not like what I know, but at least I have the comfort of knowing what it is. But there is a nervousness when I do not know who you are; your name and your cultural nationality are so important, for they tell me who you are personally and fundamentally. They give me your immediate and ultimate human identity. Because of the dual identity, the *mestizo* cannot be named adequately by the categories of analysis of either group. He or she does not fit into a singular set of historical norms for testing and identifying persons. This is threatening to both groups; we can name them and even study them, but they cannot name us or even figure out how to really study us. It is threatening for anyone to be in the presence of one who knows us very well even in our innermost being, but we do not know who they are. To be an outside-insider, as is the *mestizo,* is to have both intimacy and objective distance at one and the same time, for, insofar as we are in Mexico, we are outside the United States; but insofar as we are in the United States, we are distant from Mexico. As such, we can see and appreciate the aspects of both that neither see of themselves or each other. In this very in-out existence lies the potential for our creativity: to pool the cultural identity and biological admixture of both so as to create a new one.

The potential for newness will not be actualized automatically. The *mestizo* can simply become like one of the parent groups and continue to do unto others as they had done unto them. This approach will be the constant temptation, the great danger and threat to the emergence of new life. The temptation to abort this new life that is just beginning will always be there. However, they can equally, although with more hidden difficulties than anyone suspects, choose to live out the radical meaning of their new being. This is exciting but difficult because, even though the dominant way may be rejected totally and explicitly, subconsciously the oppressed will strive to become like the oppressor since they have already assimilated many of the characteristics of the dominant group. Will the group simply obtain power and acceptance by reverting to the ways of the parent group, or will they initiate new life? That question is the key.

As a Mexican American Christian, I am convinced that the full potential of *mestizaje* will be actualized only in and through the way of the Lord that brings order out of chaos and new life out of death. It is in his way that the salvific and liberating role of our human *mestizo* way finds its ultimate identity, meaning, direction, and challenge. Because of our history and our situation today, three key elements of the way of Jesus allow us to reread our own human story in a radically new way: the sociocultural identity of Jesus; the struggles of Jesus with the various power institutions of his time, which led to his condemnation and death sentence; and finally the ultimate triumph: society was able to kill the prophet, but it was not able to destroy or silence him.

The more we appreciate the real status of Jesus—his cultural origins as a human being, his ability to consistently bring the unexpected out of the accepted human ways, his great liberty in transgressing human taboos, even the most sacred ones, in favor of doing good for people—the more that all the christological titles become all the more powerful and fascinating. Our Christian liberation, which continues to be a scandal to the world of human values, begins not with the cross but with the very conception of Jesus and his subsequent journey and struggle through life. His entire life gives meaning, direction, and hope to our own life and struggles of today.

THE EXPERIENCE OF JESUS

Incarnation: The Scandal of the Savior's Beginning

I wonder more and more why Christologies always seem to skip over Jesus' sociocultural identity and status. This aspect of a person seems to be the all-important starting point in the life and mission of every person, and it certainly is for Jesus. The Gospel of Mark begins the good news by telling us precisely that Jesus came from Nazareth, a town in Galilee. This was the all-important starting point. It seems like the further away one moves from the Gospels, the more that Christologies become scandalized by the earthly beginnings of Jesus. Could it be that the full kenosis of the Son of God is still too shocking and scandalous to the thought and value structures of today's comfortably installed world? For many people, confessing Christ as Lord and Savior is easier than confessing that Jesus of Nazareth is the Christ. Such confessions are much less disturbing to our contemporary world of racist and classist values.

The racial-cultural identity and social status of a person are the very first and immediate revelations of who one is, according to the world. We all have stereotyped prejudices about certain colors, accents, languages, features, regions, and religions. There is a natural tendency to categorize people according to our stereotypes of them and to prejudge them as to their human worth and potential even before they have said or done anything. Looks are all-important, and they are the first revelation, according to the standards of the world, of the worth and dignity of the person. People from the outer regions of any country are usually looked down upon as rustics, while the people from urban centers look upon themselves as sophisticated.

What was the racial-cultural identity and status of Jesus? What did people think of when they first saw or heard him? What did people think before they even heard him speak or witnessed his actions? These are all important questions, for we know from the New Testament itself that God has made himself known to us in the human face and heart of Jesus. Through the full humanity of Jesus, God has allowed us to see him in a human way. There is no doubt that, during his lifetime, Jesus was regularly known as a Galilean, that most of his disciples were from Galilee, and that most of the things we remember best of his activity took place in Galilee.

Galilee plays a key role in the life and mission of Jesus as presented in the Gospels. The full human signification of the kenosis of the Son of God becomes evident when we look at the image of Galilee in Jesus' time. First of all, if it had not been for Jesus, Galilee would probably remain an unknown region of the world. Jerusalem, Greece, and Rome were all important with or without Jesus, but not Galilee. It was an outer region, far from the center of Judaism in Jerusalem and a crossroads of the several caravan routes. It was a region surrounded by various traditions, peoples, and languages. In Galilee, the Jews were looked down upon and despised by the elites of Judea, while they were also looked down upon by the rest of the world. Even though they were fervent Jews, they were often considered to be stubborn, backward, superstitious, and all the negative stereotypes one could imagine.

Furthermore, the Jewish elite of Judea looked down upon the Galilean Jews, for they considered them ignorant about the Law and the rules of the Temple, contaminated in many ways by their contacts with the pagans of the surrounding regions, and not capable of speaking correctly. They were often ridiculed because of their regional pronunciation. As marginal peasants from the countryside, they were often regarded as inferior and impure by the Judean Jewish elites.

While much archaeological debate is going on today as to the amount of cultural mixture/exchange that took place in the region, I am sure that some amount of cultural *mestizaje* would have taken place. Knowing the ordinary dynamics of people, I am sure a certain amount of biological admixture, though abhorred, was still occurring. Culturally and linguistically speaking, Jesus probably appeared as a *mestizo* between Judaism and the other cultures that flourished throughout the greater Galilean region. This point has given rise to various theories about Jesus—whether he was similar to cynic philosophers, an apocalyptic prophet, a teacher of wisdom, and so on. Early Jewish charges tried to discredit Jesus, claiming that he was the bastard son of a Roman soldier named Pantera, which could also be a colloquial term simply meaning "a Roman." Jesus is referred to in the derogatory way as "the Son of Mary" in Mark's Gospel, which could have meant his father was unknown, and the Jews infer this origin of Jesus in John 8:41 when they state, "We are not illegitimate children," or as in other translations, "We are not born out of fornication."

We are, of course, in no way denying or even questioning that Jesus was conceived by the Holy Spirit. What we are saying is that in his human appearance as viewed by those who knew him only in a worldly way and not through the eyes of faith, his earthly Galilean identity, while being very Jewish, was nevertheless somewhat ambiguous. The New Testament itself gives evidence that nothing good was expected to come out of Galilee.

The point of bringing all this out is to appreciate the human beginnings of God's mission. God becomes not just a human being, but one of the shamed, lowly, and rejected of the world—a victim of the world's sin and the sinful structures that condition our view of others. He comes to initiate a new human unity, but the all-important starting point is among the most segregated, untouchable, and impure of the world. Among those whom the world has thrown out, God will begin the way to final unity. It is among those whom the world labels as "impure" or "untouchables" that a new criteria for real purity will emerge. Those who have suffered the rejection and the insults of the world will be the first to hear the new invitation and in responding form a new and more inclusive human group.

Because the world expected nothing good to come out of Galilee, God chose it not only to be the starting point of God's human presence, but even more so to be God's very own racial-cultural identity and language. The principle behind the cultural image of the Galilean identity is that God chooses what the world rejects. What is marginal to the world is central to God. Through those whom the world has made nothing, God will reduce to nothing the power and wisdom of the world. Through the poor and nothing of the world of today's Galileans, salvation continues to begin for all the peoples of the world.

The mission of Jesus is not some sort of esoteric or aesthetic truth. He comes to live out and proclaim the supreme truth about human beings and humanity that will have immediate and long-term implications in everyday life and in the history of humanity. Those who hear his word and are converted to his way will see themselves and will equally see all others in a radically new way. This new image of self and of others will allow everyone to relate with each other as never before.

Because of his concrete human identity, Jesus had personally suffered the pains of margination, ridicule, and dehumanizing insults. He was concerned with the pains of hunger, sickness, bad reputation, rejection, shame, class struggles, loneliness, and all the real sufferings of humanity. His concern was not abstract, but real and immediate. He spoke with the Samaritan woman, and ate with the rich, the tax collectors, and public sinners alike. He did not feel repelled by the leper, and he enjoyed the company of women and little children. Jesus was truly at home with everyone, and everyone evidently felt at home with him. In his ministry, Jesus had the ability to enjoy himself in common table fellowship with everyone without exception.

Out of the cultural suffering of rejection, Jesus offers a new understanding of the kingdom. He did not come to restore the kingdom of David, but to initiate the reign of God who is the Father of everyone. The innermost identity of Jesus was his life of intimacy with God-Father. This living relationship with the Absolute cuts through and relativizes all human images of importance or nonimportance, dignified or undignified. When we know the ultimate origins of a person—that he is really the Child of God—then superficial appearances are no longer important. The ultimate origins and name of a person give us their true worth. Precisely this intimacy with God-Father is the basis of the innermost identity of Jesus, which he offers to all others. It is not the labels that the world places on people that count, but one's own innermost identity and image of oneself as reflective of the likeness of God. By discovering that God is our real Father we begin to see everything in a new way. No longer do I see others as superior or inferior to me, but as brothers and sisters of the same Father. In this realization is the basis for a totally new value system for humanity.

In fidelity to God, Jesus refuses to conform to any human law or tradition that will dehumanize and make appear as inferior any human being whatsoever. The truth of Jesus will upset humanity's criteria of judgment. Because one is, one is a child of God. But precisely because everyone can now belong, those who have set up and guarded the multiple barriers of separation that allow them to enjoy the privileges of being in at the cost of keeping the so-called inferior ones out will not only refuse the invitation but will discredit the new way and try to prevent it from coming into existence.

Crucifixion: The Scandalous End

But inviting the rejected into the kingdom is not sufficient. It is not sufficient to tell the exploited and excluded of society that they are truly free human beings who are equal to all others. One must go to the roots of the human mechanisms, both to the external and the internal structures of society, to make known the segregating and dehumanizing evil that has been institutionalized and is now hidden in the various structures of the group. Jesus makes known that he must go to Jerusalem where salvation will take place. Truth in the service of love must bring out clearly the evil that is hidden in the structures of society and which thus passes as good and even holy. Jerusalem, the beloved and venerated sacred center of his people, had now become a center of oppression through the collaboration of the Judean leadership elite with the Roman authorities. The Temple, in the words of Jesus, had become "a den of thieves," thus allowing the real criminals to appear as good while the victims appear as public sinners. This is the ongoing confusion of Babel that continues to mask and confuse both the evil and the good of the world.

Jesus appears in the New Testament as the aggressive prophet of nonviolent love who refuses to conform to the violence of the structures in full loyalty to the authentic tradition of the God of his people, of the God who sees the suffering, who hears the cries of affliction, and who wills to save; he questions the human traditions that oppress or destroy people. Jesus must go to Jerusalem because this had become the center of institutionalized power that was oppressing his people. When he arrives he goes to the very core of Judaism: the Temple. In Jerusalem, we meet the confronting Jesus who does not hesitate to question the very legitimacy of the structures that were now enslaving the masses of the people. The Temple was supposed to be a house of prayer for all the peoples of the world, but instead it had become a den of thieves. The house of the God of compassion and justice had become the place that now legitimized and covered up the oppressive ways of the establishment. Like the great prophets of his Jewish tradition, he does not hesitate to confront the abuses and deviations that had crept into the contemporary practice of his religion.

This is the story that we find in all human institutions. We need institutions in order to live in an orderly and peaceful way. Yet, all institutions have the tendency to become self-serving to the benefit of those in control. They are set up to serve people, but people end up serving them. This very tendency to absolutize must be confronted and made known if it is to be corrected. As institutions, customs, and traditions become absolutized, they function as the idols of the group. Whether we call them God or not, they function as the real gods of the group. To question them is the same as questioning God. When we challenge them, we are accused of blasphemy. Yet to the degree that these ways dehumanize or reject any human being, they must be questioned in the name of God. But Jesus does not confront the power of the world with a power of the same order. He confronts the power of the world and the violence of human beings with a power of an entirely different order: the power of unlimited love that will not give in to violence to eliminate violence.

The way of Jesus to Jerusalem and the cross is the challenging task of those who are on the margins of society. Their temptation will always be to simply become the powerful themselves, as even the disciples wanted to do. But the challenge is to be willing to die so that a new way will truly be ushered in. The authorities kill Jesus, but they cannot destroy him. In absolute obedience to the God of love, Jesus remains faithful to his way to the very end. He came to reject every type of human rejection, and even when all appear to have rejected him—even his God—he rejected no one. He died in perfect communion with his people and his God. He came to tear down barriers of separation, and no matter what humanity tried to do to stop him, they were not able to break him down. It is no surprise that the ultimate barrier of sacralized segregation, the Temple veil, is ripped apart upon his death As he lived his life in communion with everyone, so he died. All had rejected him, but he rejects no one.

Resurrection and Pentecost: The Unexpected Triumph and Glorious Beginning

God's love in and through Jesus triumphs over all the divisive hatreds and consequent violence of humanity. Jesus passes through death to life. In resurrecting him, God rejects the rejection of humanity, destroys all their charges of illegitimacy, and demolishes their idolized structures. In the resurrection, God ratified the entire way and message of Jesus. From the resurrection the entire way of Jesus and every aspect of his life takes on a liberating and salvific signification.

In the resurrection the new life initiated and offered to everyone by Jesus is now fully and definitively present. No human power can destroy it or slow it down. Jesus is the firstborn of the new creation, and in his followers a new human group now begins—definitely a new human alternative that is now present in the history of humanity. First of all, those who had nothing to offer now have the best thing to offer to everyone: new life. The rejected and marginalized Galileans have received the spirit and, without ceasing to be Galileans, now see themselves in a new way: initiators of the new humanity. Everyone is invited, but the very ones who had been excluded are now doing the inviting.

The history of the early church shows how quickly the new way spread to all peoples. It crossed all boundaries of separation. People, without ceasing to be who they were culturally, nevertheless saw themselves in such a new way that the ordinary human barriers were no longer obstacles to the new brotherhood. The crossing of cultural boundaries was not easy, for each group had its own unsuspected idols, yet the miracle is that it took place. Cultural-national groups that had been totally separated now came together—no longer Jew or Gentile, master or slave, male or female, but all one in Christ. They continued to be who they were, but they lived their nationality and religion in a radically new way. Their identity was affirmed, and their exclusiveness was destroyed. This openness led them to discover new values and criteria of judgment that brought them from competition to cooperation, from division to unity, from strangers to a common family, from a superior or inferior status to common friends, and all children of the same Father.

The radical, all-inclusive way of Christianity started among the rejected and lowly of society. This is the ongoing starting point. In the spirit, they struggle to build new human alternatives so that others will not have to suffer what they have had to suffer. They are the ones who first hear the invitation to the new universal family of God, and the converted poor and suffering of the world, who see themselves in a new way, now go out to invite—by deeds and words—all others into the new society. God continues to begin where humanity would never suspect. Out of the Nazareths and Galilees of today, salvation continues to come to the entire world.

THE GOSPEL MEANING OF OUR IDENTITY AND MISSION

"God chose what is foolish in the world to shame the wise." (1 Cor. 1:27)

Through faith we discover the ultimate identity of those rejected or marginalized by society as God's chosen people—not chosen because they are better than others, but chosen for a mission. In the very cultural identity of Jesus the Galilean and in his way from Galilee to Jerusalem, the real ultimate meaning of our own cultural identity and mission to society becomes clear—not what the world says that we are, but what God knows us to be. For those who ordinarily have a good sense of belonging, the idea of being chosen is nothing special. But for one who has been consistently ignored or rejected, the idea of being noticed, accepted, and especially chosen is not only good news, but new life. In being chosen, what was nothing now becomes something, and what was dead now comes to life.

In the light of the Judeo-Christian tradition, our Mexican American experience of rejection and margination is converted from human curse to the very sign of divine predilection. It is evident from the Scriptures that God chooses the outcasts of the world not exclusively but definitely in a preferential way. Those whom the world ignores, God goes out of his way to love in a special way. But he does not choose the poor and the lowly just to keep them down and make them feel good in their misery. Such an election would be the very opposite of good news, and it would truly be the opium to keep the poor quiet and domesticated. God chooses the poor and marginalized of the world to be the agents of a new creation.

The experience of being wanted *as one is,* of being needed, and of being chosen is a real and profound rebirth. Those who had been made to consider themselves as nothing or as inferior will now begin to appreciate the full stature of being human beings. Out of the new self-image, new powers will be released that have always been there but which have not been able to surface. Through this experience, the sufferings of the past are healed though not forgotten, and they should not be forgotten. For it is precisely out of the condition of suffering that the people are chosen so as to initiate a new way of life where others will not have to suffer what the poor have suffered in the past. When one forgets the experience of suffering, as has happened to many of our migrant groups in this country, then they simply inflict the same insults upon others that had previously been inflicted upon them. The greater the suffering and the more vivid the memory of it, the greater the challenge will be to initiate changes so as to eliminate the root causes of the evils that cause the suffering. The wounded healer who has not forgotten the pain of the wounds can be the greatest healer of the illnesses of society.

In our very margination from the centers of the various establishments, we live the Galilean identity today. Because we are inside-outsiders, we appreciate more clearly the best of the traditions of both groups, while equally appreciating the worse of the situation of both—the particular sin and grace of each one. It is precisely in this double identity that, while being marginalized by both, we in effect have something of unique value to offer both. The very reasons for the marginalization are the bases of our liberating and salvific potential not only for ourselves but for the others as well. In a privileged way, God is present in the marginalized, for distance from the powers of the world is closeness to God. It is consistently in the frontier regions of human belonging that God begins the new creation. The established centers seek stability, but the frontier regions can risk to be creative pioneers. The frontier people will be the trailblazers of the new societies. "The stone that the builders rejected has become the cornerstone; this was the Lord's doing, and it is amazing in our eyes" (Matt. 21:42).

"I appointed you to go and bear fruit." (John 15:16)

God chooses people not just to make them feel good but for a mission. To accept God's election is not an empty privilege, but a challenging mission. It is a call to be prophetic both in deeds and in words. It is a call to live a new alternative in the world, to invite others into it, and to challenge with the power of truth the structures of the world that keep the new alternative from becoming a reality.

Our Mexican American Christian challenge in the world today is not to try to become like someone else—Mexico or the United States—but to combine both into a new way that is more welcoming of everyone. Through the very mechanisms of forging a new and more cosmopolitan identity, new life begins to emerge. It must be worked at critically, persistently, and creatively, for the temptation will always be there to become simply one or the other of the previous models. The temptation will always be there to restore the kingdom rather than to usher in the kingdom of God. In our present powerlessness, we may think that this is stupid, but in our faith we know that we must take the risks and begin to initiate new ways of life that will eliminate some of the dehumanizing elements of the present one. We know that we will not eliminate them all, nor will this come about easily and without much effort, organization, and frustration, but nevertheless the efforts must be made to introduce new forms and new institutions that will continue some of the best of the past while eliminating some of the worst. We will not build the perfect society, but we must do our part to at least build a better one. We must begin with the grass roots, but we must equally go to the very roots of the problems.

This is our "divine must"! We, too, must harden our faces and go to Jerusalem. We must go to the established centers of power, whether political, economic, educational, or religious, to confront their sacred idols that prevent them from truly serving all the people. The idols of society function in favor of the established, the rich, and the powerful, and against the excluded, poor, and powerless. They mask the hidden viciousness and manipulations of the wise of the world who find many ways of exploiting the poor and the simple of the world. We really do not have a choice if we want to be disciples following Jesus on his way to the cross. This road from Galilee to Jerusalem has to be continued if evil is to be destroyed, not with new forms of evil, but with the power of truth in the service of love. We have no choice but to speak the truth that brings to light clearly the evil of the world, knowing full well that the powers of darkness will not stop at anything in order to put out the light.

"Your pain will turn into joy." (John 16:20)

It is in our fiestas that our legitimate identity and destiny are experienced. They are not just parties; in fact, they are the very opposite. They are the joyful, spontaneous, and collective celebrations of what has already begun in us, even if it is not recognized by others or verbalized even by ourselves. They are the celebration of the beginning of the ultimate eschatological identity where there will be differences, not division. They are the celebration of what has already begun in germ (redemption) but is yet to be totally fulfilled (eschatology). Yet the fiesta is a foretaste and experience, even if for a brief moment, of the ultimate accomplishment (eschatological banquet). Fiestas are a result of who we are and a cause of what is yet to become. Just as the celebrations of the people can be used to sort of drug the people and keep them in their misery, the fiestas can be used as the rallying moments that not only give the people an experience of togetherness, but can also nourish the movements of liberation.

In the fiestas, we rise above our daily living experiences of death to experience life beyond death. They are the moments of life that enable us to survive, to come together, to rally, and to begin anew. The spirit not only to survive but to bring about a new existence can be enkindled in the fiestas so as to ignite the people to action. I am convinced that there is nothing more redeeming for our people than the celebration of our religious feasts that allow us to participate in body and spirit in the entire way of Jesus from the *Posadas* through *Viernes Santo* unto the eschatological feast of *Cristo Rey*. This was certainly my experience in my twelve years as rector of San Fernando Cathedral in San Antonio.

Fiestas without prophetic action easily degenerate into empty parties, drunken brawls, or the opium to keep the people in their misery. But prophetic action without festive celebration is equally reduced to dehumanizing hardness. Prophecy is the basis of fiesta, but the fiesta is the spirit of prophecy. In the combination of the two, the tradition of faith is both kept alive and transmitted to newcomers. Through the two of them, the God of history who acts on our behalf, on behalf of the poor and the lowly, continues to be present among us, bringing his project of history to completion. Thus, precisely through our civic and religious fiestas we are kept together as a people. Through them we have continued to maintain our identity and sense of belonging. They are the deepest celebrations of our existence—meaningful to those who belong, and incomprehensible and folkloric to the outsiders. They are the lifeline of our tradition and the life sources of our new existence.

Chapter 2

The Galilean Jesus
as Faithful Dissenter

*Latino/a Christology and
the Dynamics of Exclusion*

MICHAEL E. LEE

Recent decades have seen critiques by scholars doing historical Jesus research of his portrayal in theologies inspired by the preferential option for the poor.[1] Virgilio Elizondo's landmark work, *Galilean Journey: The Mexican-American Promise*, has been criticized by some for anti-Jewish rhetoric in its portrait of Galilee, and of Jesus' conflicts with the Jewish religious authorities in Jerusalem.[2] Mary C. Boys treats Elizondo's work as emblematic of liberation theologies, asserting, "Scholarship simply does not support the sweeping generalizations they draw, and the anti-Judaism in their work is appalling."[3]

The basic tension that Elizondo identifies, however, is not his own invention. It is rooted, rather, in the Gospel narratives themselves, and raises complex issues for readers of the Second Testament. The deadly conflict between Jesus and some Jerusalem authorities poses special problems for a culturally contextualized theology like *Galilean Journey*, which wrestles with issues of marginalization in the Mexican American experience. In what follows, I argue that Elizondo's focus on the critical-prophetic nature of Jesus' ministry serves to fortify and encourage Christian efforts toward justice, and (while granting some of the points of his critics) cannot be fairly said to advocate for the superiority of Christianity over Judaism. I suggest, rather, that the critiques serve to focus our attention on the complex hermeneutics of interpreting for a post-Shoah world the first-century intra-Jewish conflicts that led to the death of Jesus. Thus, we are led to ask, how can Christians hold fast to the prophetic dimension of Jesus' ministry, portrayed in the Gospels as a confrontation with Jewish religious authorities, without falling into or being vilified for anti-Judaism?

On the one hand, if Christian accounts of Jesus omit the portrayal of his critical stance toward the religious hypocrisy, legalism, and exclusionism of elements of first-century Jewish leadership, then important dimensions of his preaching and ministry are lost. Indeed, it would seem that these lessons should be at the forefront of Christian self-examination regarding the sad consequences of later efforts to establish Christian identity in contradistinction to Judaism. On the other hand, when such themes are linked to anti-Jewish caricatures and supersessionist theological ideas, the tragic legacy of Christian mistreatment of Jews is inevitably perpetuated and their contribution to liberation threatened. I would argue, therefore, that historical Jesus research and theologies grounded in the option for the poor have important, complementary, and sometimes mutually corrective roles to play in seeking a solution to this dilemma.

Biblical scholars have identified sections where the Gospels retroject into the time of Jesus conflicts between nascent Christianity and Judaism, while literary and archaeological sources continue to deepen our understanding of the religious, cultural, and political character of the Galilean region in which Jesus spent the majority of his life. At the same time, the problem of Christian anti-Judaism requires more than just new data; it demands a hermeneutic to assist in the reception of these biblical accounts among Christian faith communities in a post-Shoah environment. In what follows, I argue that Elizondo's theology, and the U.S. Latino/a theologies that his work has helped to initiate, offer important insights on questions of marginalization, alienation, and power, and provide valuable hermeneutical resources for the ongoing reception of Gospel accounts of Jesus' ministry and its attendant conflicts.[4] I suggest that Elizondo's principles be turned around to assist in the interpretation of Elizondo's own work, so that its ongoing reception remains true to its liberative spirit.

Elizondo frames his analysis of the Galilean Jesus in his account of the dynamics of *mestizaje*, that often-violent encounter of cultures at the heart of the Mexican American experience.[5] He recognizes the powerful forces of exclusion faced by *mestizos/as* in a borderland existence, including a double rejection by those on both sides of the given border. Elizondo finds hope in Jesus the Galilean who experiences this double rejection, and whose ministry as it is narrated in the Gospels incarnates three principles that serve to overcome such exclusion: (1) the Galilee principle: God loves what human beings reject;[6] (2) the Jerusalem principle: God calls and empowers the marginalized to resist the powers of exclusion and domination;[7] and (3) the Resurrection principle: only the power of love can conquer evil.[8]

This essay argues that, viewed within the larger context of the *mestizo/a*'s double rejection and the aforementioned principles, the basic insights of *Galilean*

Journey work against anti-Jewish readings by interpreting Jesus' conflict with Jewish authorities as the prophetic battle against exclusion waged by a Galilean firmly rooted within the Jewish tradition. Drawing from his experience of traditional Mexican American fidelity to ecclesial and social bodies despite marginalization, Elizondo ultimately envisions Jesus as a faithful dissenter. In this way, Jesus offers a path to resist all forms of exclusion, epitomizing Elizondo's view that resistance springs from fidelity and love of one's own tradition.

The essay begins by analyzing the structure and content of *Galilean Journey* as a constructive theological project, which draws a mutually critical correlation between Elizondo's interpretation of the contemporary situation of Mexican American *mestizaje,* and his understanding of the significance of the Galilean dimension of the identity of Jesus. Then I briefly consider critiques that *Galilean Journey* evidences anti-intellectual romanticism, anti-Jewish rhetoric, or anti-historical anachronisms. Finally I examine how Elizondo's distinctive hermeneutical location shapes the aforementioned principles, which I argue serve to adjudicate the claims made against the text. Elizondo's principles, I propose, draw our attention to traces of the logic of exclusion in the accusations themselves. Overall, my goal is to revisit the portrait developed in *Galilean Journey* of Jesus as a faithful dissenter who speaks and acts against the dynamics of exclusion suffered by marginalized Jews and certain others in first-century Israel, and to demonstrate its ongoing significance for people of diverse races, cultures, and religions today.

GALILEAN JOURNEY: REJECTION OF THE *MESTIZO* TRANSFORMED INTO PRINCIPLES OF HOPE

The power of Virgilio Elizondo's *Galilean Journey* is rooted in its creative correlation of the Gospel Jesus with Elizondo's own Mexican-American experience.[9] Following David Tracy's understanding of theology as the mutually critical correlation between an interpretation of a faith tradition and an interpretation of a contemporary situation, I would characterize *Galilean Journey* not as a work of historical Jesus research, but as a foundational correlational text of Latino/a systematic theology with important christological implications in its own right.[10]

Elizondo explicitly identifies the Mexican-American experience as the setting for his theological reflection. Methodologically, the historical influence of Latin American colleagues on Elizondo draws our attention to the see-judge-act method inherited from Catholic Action and powerfully utilized in the episcopal documents of Medellín and a number of liberation theologians.[11] In Elizondo's work, this method first yields a "seeing" of the basic sociocultural reality of Mexican-Americans, the situation that he calls *mestizaje.* Second, Elizondo interprets this situation in light of the Gospels, and (true to his correlational approach) highlights corresponding aspects in the sociocultural situation of the Gospels and of Jesus himself.[12] Third, Elizondo formulates the aforementioned principles as implications of God's work in Jesus of Galilee for Christian action or discipleship today.[13] In what follows I will briefly summarize each of these themes, and suggest their significance for theology today.

SEEING THE REALITY OF THE MEXICAN-AMERICAN EXPERIENCE: *MESTIZAJE*

Without question, Elizondo's focus on *mestizaje* as a reality demanding theological reflection represents one of the most significant and enduring contributions of *Galilean Journey*.[14] *Mestizaje* involves the (often violent) meeting of two cultures and possesses a dual nature for Elizondo. The term connotes both the suffering inherent in conquest and marginalization, and the positive potential linked to the creation of new identities. Elizondo asserts that Mexican-American identity is a product of two *mestizaje*s: (1) the Spanish-Indigenous encounter that originated in the European conquest of Mexico and helped produce the Mexican people and their culture, and (2) the Nordic-Protestant wresting of northern Mexico into U.S. hands and the creation of the Mexican-American reality. The genius of Elizondo's approach lies in his recognition of both the deplorable nature of the conquests and the painful struggles that have produced *mestizaje*, and his illumination of the resilient beauty of the Mexican and Mexican-American peoples and cultures that have appeared in their wake.

Elizondo outlines the cruel power dynamics that often attend *mestizaje* in three "anthropological" laws: group inclusion/exclusion, social distance, and elimination of opposition.[15] The first indicates the dangerous tendency of human beings to separate and classify each other, and to create polarities of us versus them in the name of group purity.[16] Second, when reified in social structures of domination, these in-out, superior-inferior polarities create social distances that order and condition even genuinely positive interpersonal relationships. Witness how acts by the dominant group may, even unconsciously, involve paternalism or an implicit call to assimilation. Third and finally, Elizondo says, "Anyone who threatens to diminish or destroy the barriers of group separation must be eliminated."[17] Grounded as they are in the commitment to group purity, Elizondo's laws capture the fear and animosity that too often result from *mestizaje*.

Elizondo asserts that the *mestizo/a* blurs codes of group purity, and that this leads to a pattern of double rejection. He evocatively describes the situation of Mexican-Americans who are not "Mexican" enough to achieve full acceptance by relatives and friends in Mexico, and are not "American" enough for those in the United States. This rejection manifests itself economically, politically, culturally, psychologically, and religiously so that even the overcoming of oppressive obstacles is fraught with ambiguity. Despite these problems, however, Elizondo identifies creative possibilities in *mestizaje*, especially in the powerful religious symbols of Mexican-American culture.

Surprisingly perhaps, Elizondo does not attempt to excavate or construct an aboriginal or autochthonous religiosity in opposition to colonially imposed Christianity, a move that might reify the very barriers he denounces. Instead, he exalts the beauty of Mexican-American religiosity, and specifically that of his own Roman Catholic tradition, as a rich resource and site of resistance and survival. For Elizondo, "Christianity was not so much superimposed upon as implanted and 'naturalized' in the Mexican-American way of life."[18] Having detailed the cruel dimensions of the double *mestizaje* of Mexican-Americans, Elizondo does away with benign views of the conquest. However, rather than reject the religiosity that emerges from the conquest, he extols its beauty and creative possibilities. Accordingly, Elizondo identifies elements in Mexican-American religiosity—its images, rituals, devotions, saintly figures, and so on—that serve not only as symbols of struggle, suffering, and death but also as symbols of a new creation.[19] These popular traditions mediate a sense of ultimate belonging. Since his Mexican-American religiosity is profoundly Christian, Elizondo turns to the figure of Jesus, particularly Jesus the Galilean Jew, in order to articulate the characteristics of this new creation and to elicit new understandings of Christian sacred texts concerning Jesus Christ.

THE GALILEAN JESUS AND JUDGMENT: READING CULTURE AND A CULTURAL REREADING OF THE GOSPELS

Elizondo's exploration of *mestizaje* and the value he places on Mexican-American religiosity establishes *Galilean Journey* as an important and creative theological work. It is the manner in which he utilizes these insights to carry out a cultural rereading of Jesus as a Galilean, however, that defines his contribution to Christology, and this contribution must be situated correctly so that Elizondo's work is not confused with historical Jesus research. While his work explores the historical world, actions, and words of the first-century Jesus of Nazareth, *Galilean Jesus* is neither a work of biblical scholarship, nor a part of "third quest" historical Jesus research.[20] Elizondo clearly states that he views his work as pastoral theology.[21] He explicitly describes his task as a culturally conditioned reading of the Gospels that turns to the Second Testament in order to shed light on the contemporary situation of Mexican-Americans, but which also draws from the Mexican-American experience in order to "turn up previously hidden aspects of the gospel message."[22]

Elizondo's description of his correlational method places him in what Elizabeth Johnson identifies as the "second wave of renewal in Catholic Christology" that comes to the fore after the Second Vatican Council.[23] Rather than using the Chalcedonic formula of Jesus Christ's full divinity and humanity as a starting point, theologians of this post-Conciliar generation turn to the scriptural narratives about Jesus' historical ministry.[24] What results is a reading of Jesus that is not less faithful or traditional, but one that, in light of modern historical consciousness, is focused on the "history of Jesus" so as to render a more faithful discipleship among believers today. As Johnson articulates it,

> If Jesus is the revelation of God and stood for definite purposes and upheld certain values, then the significance of that for believers is inestimable. What he does in the concrete, matters; it embodies the way of God in this world which patterns our way as disciples today. . . . Jesus does not just have a human nature in the abstract, but a very concrete human history. We need to put that story into dialogue with our own lives today.[25]

Although Elizondo makes assertions regarding the historical reality of Jesus of Nazareth, *Galilean Journey* does not attempt to reconstruct the life of the "historical Jesus," and does not try to discern the intentions of the biblical authors. Instead, it rereads the Gospel narratives concerning Jesus' cultural reality in the borderland area of Galilee from the perspective of those who live in the borderland today. When Elizondo develops the notion of Galilee as a symbol of multiple rejection, he draws not just from the biblical texts and the work of biblical archaeology and history, but from the very experience of multiple rejection that is part of the contemporary Mexican-American *mestizaje*. In this way, Elizondo's provocative image of Jesus the Galilean as a "borderland reject"[26] correlates (1) the Christian confession of Jesus Christ as a fully human being—incarnated in the specific body, time, place, and culture of a first-century Galilean; (2) the biblical account of Jesus' ministry occurring primarily in the marginal area of Galilee; and (3) the Mexican-American experience of borderland marginalization.

For Elizondo, taking Jesus' humanity seriously demands attention to his cultural reality as a Galilean. Theologically, the incarnation is not God-become-(abstract) flesh, nor is it God-become-human with a vague sense of history. The incarnation involves God becoming a human being with the cultural reality of a first-century Galilean, and that is crucial for understanding what God reveals to humanity in Jesus Christ. One aspect of this revelation lies in the fact that the cultural reality of the Galilean Jesus is marked by the kind of double rejection experienced by *mestizos/as* today. Elizondo draws the following comparison:

> The image of the Galileans to the Jerusalem Jews is comparable to the image of the Mexican-Americans to the Mexicans of Mexico. On the other hand, the image of the Galileans to the Greco-Romans is comparable to the image of the Mexican-American to the Anglo population of the United States. They were part of and despised by both.[27]

We have already seen that Elizondo emphasizes not only the destructive potential of *mestizaje* in the anthropological laws of group inclusion/exclusion, social distance, and elimination, but also its creative potential for bringing about new life. This is epitomized in the ministry of Jesus, which manifests the scandalous, transgressive nature of *mestizaje* by valorizing what has been rejected by human beings as most beloved by God. Elizondo asserts that the Galilean ministry of Jesus announces a good news that subverts the polarizing barriers of human exclusion, and in doing so, finds itself in direct confrontation with the powers that most benefit from the entrenched status quo.

In chapter 4 of *Galilean Journey*, Elizondo argues that the Galilean ministry of Jesus—preaching, healing, and table fellowship with powerful and marginal persons alike—was the result of Jesus' rejecting the very rejecting he faced as a Galilean, and announcing the universal love of God-Abba to other "rejects" of this time and place. This led to the confrontation with systems of rejection and eventually the cross (chap. 5), and then to the hope of resurrection and Pentecost (chap. 6).

If Galilee represents the margins, then Jerusalem, and specifically the rejection of Jesus and his message by some of the Temple authorities, represents the oppressive center. Accordingly, the movement of the Gospel narratives themselves from Galilee to Jerusalem and their ultimate culmination in the resurrection provides the pattern for Elizondo's constructive theological statement in the Galilee principle, the Jerusalem principle, and the Resurrection principle.[28]

THE GALILEAN JOURNEY AS ACTION: THREE PRINCIPLES AND THE LEGACY OF LATINO/A THEOLOGY

Elizondo's three principles signal the engagement of his christological reflection with the "preferential option for the poor" and Christian discipleship as prophetic praxis, important motifs in contemporary theological reflection. The Galilee principle—"what human beings reject, God chooses as his very own"— succinctly summarizes the preferential option for the poor,[29] and functions as a fundamental guide for Christian discipleship.[30] The Jerusalem principle lifts up the agency of oppressed people as a way to avoid fatalism and paternalism in their confrontation with structural evils, including racism and the abuses of liberal capitalism. And the Resurrection principle—"only love can triumph over evil, and no human power can prevail against the power of unlimited love"[31]—culminates Elizondo's theological correlation, marking out parameters for Christian discipleship grounded in the disciple's encounter with the risen Jesus of Galilee.

Galilean Journey has fueled the development of U.S. Latino/a theologies for thirty years, particularly in the study of popular religiosity, *mestizaje,* and the everyday reflection of Latino/a communities on Jesus Christ.[32] Latino/a theological reflection on Jesus has focused on the Galilee principle of valorizing the marginalized, the Jerusalem principle of prophetic resistance, and the Resurrection principle of new creation.[33] Latino/a authors have made some of their most distinctive contributions elaborating the notion that Jesus dignifies the marginalized and shares an identity with them. In *Jesus Is My Uncle,* Luis Pedraja portrays a Jesus who responds to the cultural alienation felt by U.S. Latinos/as.[34] Locating marginalization in culture and language, as well as economics, U.S. Latino/a theologians complement Latin American liberation theology as a genuine reflection on the particularity of the U.S. Latino/a situation. This comes through in the work of Miguel De La Torre, who explores the *Ajiaco* Christ of Cuban christological reflection, devotion, and artistic depiction.[35] Such portrayals capture how Latino/a theology interprets the preferential option for the poor through what Elizondo calls the Galilee principle, the identification of God with the marginalized person as embodied in both the person and ministry of Jesus Christ.

The Jerusalem principle asserts that God's love for the rejected should not pacify but rather empower the marginalized to transform the structures of rejection. Accordingly, U.S. Latino/a theology has always had a strong prophetic critique and a vision of Jesus as liberator, emphasizing active Christian discipleship expressed in communal and social resistance to oppressive structures. Though the legacy of Iberian colonial Christian devotion can seem to some a profoundly interiorized, emotional, and fatalistic spirituality, U.S. Latinos/as have transformed these elements into grounds for social resistance. Even a cursory glance at the many *Via Crucis* devotions around the United States demonstrates how Latino/a communities wed profound Christian religiosity with protest of social evils and exploitation.[36] Jesus is not just the victim with whom one identifies, but the liberator whose mission the disciple carries forward. For many U.S. Latinos/as, Jesus' prophetic critique also empowers women, struggling for liberation from oppression as subalterns within a marginalized population.[37]

As seen in this reference to the *Via Crucis,* U.S. Latino/a reflection on Christ highlights the liberative dimensions of aesthetic-transformative practice. Themes such as beauty, celebration, and a relational anthropology give witness to the Resurrection principle of love as that which triumphs over evil.[38] Despite deep and lingering marginalization and exclusion, U.S. Latino/a theology resonates with the language of new hope, new creation, and new reconciliation.[39] Though much work remains to be done, the richness and variety of Latino/a theologies reflect and expand upon the important legacy of Elizondo's *Galilean Journey*. The future reception of this classic, however, is threatened by serious allegations, which require honest scrutiny if *Galilean Journey* is to continue to bear fruit.

JOURNEY IN THE WRONG DIRECTION?
GALILEAN JOURNEY AND ANTI-JUDAISM

Critics of *Galilean Journey* invariably focus their most vehement opposition on two short sections—"Galilee: Symbol of Multiple Rejection" and "Jerusalem: Symbol of Established Power"[40]—built around geographical and metaphorical polarities that Elizondo seeks to overcome, and to which his constructive theological-pastoral proposals respond. Though brief, detractors argue that the errors found in these sections overshadow the work as a whole.

Critics find particular fault with the manner in which *Galilean Journey* construes Jesus' Galilee against what appears to be its polar opposite, the oppressive center of Jerusalem. Some accuse Elizondo of anti-intellectual romanticization of Galilee, an anti-Jewish juxtaposition of Jesus and the Jewish authorities of Jerusalem, or nonhistorical and ideologically driven eisegesis, reading his contemporary theory of *mestizaje* into the ancient world of Galilee. Any ongoing reception of Elizondo's text must take these critiques seriously. Ironically, their implications lead to the very types of exclusion that Elizondo ostensibly condemns. Among the various critics of *Galilean Journey,* the most pertinent voice for its future reception in Latino/a circles has to be that of Jean-Pierre Ruiz.[41]

Ruiz briefly analyzes *Galilean Journey* in the context of a larger conversation among biblical scholars and systematic theologians. Lamenting the fragmentation and isolation of work in these areas, Ruiz, citing Stephen Fowl, notes sadly how historical criticism of the Bible has "largely become separated from the theological ends it was initially meant to serve. While most biblical scholars of both Testaments still continue to identify themselves as Christians, they generally are required to check their theological convictions at the door when they enter the profession of biblical studies."[42] Furthermore, Ruiz asserts that historical-critical approaches have been challenged by feminist and other explicitly contextual interpretations of the Bible "that have unmasked it as a set of contextual discourses that reflect the interests and the presuppositions of economically privileged western European Christian male readers." While *Galilean Journey* would seem a salutary example of both biblical-theological cooperation and the unmasking of biased discourses, to Ruiz it represents the unconscious reinforcement of deleterious and hegemonic discourses due to its naïve use of source material.

Ruiz levies two central accusations against Elizondo's work in *Galilean Journey*: (1) anti-intellectualism in its construction of Galilean Judaism, and more perniciously, (2) unexamined anti-Judaism flowing from sources in German biblical scholarship promoting a stark distinction between Jesus and Galilean Judaism on the one hand, and Jerusalem and the Jewish authorities on the other.[43] In light of these accusations, Ruiz calls for a reexamination of *Galilean Journey*'s "hidden assumptions" and the "unexamined implications of its discourse about mestizaje."

In what he terms "a rare and unfortunate combination for a volume that began as a doctoral dissertation," Ruiz detects a "ruralist romanticism verging on anti-intellectualism" in Elizondo's description of the Galilean Judaism that nurtures Jesus' worldview. He says Elizondo contrasts the "refreshing originality" of Galilean Judaism characterized by "the commonsense, grass-roots wisdom of practical expertise," with the "intellectual preoccupation" of Jerusalem. And he attacks Elizondo's assertion that "Galilean faith in the God of the fathers was thus more personal, purer, simpler, and more spontaneous. It was not encumbered or suffocated by the religious scrupulosities of the Jewish intelligentsia."[44] Ruiz, however, discerns another, much deeper problem in *Galilean Journey*. He argues that some of the biblical scholarship supporting Elizondo's overstatement of the tensions between Galilee and Jerusalem evidences the specter of an unexamined anti-Judaism.[45]

Ruiz's central indictment on this score is, "At the heart of Elizondo's inadvertent anti-Judaism is his uncritical embrace of Western European exegetical discourses that were themselves irreparably racialized."[46] The key piece of evidence is the fact that Ernst Lohmeyer's *Galiläa und Jerusalem* (1936) appears in Elizondo's bibliography.[47] In this work, Lohmeyer sets Galilee against Jerusalem as part of a two-site origin theory of Christianity,[48] contrasting a universalistic, Son of Man eschatology associated with Galilee with a nationalistic, Jewish eschatology emerging from Jerusalem. Once the two sites are juxtaposed in this manner, Ruiz asserts that a supersessionist and ultimately anti-Jewish/anti-Semitic view of Christianity as triumphing over Judaism follows. This leads Ruiz to the startling claim that "here then, are the twisted roots of Elizondo's 'Galilee principle' and his 'Jerusalem principle.'"[49]

Ruiz views *Galilean Journey* as a tragic instance of irresponsible theological research, a negative example that underscores his call for greater cooperation between systematic theologians and biblical scholars. To be clear, Ruiz does not accuse Elizondo of being an anti-Semite, but rather criticizes what he sees as an inadvertent anti-Judaism in *Galilean Journey* owing to its naïve or ignorant use of sources. Thus, Ruiz concludes his essay by admonishing systematic theologians to bear in mind the contextuality of exegetical discourses, which, by implication, is a standard met neither by Elizondo nor by the many theologians who have drawn upon *Galilean Journey* for inspiration.

Though the charge of anti-Judaism (latent or otherwise) represents the most serious criticism of *Galilean Journey,* it is sometimes accompanied by questions of hermeneutical method. Jeffrey Siker seconds Ruiz's criticism that *Galilean Journey* enacts an underlying anti-Judaism in its portrayal of Jerusalem's Judaism as an ossified, legalistic religiosity.[50] He goes beyond Ruiz's charge of ruralist romanticism, however, arguing that Elizondo simply makes claims without foundation. The problem is a hermeneutical one for Siker. He views Elizondo as reversing the "proper" interpretive strategy of "moving from the historical Jesus to a theological appropriation of Jesus," charging that "it appears that Elizondo is really working the other way around, applying the reality of modern mestizo culture in an anachronistic manner onto the map of first-century Galilee and claiming it as an historic reality."[51] Thus, he portrays Elizondo's hermeneutical strategy as an ideologically driven effort to provide a scriptural basis for a theological interpretation of *mestizaje.*

Siker believes that Elizondo does not rely on historical Jesus research in his reconstruction of Galilee, and so questions the entire notion of a *mestizo* Jesus. For Siker, "This anachronistic rendering of first-century Galilee in the image of the borderlands of the American Southwest can undergird Elizondo's theological project only if he is willing to advocate what increasingly appears to be an historical fiction, Galilee as the land of *mestizaje.*"[52] What further complicates the scenario is Siker's understanding of *mestizaje.* He states, "Elizondo poses the idea of *mestizaje* in Hegelian terms as the transcendent synthesis of what appear now to be two lesser realities."[53] The implications of Siker's diagnosis lead to a similar conclusion as that asserted by Ruiz: not only is *Galilean Journey* bereft of support from biblical research, but given the nefarious nature of its latent anti-Judaism, both the text and the theological enterprise of relating the Galilean Jesus to the notion of *mestizaje* are called into question.

Guide for the Journey: Jesus, Galilean Jew and Faithful Dissenter

Elizondo's critics, then, not only raise substantive questions about *Galilean Journey*, but also pose broader questions regarding the relationship between biblical-historical research and the contemporary appropriation of sacred texts by theologians and communities of faith. Though voicing a relative sympathy for his wider theological program, the basis of their concerns resides in what they perceive to be misguided or erroneous claims about the historical Jesus and the Galilee in which he lived. Thus, historical Jesus research is assumed to provide constructive counterevidence and much needed norms for what can and cannot be said about Jesus.[54] Of course, historical Jesus scholarship is not without its own problems. From ongoing debates among scholars who study Jesus and first-century Galilee, to critics of the entire enterprise who view the historical Jesus as the wrong object of study, historical research on Jesus must not be seen monolithically or simplistically as a clear standard against which all claims about Jesus can be judged. Moreover, as contemporary hermeneutics has demonstrated, the reader's own "horizon of understanding" must be factored in as a crucial component in the process of interpretation. Indeed, I believe this has been the area of Elizondo's primary contribution to theological discourse.[55]

Accordingly, while the final section of this essay addresses the aforementioned criticisms of *Galilean Journey*, it also outlines what I see as fundamental hermeneutical and methodological parameters for the proper use of historical Jesus (and Galilee) research, and suggests how these may be used as correctives to the problematic aspects of Elizondo's thought. My claim is that, on the one hand, Elizondo's critics and more recent historical research on Jesus and Galilee both provide important correctives to aspects of *Galilean Journey*. On the other hand, however, I use Elizondo's three "principles," which undermine the logic of exclusion, to address some of the concerns raised above, and to highlight certain problematic aspects of the critiques themselves.

READING JESUS: HISTORICAL, HISTORIC, AND HISTORICIZED

Historical research on Galilee and Jesus helps to clarify two shortcomings identified by the aforementioned critics of *Galilean Journey*. First, recent studies undermine the polarities embodied in two outdated and extreme portraits of Galilee at the time of Jesus.[56] It appears the region was neither the staunchly Jewish enclave with no outside cultural exchange or influence favored by some commentators, nor the cosmopolitan, pluralistic region with a limited or non-Jewish identity promoted by others.[57] The more likely scenario is of a Galilee that, though possessing a diverse population and including the imperial cities of Tiberias and Sepphoris, remains profoundly Jewish in identity and rooted in the symbol system of Jerusalem.[58] And for all of the cultural interaction that may have occurred, Galilee seems to have been a tense and conflictual setting, not a sunny cosmopolitan oasis. Thus, to the degree that Elizondo sees Galilee in the latter terms, this scholarship represents a helpful corrective.

Second, recent studies have provided valuable information about Galilean tensions with Judea and the Temple authorities of Jerusalem. Recognizing that these tensions have been exploited by anti-Jewish theologies, contemporary scholarship largely insists that they must be interpreted in the context of intra-community struggles typical of a vibrant and complex first-century Judaism. How to do so remains a debated topic. Richard Horsley situates Jesus and the early Jesus movement within a stream of Galilean resistance movements in the Late Second Temple period.[59] Arguing that Galilee's development is historically distinct from that of Judea, Horsley stresses traditions of Galilean independence within Israel and resentment of the Jerusalem establishment, while emphasizing its profound Jewish identity. Sean Freyne envisions much closer relations between Galilean Jews and their counterparts in Judea, arguing for an orthogenetic relationship with Jerusalem grounded in a shared worldview and symbol system.[60] He insists that this shared worldview implies a Jesus deeply familiar with the Jewish Scriptures of his day.[61] From stories of conquest and settlement to the universalizing vision of the Isaian corpus, Jewish tradition nurtures creative and critical elements in Jesus' ministry and preaching. In this way, Jesus' conflicts with some of the Temple authorities find their proper context in his synthesis of various strands of Jewish thought.[62]

Though disagreements abound regarding the particulars, contemporary historical scholars studying Jesus and Galilee generally agree that Jesus' conflicts with Jerusalem authorities do not lead to the conclusion that he is condemning or moving beyond Judaism. This consensus serves as an important corrective to the tenor of some of Elizondo's comments about the novelty of Jesus' preaching or message,[63] which can sound as if Jesus is breaking with Judaism itself. Historical research on Jesus allows us to frame his position as that of a critical and prophetic "insider" who is faithful to Judaism—a position, as will be demonstrated, that is analogous to what Elizondo ultimately assumes himself.

Thus, I would agree on the one hand that historical research on Jesus and Galilee provides an important corrective to contemporary formulations about Jesus, including those of Elizondo. At its best, this research enacts a negative function, guiding what cannot said about Jesus without dictating what can be said,[64] and providing leads for new theological ideas. On the other hand, this important function does not diminish serious difficulties with both the nature and the object of these studies themselves. As Terrence Tilley notes, several critics of the so-called Third Quest seem to highlight the need for new approaches.[65]

Seen in authors as varied as Elisabeth Schüssler Fiorenza, James D. G. Dunn, and Larry Hurtado, these authors seem to shift the focus from the historical Jesus to what Tilley calls the "historic Jesus," the person remembered by his followers who enact that memory in story, worship, ritual, and action.[66] Tilley summarizes the methodological significance of this shift:

> The fundamental methodological point we can take from their work is crucial: practices like living in and living out the *basileia tou theou*, worship, and remembering in the community do not merely count in understanding the significance of Christological claims, but in fact constitute the context of discipleship, the context in which the imaginative and faithful Christological claims in the developing tradition can even have significance.[67]

If Tilley's thesis is correct, Elizondo's claims as articulated in the principles he espouses are better tested by examining how they are lived out in believing Latino/a communities, and by comparing this with the practical manner in which Jesus' followers enact his memory—be it through worship, the transmission of stories through oral tradition, or actions motivated by the confession of Jesus as Christ. While this comparison to the "historic" Jesus enacted by his followers in story, worship, ritual, and action does not replace "historical" Jesus and Galilee research, it does offer a more nuanced and, I would argue, appropriate standard for judging Elizondo's claims than what critics of *Galilean Journey* have offered to date.

New programs of "historic" Jesus research may indeed open up fruitful avenues of analysis. They nonetheless require a hermeneutics committed both to reading "behind" the text, which characterizes the critics of *Galilean Journey*, cited above, and to reading "in front of" the biblical text,[68] which I would argue more properly characterizes Elizondo's approach. My point is that in *Galilean Journey* Elizondo does not seek to describe the historical Jesus, but rather focuses on the theological import for the reader of the Gospels' portrayal of Jesus as a Galilean. Elizondo reminds us that Galilee, as it is theologically and symbolically evoked in the Gospels, represents a marginality that resonates with the marginal location of U.S. Latinos/as who read the Gospels today. This perspective constitutes the particular hermeneutic of *Galilean Journey* and demarcates its unique contribution. Thus, while historical research may provide cautionary or regulative principles of interpretation or be used to suggest new theological connections, it must be employed cautiously, always explicitly acknowledging the historian's own interpretive horizon.[69]

In this connection, the interpretive locus of marginalized peoples adds an important dimension to the "historical" vs. "historic" Jesus debate. I would argue, in fact, that Elizondo's three principles "historicize" the Jesus found in the Gospels (to borrow the term from Ignacio Ellacuría),[70] and play a crucial role in his correlational interpretive framework. It is through the mediation of such interpretive devices that the experience of marginalization, typical of South-Texas Mexican-Americans of Elizondo's generation, is able to illuminate and to actualize the untapped semantic potential of the marginalization of Jesus portrayed in the Gospels. Just as the Gospels historicize in their own narrative and historical worlds the good news announced by Jesus through portraits that highlight the way he resists and overcomes marginalization, so Elizondo's interpretation illumines and historicizes the untapped semantic potential of those portraits for faithful discipleship today. Therefore, while discussions about the "historical" and "historic" Jesus serve to draw our attention to the relationship between the world "behind" the text and the reader "in front of" it, they are enriched when we ask how the Jesus found in each location is "historicized." With this principle in mind, let us return to the criticisms of *Galilean Journey,* noting that, while they point to important issues in Elizondo's work, if taken too far they enact the very logic of exclusion against which they protest.

FAITHFUL DISSENT: SPEAKING AGAINST ONE'S OWN

Jean-Pierre Ruiz correctly criticizes *Galilean Journey* for espousing a kind of ruralist romanticization in its portrayal of first-century Galilee. Given the sad history linking negative portrayals of the Jerusalem/Jewish intelligentsia to anti-Semitic scholarship, he is right to address this issue. Sweeping statements contrasting the fresh originality of Galilean faith with the hypocrisy of the Jerusalemite religious rulers do not belong in a scholarly treatment of Jesus and contribute little to our understanding. On the other hand, Ruiz's accusation that the text is anti-intellectual seems to suggest that Elizondo demeans the intellectual task itself. Similarly, he appears to suggest that Elizondo's portrayal of Jesus as critical of Jewish religious leaders places Jesus outside the circle of Judaism itself.

I would argue, instead, that Elizondo's "rural romanticism" constitutes an extension of the Galilee principle, his theological articulation of the preferential option for the poor. *Galilean Journey* attacks the exclusionary anthropological laws of *mestizaje,* finding beauty and dignity in the *mestizo* who has been marginated and excluded. The fact that Elizondo lifts up the dignity of the rural peasant is an important trope, representing a point of view found among those who have been marginalized, the self-defense of those who have been told that they do not have the intellectual capacity to match wits with their oppressors. A wealth of examples from Latino/a culture provide a trajectory within which to situate Elizondo's statements.[71] In this world, as Paul would suggest to his mainly non-Jewish followers from the middle and lower classes, the fool confounds the wise. Ironically, in doing so they show where true wisdom abides, which is crucial. Thus, what may seem to some like anti-intellectualism turns out from another perspective to be a faithful reliance on a God that confounds the wise, and unites learning with true wisdom. While I grant that Elizondo's portrayal requires pruning, I would argue that it captures something real in the perspective of the peasant at the margins.

Correspondingly, Elizondo's critique of part of the Jerusalem Jewish intelligentsia of first-century Israel is not a deprecation of the intellect itself, but a statement about its proper use. The seemingly contradictory trajectories of Elizondo's own biography make the point: he criticizes an exclusivist intelligentsia while writing his own doctoral dissertation; he is a parish priest from San Antonio on a one-year sojourn in Paris, one of the great intellectual centers of the last eight hundred years, funded mainly by the meager savings of his working-class mother. In the end, I would argue that Elizondo's critique of the Jewish intelligentsia in Jerusalem is no more "anti-intellectual" than that of Ruiz, when the latter (rightfully) questions the "centrist" bias of much contemporary biblical criticism. Both highlight how "intelligentsia" can lose touch with and marginalize others. What remains to be seen, however, is whether Elizondo's criticism of the Jewish intelligentsia of Jesus' time evidences an anti-Jewish bias.

Nineteenth-century anti-Jewish readings of the Gospels divorce Jesus from his Jewish heritage and Hellenize the early Jesus movement in making the case for a supersessionist Christianity. Elizondo, however, makes no argument for the superior origins of Christianity over against Judaism. He does not advocate Lohmeyer's two-site origin theory, much less Grundmann's notion of a pagan or Aryan Jesus. *Galilean Journey* falls into danger when it amplifies aspects of the conflict between Jesus and the Jerusalem authorities, and vague statements about the Jewish law becoming a burden or about the legalistic scrupulosity of Pharisees not only beg verification, but beckon harmful stereotypes. Still, despite these shortcomings, Elizondo does not divorce Jesus from his Jewish identity. Rather, he emphasizes Jesus' identity as a Jew who, while remaining firmly rooted in his tradition, must face the double marginalization of a *mestizo*.

> As a Galilean confronting Jerusalem, Jesus confronted a structured system to which at the same time he did and he did not belong: he was not one of the in-group, but neither was he a total outsider. In his Galilean identity, he questioned the official structures. *But still, he was a Jew; he questioned the system from within.* . . . As a Galilean he demonstrates the role of a marginal person who by reason of being marginal is both an insider and an outsider—partly both, yet fully neither.[72]

Rejection by one's own constitutes a central theme in Elizondo's treatment of *mestizaje*. Accordingly, I would argue that scholarly evaluation of Elizondo's treatment of the Jewishness of Jesus and his Galilean context must move beyond its present, somewhat narrow focus on the self-identity of Jesus to include the perception by others of the Jewishness of Jesus—specifically, the views of those among the first-century Jewish intelligentsia and leadership in Jerusalem. The claim that Jesus was critical of the authorities in Jerusalem does not make Jesus any less Jewish.[73] Baldly stated, the claim that it does can be said to echo the logic of first-century and contemporary elites who interpret such protests as heretical. On the other hand, Elizondo brings the insight from the borderland that, while those on the border may identify with the center, those living at the center(s) often reject people from the border in the name of purity. Elizondo's Jerusalem principle, then, provides us a model for critical-fidelity grounded in the prophetic ministry of the Galilean Jesus and its historical rejection by the Jerusalemite authorities. In fact, neither the Jerusalem principle nor its sources lead inevitably to an anti-Jewish or an anti-intellectual Jesus.

In light of this discussion on "historicizing" Jesus, the final charge that Elizondo's theological ruminations on *mestizaje* reverse the "proper" strategy of assessment seems unfounded. First-century Galilee, like all places, is a constructed and contested space, and Jesus' own ministry has been examined fruitfully using that notion.[74] Though historical research has much to offer, it is subject to the same problems of construction as contemporary theology and offers no more an "objective" place on which to base its conclusions.[75] Elizondo does not superimpose *mestizaje* on Galilee, but rather rereads the Gospel narratives from the perspective of *mestizaje*, bringing a fresh perspective that actualizes the untapped semantic potential of the marginalized Galilee portrayed in the Gospels. Elizondo's work, like that of other explicitly contextual theologies of marginalized peoples, offers distinctive insights into issues of power and exclusion particularly from that location of marginalization that has too often been overlooked by elite interpreters.[76]

Finally, the accusation that Elizondo's understanding of *mestizaje* involves a Hegelian sublation of inferior races is an unfortunate example of a dangerous logic of exclusion, particularly the mistaken assertion that Elizondo's focus on raising up the dignity of those facing double rejection is based on the exclusion of others. Elizondo argues that a society is enriched when it embraces the "mixture" of the *mestizo/a,* but he never suggests that this should happen at the expense of others. Ultimately, Elizondo's view of *mestizaje* corresponds to the Resurrection principle that "only love can triumph over evil," and that love rejects all forms of exclusion.

CONCLUSION

Christian claims that Jesus opposed the Jewish authorities have too often tragically focused on the former term, "Jewish," when they should emphasize the latter, "authorities." Jesus was a faithful Jew whose prophetic critique springs precisely from fidelity to the religious tradition of which he was a part. The Gospels attest that Jesus assumed a critical prophetic stance toward the wrongful excesses of some of the authorities of his day, a stance similar to that of Jesus' prophetic predecessors: Isaiah, Jeremiah, and Amos. This is the tradition of Paul's confrontation with Peter, Catherine of Siena's admonishment of the Avignon papacy, and Martin Luther King's scolding of clergymen who would side with the segregationists. The assertion that Jesus criticizes the religious authorities of his own tradition need not, indeed must not, be understood to imply that Jesus is moving outside of his tradition. Ironically, claiming so enacts the logic of his adversaries among the elite. By equating faithful dissent with the betrayal of one's tradition, this trope perpetuates the age-old strategy of exclusion directed against the *mestizo/a,* the borderland figure abandoned by both sides.

The deepest pain of the *mestizo/a,* so powerfully articulated by Elizondo, consists in feeling loyalty and a sense of identification with two groups, and being rejected by both. For some, rejection flows from characteristics not voluntarily possessed: one's culture, race, gender, and so on. For others, exclusion follows from a stance: called a traitor for protesting a nation's unjust war, or a heretic for excoriating a church's injustice and scandal. Purity codes, be they racial/ethnic or ideological, enact logics of exclusion grounded in one-dimensional portraits of those who protest as "the other."

In this article, I have argued that scholars of the historical Jesus and Galilee offer important correctives to aspects of the views of Virgilio Elizondo and other contemporary theologians. On the other hand, I have insisted that theology has an important, sometimes corrective role to play as well. While John Meier describes Jesus as a "marginal Jew in a marginal province at the eastern end of the Roman empire,"[77] Elizondo offers insight into the significance of that marginality from the margin itself. Elizondo reminds us that "marginal" is not an innocent term, and that "marginal" means "marginalized." He correlates the double rejection of U.S. Latinos/as with the situation of the Jewish Jesus of Galilee, whom the Gospels portray as the object of a double rejection that leads to his execution.

My hope is that scholars of both the historical Jesus and the preferential option for the poor will continue to mutually enrich each other's work, and work together to end the scourge of anti-Judaism in Christian theology. In this essay, I have argued that biblical scholarship offers a helpful corrective to certain aspects of *Galilean Journey.* On the other hand, I have tried to show how, by lifting the veil on the logic of exclusion, Virgilio Elizondo amplifies the words and illumines the lives of contemporary prophets, authentic disciples of the Galilean Jesus carrying on his ministry in the marginalized Galilees of the world today.

NOTES

1. See, for example, the critique of Jon Sobrino in John P. Meier, "The Bible as a Source for Theology," in *Catholic Theological Society of America, Proceedings of the Forty-Third Annual Convention,* ed. George Kilcourse, Toronto, June 15–19, 1988, 53:3.
2. Virgilio Elizondo, *Galilean Journey: The Mexican-American Promise,* 2nd ed. (Maryknoll, NY: Orbis Books, 2000).
3. Mary C. Boys, *Has God Only One Blessing? Judaism as a Source of Christian Self-Understanding* (New York: Paulist, 2000), 314 n. 19.
4. Here, the work of feminist theologians, in its self-criticism and (re-)constructive vision, illustrates analogous possibilities. For example, see Judith Plaskow, "Anti-Judaism in Feminist Christian Interpretation," in *Searching the Scriptures: A Feminist Introduction,* ed. Elisabeth Schüssler Fiorenza (New York: Crossroad, 1993), 116–29; Elisabeth Schüssler Fiorenza, *Jesus, Miriam's Child, Sophia's Prophet: Critical Issues in Feminist Christology* (New York: Continuum, 1994).
5. Noting this violence helps to overcome a romanticization of the term. On its limits, see Roberto Goizueta, "¿La Raza Cósmica? The Vision of José Vasconcelos," *Journal of Hispanic/Latino Theology* 1, no. 2 (1994): 5–27.

6. Elizondo writes, "What human beings reject, God chooses as God's very own" (*Galilean Journey*, 91).

7. Elizondo asserts, "God chooses an oppressed people, not to bring them comfort in their oppression, but to enable them to confront, transcend, and transform whatever in the oppressor society diminishes and destroys the fundamental dignity of human nature" (ibid., 103).

8. Elizondo writes, "Only love can triumph over evil, and no human power can prevail against the power of unlimited love" (ibid., 115).

9. Throughout this analysis of the text proper, I prefer to use Elizondo's own phrase "Mexican-American" rather than "Hispanic" or "Latino/a."

10. For a succinct elucidation of the method, see David Tracy, "Theological Method," in *Christian Theology*, ed. Peter C. Hodgson and Robert H. King (Philadelphia: Fortress, 1985), 35–60. A fuller account, including the development of the notion of the theological classic, may be found in David Tracy, *The Analogical Imagination: Christian Theology and the Culture of Pluralism* (New York: Crossroad, 1981).

11. Clodovis Boff articulates this method as a triad of utilized "mediations." So, see-judge-act translates into the use of socioanalytical, hermeneutic, and practical mediations. See "Epistemology and Method of the Theology of Liberation," in *Mysterium Liberationis: Fundamental Concepts of Liberation Theology*, ed. Jon Sobrino and Ignacio Ellacuría (Maryknoll, NY: Orbis Books, 1990), 57–85. For an ecclesiastical example of the method, see the pastoral letters of Salvadoran Archbishop Oscar Romero in Oscar Romero, *Voice of the Voiceless: The Four Pastoral Letters and Other Statements*, trans. Michael J. Walsh (Maryknoll, NY: Orbis Books, 1985).

12. Here Elizondo's innovative work fulfills the 1965 mandate of Vatican II stated in the *Pastoral Constitution on the Church in the Modern World*: "In every age, the church carries the responsibility of reading the signs of the times and of interpreting them in light of the Gospel, if it is to carry out its task" (*Gaudium et Spes*, 4).

13. Elizondo never explicitly refers to the see-judge-act model, but I believe it is a fruitful way to interpret the three major parts of the text: "The Mexican-American Experience" (see), "The Gospel Matrix" (judge), and "From Margination to New Creation" (act). See Elizondo's essay in this volume for his indebtedness to this pastoral model.

14. Elizondo develops this category more fully in his *The Future Is Mestizo: Life Where Cultures Meet*, 2nd ed. (Boulder: University Press of Colorado, 2000).

15. Elizondo, *Galilean Journey*, 17–18.

16. It is interesting to note how Elizondo's first law resonates with the basic insight of Edward Said's highly influential work, *Orientalism* (New York: Pantheon, 1978). This is not to imply any overt relationship, but rather to signal how subsequent Latino/a theologians will read *Galilean Journey* in relation to postcolonial theory.

17. Elizondo, *Galilean Journey*, 18.

18. Ibid., 32.

19. Certainly, foremost among these is La Morenita, Our Lady of Guadalupe, whom Elizondo has named elsewhere as "mother of a new creation." See Elizondo, *Guadalupe: Mother of the New Creation* (Maryknoll, NY: Orbis Books, 1997).

20. Outstanding examples include the multivolume project that began with John P. Meier, *A Marginal Jew: Rethinking the Historical Jesus* (New York: Doubleday, 1991), and the work of a leading member of the Jesus Seminar: John Dominic Crossan. See, e.g., Crossan, *The Historical Jesus: The Life of a Mediterranean Jewish Peasant* (San Francisco: HarperSanFrancisco, 1991).

21. Elizondo, *Galilean Journey,* 47.
22. Ibid.
23. Elizabeth A. Johnson, *Consider Jesus: Waves of Renewal in Christology* (New York: Crossroad, 1990), 49. Johnson describes the "first wave" of renewal as occurring in the 1950s and 1960s "when theologians pondered the dogmatic confession of Jesus Christ's identity" that yielded a "deeper appreciation of the genuine humanity of the Word made flesh, and of the dignity and value of every human being."
24. Examples cited by Johnson include Karl Rahner (in his later years), Edward Schillebeeckx, Hans Küng, Walter Kasper, Gerald O'Collins, James Mackey, Monica Hellwig, and William Thompson.
25. Johnson, *Consider Jesus,* 50.
26. Elizondo, *Galilean Journey,* 54. Methodologically, Elizondo's openness to biblical explanatory methods moves away from Gadamer's comprehensive rejection of method and more closely to the "arc of understanding" found in the work of Paul Ricoeur.
27. Ibid., 52.
28. See Elizondo's essay in this volume for a clarification of his treatment of Jerusalem.
29. Elizondo, *Galilean Journey,* 91. Perhaps the theologian who has developed this notion the most in the past few decades is Elizondo's good friend Gustavo Gutiérrez. In addition to his landmark work, *A Theology of Liberation* (1973; Maryknoll, NY: Orbis Books, 1988), see Gutiérrez's concise explanation in "Option for the Poor," in *Mysterium Liberationis: Fundamental Concepts of Liberation Theology,* ed. Jon Sobrino and Ignacio Ellacuría (Maryknoll, NY: Orbis Books, 1990), 235–50.
30. Elizondo, *Galilean Journey,* 103.
31. Ibid., 115.
32. The following is indebted to the summary of Hispanic Christology done by Michelle A. Gonzalez, "Jesus," in *Handbook of Latina/o Theologies,* ed. Edwin David Aponte and Miguel A. De La Torre (St. Louis: Chalice, 2006), 17–24. Her tripartite division of this work is *mestizo* Jesus, liberating Jesus, and accompanying Jesus.
33. Of course, this designation is merely heuristic. In fact, most of the authors combine all three themes in some way. Another dimension of Hispanic research has focused on the reception of Jesus as expressed in symbols of popular religiosity. See, e.g., Orlando Espín, *The Faith of the People: Theological Reflections on Popular Catholicism* (Maryknoll, NY: Orbis Books, 1997), 77–82.
34. Luis G. Pedraja, *Jesus Is My Uncle: Christology from a Hispanic Perspective* (Nashville: Abingdon, 1999).
35. Miguel De La Torre, *The Quest for the Cuban Christ: A Historical Search* (Gainesville: University of Florida Press, 2002).
36. Karen May Davalos, "'The Real Way of Praying': The Via Crucis, *Mexicano* Sacred Space, and the Architecture of Domination," in *Horizons of the Sacred: Mexican Traditions in U.S. Catholicism,* ed. Timothy Matovina and Gary Riebe-Estrella (Ithaca, NY: Cornell University Press, 2002), 41–68.
37. Ada María Isasi-Díaz, "Christ in Mujerista Theology," in *Thinking of Christ: Proclamation, Explanation, Meaning,* ed. Tatha Wiley (New York: Continuum, 2003).
38. Perhaps the most powerful example of this theme, and indeed a theological synthesis of all of the above-mentioned themes, can be found in Roberto Goi-

zueta, *Caminemos con Jesús: Toward a Hispanic/Latino Theology of Accompaniment* (Maryknoll, NY: Orbis Books, 1995).

39. Of course, not all talk of new creation is innocent. For a critique of biological determinism latent in the language of *mestizaje* and its recovery, see Rubén Rosario Rodríguez, *Racism and God-Talk: A Latino/a Perspective* (New York: New York University Press, 2008).

40. Elizondo, *Galilean Journey,* 51–53 and 68–70, respectively.

41. Jean-Pierre Ruiz, "Good Fences and Good Neighbors? Biblical Scholars and Theologians," *Journal of Hispanic/Latino Theology* (May 2007). (Because it is now an electronic journal, no citations of the article will contain page numbers.)

42. Ibid.

43. For this second accusation, Ruiz follows much of the argument laid out in Boys, *Has God Only One Blessing?*

44. Elizondo, *Galilean Journey,* 51–52.

45. Indeed, it leads Ruiz to assert that "odd anti-intellectualism cum anti-Judaism is a persistent motif in *Galilean Journey.*"

46. Ruiz, "Good Fences and Good Neighbors." Here, Ruiz is indebted to the broader analysis of Shawn Kelley, *Racializing Jesus: Race, Ideology and the Formation of Modern Biblical Scholarship* (New York: Routledge, 2002).

47. Elizondo elsewhere cites Lohmeyer in the text as part of a triad of recent scholars (along with R. H. Lightfoot and W. Marxsen) who have pointed to Galilee as a significant theological motif in the Gospels (*Galilean Journey,* 50).

48. Here Ruiz refers to the work of Susannah Heschel, *Abraham Geiger and the Jewish Jesus* (Chicago: University of Chicago Press, 1998).

49. Ruiz, "Good Fences and Good Neighbors." Lest there be any doubts about the implications of this tie, Ruiz adds that shortly after Lohmeyer's work appeared, Walter Grundmann (who does not appear in Elizondo's bibliography) suggested that Jesus' taking of the title "Son of Man" proved his Galilean and thus his Aryan origin.

50. As with Ruiz, Siker understands the Galilee-Jerusalem distinction as ultimately supersessionist. "Elizondo's image of a decrepit and ossified Judaism in Jerusalem buys into a now discredited Christian caricature of Judaism as the dying religion that gave way to nascent Christianity." See Jeffrey S. Siker, "Historicizing a Racialized Jesus: Case Studies in the 'Black Christ,' the 'Mestizo Christ,' and White Critique," *Biblical Interpretation* 15 (2007): 43.

51. Ibid., 40.

52. Ibid., 41.

53. Ibid., 46.

54. This is true particularly in the case of Boys and Siker. And while Ruiz warns against the naïve appropriation of historical research and its underlying racialized discourses, he offers neither constructive counterevidence, nor an alternative construction.

55. For a concise summary of the relevant developments in hermeneutics, see Richard E. Palmer, *Hermeneutics: Interpretation Theory in Schleiermacher, Dilthey, Heidegger, and Gadamer* (Evanston, IL: Northwestern University Press, 1969).

56. For a very helpful summary of current research on Galilee, see Mark Rapinchuk, "The Galilee and Jesus in Recent Research," *Currents in Biblical Research* 2, no. 2 (2004): 197–222.

57. There are differing ways to portray this reality. For example, Douglas Edwards argues that the villages of Galilee had access to urban markets and engaged in intra- and interregional trade, while Richard Horsley envisions a more

traditional agrarian society, but with a greater population diversity than Judea. See Douglas Edwards, "The Socio-Economic and Cultural Ethos of the Lower Galilee in the First Century: Implications for the Nascent Jesus Movement," in Lee I. Levine, *The Galilee in Late Antiquity* (New York: Jewish Theological Seminary of America, 1992), 53, and Richard A. Horsley, *Galilee: History, Politics, People* (Valley Forge, PA: Trinity Press International, 1995), 243.

58. Debate continues over whether to characterize Sepphoris and Tiberias as predominantly Jewish or Gentile. Batey argues for a reevaluation of Jesus' sayings because of Nazareth's proximity to a Greco-Roman city like Sepphoris, while Myers and Chancey see little evidence of its Hellenized character in the first century. See Richard Batey, "Sepphoris and the Jesus Movement," *New Testament Studies* 46 (2001): 402–9; Eric M. Myers and Mark Chancey, "How Jewish Was Sepphoris in Jesus' Time?" *Biblical Archaeology Review* 26, no. 4 (July–August 2000): 18–33, 61.

59. See Richard Horsley, "Popular Messianic Movements around the Time of Jesus," *Catholic Biblical Quarterly* 46 (1984): 471–95; and "'Like One of the Prophets of Old': Two Types of Popular Prophets at the Time of Jesus," *Catholic Biblical Quarterly* 47 (1985): 435–63.

60. Sean Freyne, "Urban-Rural Relations in First-Century Galilee: Some Suggestions from the Literary Sources," in *The Galilee in Late Antiquity*, ed. Lee I. Levine (New York: Jewish Theological Seminary of America, 1992); and "Behind the Names: Galileans, Samaritans, *Ioudaioi*," in *Galilee through the Centuries: Confluence of Cultures*, ed. Eric M. Meyers (Winona Lake, IN: Eisenbrauns, 1999), 39–56.

61. In making this claim, Freyne intones Gerd Theissen's criteria of historical plausibility, relying on influence and context, as superior to the older principle of dissimilarity that stressed the uniqueness of Jesus over against his Jewish traditions. Sean Freyne, *Jesus, A Jewish Galilean* (New York: T&T Clark International, 2004), 11–12.

62. As Freyne avers, "These various strands provide a broader and richer set of association for Jesus' word and deed against the temple, without in any sense removing him from his own tradition as this had been articulated by prophetic voices. . . . It was a potent mix of wisdom and apocalyptic, creation and restoration, and Jesus' particular synthesis of the various stands, allied to his passionate concern for the poor, who had been marginalized by the temple system, help to make the incident both predictable and intelligible" (ibid., 162–63).

63. E.g., Elizondo states, "It is equally evident that from the very beginning [Jesus' followers] had difficulty accepting and understanding his ways, especially in the light of their laws, customs, and tradition." Later in that section, he claims, "Yet from the very beginning he begins to break with many of their traditions. Every 'tradition' that was supposed to be a way of forcing the kingdom to come is questioned or transgressed by Jesus—the purity laws, the pious practices, the religious observances" (*Galilean Journey*, 65).

64. For example, John Meier identifies four ways that the appropriation of historical Jesus research may serve the interests of theology by working against attempts to reduce faith in Christ to a content-less cipher, to swallow up the real humanity of Jesus in a docetic manner, to domesticate Jesus, and to co-opt Jesus for political programs (*A Marginal Jew*, 1:199).

65. See Terrence W. Tilley, "Remembering the Historic Jesus—A New Research Program?" *Theological Studies* 68 (2007): 3–35. He develops these ideas in his own constructive project, *The Disciples' Jesus: Christology as Reconciling Practice* (Maryknoll, NY: Orbis Books, 2008).

66. Significant works by these authors include: Elisabeth Schüssler Fiorenza, *Jesus and the Politics of Interpretation* (New York: Continuum, 2000); James G. D. Dunn, *Jesus Remembered, Christianity in the Making*, vol. 1 (Grand Rapids: Eerdmans, 2003); Larry Hurtado, *Lord Jesus Christ: Devotion to Jesus in Earliest Christianity* (Grand Rapids: Eerdmans, 2003).

67. Tilley, "Remembering the Historic Jesus," 34.

68. The nomenclature here comes from that landmark work of hermeneutics, Hans Georg Gadamer's *Truth and Method*, 2nd rev. ed. (New York: Continuum, 1999).

69. Thus, rather than adopt Gadamer's more thoroughgoing rejection of interpretive methods (after all, for Gadamer, Truth and Method really means Truth or Method), I would subscribe to the manner that Paul Ricoeur's arc of understanding-interpretation-understanding both allows for the contribution of critical-interpretive methods in dealing with our distance from texts while recognizing the reader's or community's interpretive horizon. E.g., see Paul Ricoeur, *Interpretation Theory: Discourse and the Surplus of Meaning* (Fort Worth: Texas Christian University, 1976).

70. Ellacuría defines this neologism as "Demonstrating the impact of certain concepts within a specific reality is what is understood here as their historicization. Hence, historicization is a principle of de-ideologization." "La historización del concepto de propiedad como principio de desideologización," in *Veinte años de historia en El Salvador 1969–1989* (San Salvador: UCA Editores, 1993), 591. For a further explanation of this term in Ellacuría's complex philosophy, see Kevin F. Burke, *The Ground beneath the Cross* (Washington, DC: Georgetown University Press, 2000), and Michael E. Lee, *Bearing the Weight of Salvation* (New York: Crossroad, 2007).

71. Consider the Puerto Rican rhapsodizing of the *jíbaro* figure, or comedic tales of Juan Bobo (a synonym for fool), the cinematic portrayals by the Mexican icon Cantinflas, or even the retelling of Juan Diego's confrontation of episcopal authority.

72. Elizondo, *Galilean Journey*, 107 (italics added).

73. John Meier's summary is instructive. "Jesus, the poor layman turned prophet and teacher, the religious figure from rural Galilee without credentials, met his death in Jerusalem at least in part because of his clash with the rich aristocratic urban priesthood. To the latter, a poor layman from the Galilean countryside with disturbing doctrines and claims was marginal both in the sense of being dangerously antiestablishment and in the sense of lacking a power base in the capital. He could be easily brushed aside into the dustbin of death" (*Marginal Jew*, 1:9).

74. See Halvor Moxnes, *Putting Jesus in His Place: A Radical Vision of Household and Kingdom* (Louisville, KY: Westminster John Knox Press, 2003).

75. Even archaeology is ambiguous in this respect. See Marianne Sawicki, *Crossing Galilee: Architectures of Contact in the Occupied Land of Jesus* (Harrisburg, PA: Trinity Press, 1998).

76. For a feminist correlate to this principle, see Mary McClintock Fulkerson, *Changing the Subject: Women's Discourses and Feminist Theology* (Minneapolis: Fortress, 1994). Elizondo himself, through his work as founder of the Mexican American Cultural Center and pastor of San Fernando Cathedral in San Antonio, has been profoundly affected by the insights of "ordinary" Latinos/as.

77. Meier, *Marginal Jew*, 1:25.

Chapter 3

Identifícate con Nosotras

A Mujerista *Christological Understanding*

ADA MARÍA ISASI-DÍAZ

The Kyrie Eleison, a well-known prayer heard for centuries in the Roman Catholic eucharistic liturgy, becomes a very different cry for mercy when it is uttered by those of us who are marginalized by society and suffer discrimination. A petition to an almighty and sovereign God to show mercy and forgive us our sins is transformed, in the *Misa Nicaragüense,* into a cry to Christ Jesus to identify himself with us and to be in solidarity with us instead of with those who destroy us.[1] Vague requests for mercy become concrete: Christ Jesus, acknowledged as Lord but also addressed as a personal God—*Dios mío*—is asked to stand with us, to become one with us.[2] This request for him to join our ranks is not born out of a desire for personal solace and comfort. A private need would not result in a call for solidarity, which usually refers to a public stance taken to identify with and support others. What is at stake in this Kyrie is the need of the community for peace, the opposite, in this song, of being "squelched and devoured" by the oppressive class.[3]

WHAT IS *MUJERISTA* THEOLOGY?

This prayer, this song, points to the *mujerista* understanding that theology is a praxis—that is, reflection-action that in a spiraling motion integrates the faith of Latina women with the struggle for liberation-fullness of life in which we are engaged in our daily living. Our religious beliefs direct and support action on behalf of liberation for ourselves and our people. Our actions, in turn, lead us to clarify what we believe: what it means for us in our everyday struggles against oppression to believe, for example, in Jesus as the Christ. *Mujerista* theology, recognizing the importance of religious beliefs in the lives of Latinas, seeks to elaborate a theology that does not ignore the political and social realities of our life as a marginalized community within the United States. This reality of being marginalized within the most powerful country in the world nowadays is not simply a matter of location, of our mailing address. The marginalization of Latinas plays a substantial role in our theological-ethical enterprise and provides key elements to our theological praxis. Who is God for us who are pushed to the margins? How do we encounter God at the margins? Who is Christ for us, and how do we present Christ from the margins and to the margins?

What Latinas believe about Christ is not a matter of an applied doctrine, an application of what the churches teach. Our Christology is a praxis; what we believe about Christ comes out of our reality as marginalized Latinas, which is one of struggle for fullness of life. What we believe is, at the same time, a force that sustains this struggle. It is from within this praxis that *mujerista* Christology seeks to answer the question Jesus posed to his disciples, "Who do you say that I am?" (Mark 8:29). Jesus' insistence on a personal answer from his disciples makes clear that what we must elucidate are not christological dogmas but rather the meaning Jesus has for Latinas in our daily lives at the beginning of the twenty-first century. Our Christology, as all Christology whether stated or not, is a historical one. We know Jesus is with us because he joins us in our struggle for liberation-fullness of life.

Our insistence on the historical character of *mujerista* Christology and on Christology as a praxis leads to a third understanding: Christology, as with all religious beliefs, follows our ethical stance. In other words, human beings, previous to any religious thinking, form ideas about what is right and what is wrong, what is good and what is bad, or, in religious language, what is sin and what is grace. Our consciences begin to be shaped well before the so-called age of reason, usually set around the age of seven. From a very early age we begin to learn from those around us what is good and what is bad. By the time we begin to include the simplest understanding of Jesus in our thinking, the main patterns by which our consciences judge what we are supposed to do are already formed. These understandings shape what we believe about Jesus.[4] In other words, when we begin to explicitly think religiously, we ascribe—to Jesus or to God or to whatever concept of the divine we are beginning to form—the ideas we have elaborated about the good. At the personal level, answers to questions like, "Who is Jesus?" "What does Jesus want me to do?" "What would Jesus do if he were here?" are not based on our knowledge of Jesus. It is the other way around: the answers we give these questions reveal to us what it is that our consciences are telling us. In this sense, what we believe about Jesus is a mirror for our consciences. For Christians this translates into the claim that, regardless of our protests to the contrary, belief follows practice, belief follows the patterns of goodness that have been deeply sown in our hearts and minds and that guide our daily lives.

A fourth understanding of *mujerista* theology is made explicit by the old custom of melding "Jesus" and "Christ" into one word: *Jesucristo*. The traditional understanding among theologians, although not among the common folk, is that "Jesus" refers to the historical person and "Christ" to what the church has taught us to believe about that Jesus. I propose that we take seriously the fusion of the two "names" and that we abandon the thought that we can find in the past what we need to know and believe today about Jesus and about Christ. In *mujerista* Christology we try to move away from the naïve understanding that we can historically reconstruct who Jesus was, how he understood himself, and what he did. We also try to move away from making normative those christological formulae from the past so heavily laden with historical and cultural understandings. We are indeed respectful of church teaching about Christ, but that is not our emphasis. The custom of folding into one word the name "Jesus" and the title "Christ"—*Jesucristo*—provides *mujerista* theology with the creative space needed to elaborate a Christology that responds to what Latinas believe about the message of Jesus of Nazareth precisely because it sustains and motivates us in our everyday struggles against what limits liberation-fullness of life and for all that promotes justice and peace. In this we follow the established tradition of the Gospel writers who created narratives about Jesus that responded to the questions and issues that were alive in the communities for which they wrote. Our attempt to elaborate a *mujerista* Christology is part of our work to provide Latinas with a religious narrative that can help us not only to understand our Christian faith but also to deal with the struggle for liberation-fullness of life that we face every day. This struggle calls us to be creative, to offer explanations of who *Jesucristo* is for us in ways that have a certain logical flow and coherence. We have always refused to spend time deconstructing theological approaches or church teachings. The precariousness of our communities is such that we feel an urgency to create understandings that are useful in the work of liberation rather than thinking about what was conceptualized in the past. *Mujerista* Christology listens carefully to the voices of grassroots Latinas, knowing that they are admirably capable of reflecting on what they believe and of explaining it in ways that contribute to liberation-fullness of life.

Our Christology revolves around three key elements that emerge from the daily praxis of Latinas in the United States, that is, they are rooted in the way Latinas face everyday struggles for their fullness of life. First, Latinas hunger for deep, personal relationships to sustain us in our daily struggles. Second, we need God to help us take care of our people, not expecting God to solve our problems but rather asking God to be our faithful companion in our struggles. Finally, we know that only insofar as we become part of God's family can we really say that we believe in *Jesucristo*.

FAMILIA DE DIOS—THE KIN-DOM OF GOD

The concept of the "kingdom of God" has undergone many transformations since it was first conceived by the Jewish people. Initially it was a concept based on the kingships that had enslaved them, Egypt and Babylon. It was the Iranian influence that provided "a transcendent feel, with the introduction of the end time, the idea of justice, and right living, which would bring about the security of the nation [Israel]."[5] Originally this understanding of transcendence did not project the "kingdom"—a new world order—into a different-world reality. "However, by the end of the first century CE a clear distinction emerged between this world, its end, and the setting in place of a new world order. For many people things that were believed to be possible in this world became transposed onto another place and time that were eternal and unchanging."[6] This change in the way the kingdom of God was understood added to despair about its realization in this world that followed the destruction of the Temple in Jerusalem in 70 CE. Furthermore, the projection of the realization of the kingdom of God into the next world allowed it to be conceived of as achievable only by God and achievable once and for all. "The psychic landscape changed significantly from a circle of hope, committed action, change, and back to hope to divine intervention and unchanging absolutes."[7] As a result, from then on, the kingdom of God became an excuse for "nonengagement with the real stuff of life."[8]

Unfortunately the split this created between this-world reality and the kingdom of God (kidnapped from this world and taken to a world yet to come) became useful for those in charge of the newly developing church. They determined the meaning and correct interpretation of all that was "Christian." When in 313 CE the Edict of Milan legalized Christianity, the new religion began to gain political and economic power in addition to the religious power and power over consciences it already held. The church became the only access to the kingdom of God in the world to come and its most powerful symbol in this world. Placing itself above the reality of this world and insulating itself against the vast majority of its members, the church came to link its life with the life of the established order, which it grew to resemble. Though it repeatedly claimed that its role was only religious, the church throughout its history has legitimized and supported those who have social, economic, and political power. Historically it has become more and more a tool in the hands of the dominant groups in society, and the image and understanding of Christ has been affected sadly in the same way. Historically the image of Christ proclaimed by the church has seemed to float above human reality, nullifying the most precious meaning of the incarnation of God in Jesus of Nazareth. Christ little by little came to resemble monarchs and pontiffs with absolute power to whom the people only had access on bended knees. This Almighty Lord Jesus Christ was more like a feared judge demanding ever more from the people than he was like a loving mother welcoming and nurturing her children. It was only with the Second Vatican Council in the second half of the twentieth century that one finds meaningful movement in redrawing the meaning of the church and of the kingdom of God, with its great implications for Christology. The most relevant statement from the Second Vatican Council in reference to the relationship between the natural order and the supernatural order where the "kingdom of God" had been ensconced is found in *Gaudium et Spes*, no. 39. The text does not go far enough in relating the growth of the kingdom of God to temporal progress, but, at least, the Conciliar document affirms "a close relationship between temporal progress, and the growth of the Kingdom . . . Those engaged in the latter not only cannot be indifferent to the former; they must show a genuine interest in and value it."[9] This step taken by Vatican II opened the door for considering theologically "temporal progress as a continuation of the work of creation" and, therefore, for seeing temporal progress as linked to the redemptive act of the life and mission of Jesus of Nazareth.[10]

The theological understandings that "the human work, the transformation of nature, continues creation only if it is a human act, that is to say, if it is not alienated by unjust socio-economic structures,"[11] developed by Latin American liberation theology opens the possibility for rescuing the kingdom of God from the supernatural order. Various liberation theologies elaborated in the second half of the twentieth century make it clear that the "kingdom of God" was the expression that Jesus used as the central metaphor for talking about his mission, for which he died on the cross. Every aspect of the life of Jesus related by the Gospels, every word ascribed to Jesus by the Gospels gyrates around the kingdom of God. In what he did and in what he said, Jesus was always announcing the kingdom of God or denouncing the antikingdom, that is to say, the conditions that not only could not be present in the kingdom of God but that make the realization or coming of the kingdom of God impossible. Liberation Christologies, on the whole, tend to make of Jesus the "definitive mediator of the Reign of God," claiming that he was "the person who proclaims the Reign, who posits signs of its reality and points to its totality."[12] To claim that Jesus was the definitive mediator, they have to posit that who Jesus was and what Jesus said and did are central to the kingdom of God. But much more, it is not only a matter of Jesus and his life being central but also that they are essential. The claim is often made that only Jesus could grasp and live to the fullest what it means to be human. His role as definitive mediator, then, is not outside the realm of what is human, but rather is "the fullness of the human."[13] And this is precisely what we mean when we say that Jesus is Christ: that he lived to the fullest his humanity and the mission that it entailed. Because what Jesus did in reference to the kingdom of God is within the human realm; other persons can also be mediators, can also be Christs. As a matter of fact, to understand what Jesus meant by the "kingdom of God" and how he worked to make it a tangible reality, we have to understand that he stood in line with many other mediators of the kingdom, from Adam and Eve to his own mother, Mary of Nazareth. Furthermore, to understand Jesus and the kingdom of God he proclaimed with his life and deeds, we have to look carefully at the mediators of the kingdom that have lived since Jesus, who have committed themselves irrevocably to the kingdom of God, from the early men and women who were deacons, martyrs, and confessors, to contemporary witnesses of the faith martyred or still alive.

All who commit themselves to proclaim with their lives and deeds the kingdom of God are mediators of the kingdom. Each and every one of us has the capacity and possibility of being another Christ, an *alter Christus*. Whether we are mediators of the kingdom of God does not have to do with our capacity to be mediators but rather with the choices we make in our lives, with our commitments, and also with the circumstances in which we live. Our mediation of the kingdom of God is related to the fact that understanding reality always includes dealing with reality. The kingdom of God does not exist apart from us who believe in it, nor does it pass through us without being affected by us and affecting us as well. All reality that we come into contact with is changed in some way by how we deal with it or ignore it because all that we do helps "to sustain a conception of the world or to modify it."[14] The same is true of the kingdom of God.

How does *mujerista* theology deal with the understanding that Jesus was the definitive mediator of the kingdom of God? If this claim indicates that no one can do it as he did it, then we can only agree, for no one can be someone else or do what others do the way they do it. But we can likewise claim that no one else, including Jesus, can do what each of us can do in mediating the kingdom of God. In this sense each of us is unique, as Jesus was. Each of us also mediates the kingdom of God in an essential way and in a way that would not happen without us. This is so because each and every one of us is an image of God, or *imago Dei:* each and every one of us carries seeds of divinity that make who we are capable of being and what we are capable of doing essential to the unfolding of the kingdom of God. This is precisely one of the key reasons that we can rescue the kingdom from the other world and incarnate it once again in our midst. This is one of the most important reasons that we see our struggles in this world as part of the overall work of creation of God. It continues in us and with us.

In the first-century Jewish world, the metaphor of kingdom was the best way Jesus and his early followers found to indicate how people could encounter a benevolent God, one who would rule in their favor and for their sake. Kingdom was the best way in which they could talk about what values were determinant factors in the life of Jesus' followers. But in today's world the metaphor of the kingdom has become irrelevant because the reality that grounds the metaphor, actual kingdoms, rarely exists anymore. Thus, the reference point of the metaphor is foreign to the experience of vast numbers of persons. For this reason alone, church officials and theologians should use a different expression to signify the purpose of Jesus' life and mission. However, there is more. The metaphor of kingdom is not only irrelevant; as it has traveled through time, it has lost much of the meaning it had for Jesus and his early followers, often providing room for antikingdom values. In *mujerista* theology we believe that the metaphor of kingdom is not appropriate since obviously it refers only to male sovereigns and reinforces once more the male image of God, still the most prevalent one in the church. In *mujerista* theology we believe kingdom is an ineffective and danger-ous metaphor, for it suggests an elitist, hierarchical, patriarchal structure that makes possible and supports all sorts of systemic oppressions. Given this reality, one of our tasks is to suggest other metaphors that speak cogently and effectively to twenty-first-century persons.

To change root metaphors, one has to go into the content of the original one: what were the values ensconced in the metaphor of kingdom of God when Jesus and his early followers used it? "Kingdom of God" was Jesus' way of speaking about *shalom,* about fullness of life. *Shalom* was not a private reality that each individual had to find or construct. Rather, *shalom* was a reality for which people needed to work together. Therefore, Jesus made love of neighbor central to life in the kingdom of God. Love is communal, the task of a people and not solely of individuals. *Shalom*—fullness of life—then, is the value at the heart of the meta-phor that Jesus used and therefore has to be the central value in any metaphor we use to talk about Jesus' understanding of his life and mission. Today, in *mujeri-sta* theology, *shalom* goes by the name of "liberation"—a holistic liberation that happens at all levels of life: socially, politically, personally, spiritually.[15]

In *mujerista* theology we suggest replacing "kingdom" with "kin-dom." We suggest moving from a political metaphor to which we have hardly any way of relating to a more personal metaphor that lies at the core of our daily lives. The idea of kin-dom of God, of the family of God, we suggest, is a much more rel-evant and effective metaphor today to communicate what Jesus lived and died for. This suggestion of the kin-dom of God in many ways is a response to the ongoing concern for the loss of family values and the loss even of a true sense of family in present-day society. Kin-dom of God as the core metaphor for the goal of Jesus' life will help us to reconstitute our sense of family. Moreover, the picture of kin-dom of God that Jesus gives us is a broad one that has to do not exclusively with blood relatives but also with those who are united by bonds of friendship, of love and care, of community. *Mujerista* theologians bemoan the loss of family, but we do not bemoan the loss of what has been called the tradi-tional nuclear family. This so-called traditional nuclear family represents a very private and individualized group more set on defining and protecting its bound-aries than in relating and welcoming all those who make life possible and pleasant for its members. The traditional nuclear family is a patriarchal setting where the man is considered the head, the one (perhaps the only one) most capable of rep-resenting and defending the family, of guiding and deciding for the family. This is why it is so difficult for society to imagine a family without a man or without a woman to complement the man. This is why we seem incapable of imagining same-sex parents or other than a biological parent carrying out the responsibilities of parenting. The traditional nuclear family in this highly technological industrial period in the United States in the first years of the twenty-first century is a family where relationships are less important than production and accumulation of capital and where if children are not better off economically than their parents, it is presumed that the family has failed. In *mujerista* theology we do not bemoan the disappearance of the traditional nuclear family.

The sense of *familia* that we have in mind when we talk about God's family, the kin-dom, is one in which a true sense of home exists, a sense of belonging and the safety to be and become fully oneself. *Familia* provides for us a sense of unity and cohesiveness that promotes a healthy sense of self-identity and self-worth so important for the development of the person. *Familia* for us "is the central and most important institution in life."[16] Whether personally *familia* is a life-giving structure for us, or unfortunately not a valuable one for whatever reason, *familia* is one of the key markers of our Latina communities. *Familia* not only is a marker of our position in life but also provides a clear indication of how we face life. *Familia* for us is a duty but also, for most of us, a never-failing support system. From a very young age, Latinas begin to understand that because of our families we do not have to face the world alone. We are also taught that precisely because the *familia* stands with us, we have a moral responsibility to each of its members who have invested so much in us by claiming us as their own. Who we are and what we do has personal repercussions for them. It is in the midst of *familia* and because of *familia* that at a very young age we are introduced to the ethical world of responsibilities and obligations, a world where one is because one is in relationship to others. In our families we learn that persons are more important than ideas and that, therefore, we have to take time and care to cultivate relationships.

Latinas' sense of *familia* is an expansive and broad one, extending into the community in a formal way. Through the institution of *compadrazgo* and *comadrazgo,* a system of relationships is established between godparents and their godchildren and the parents of their godchildren. But this system reaches beyond religious occasions such as baptisms and confirmations to secular activities and enterprises. Sponsors of dances, businesses, and sports teams are called *madrinas* (godmothers) or *padrinos* (godfathers), for they not only provide monetary support but also supply vital connections with others to protect and promote the well-being of their godchildren. The *compadrazgo* and *comadrazgo* institution creates and sustains an effective infrastructure of interdependence that has the family at the center and extends family values such as unity, welfare, and honor in all directions into the community.

Familia relies on interdependence, not subsuming the person but making one realize that the members of our families enable us to be who we are. *Familia* provides the security needed to extend ourselves into the community and form the kind of personal relationships that are vital to us without losing our sense of self. In our families we learn that "as in a prism, . . . reflection is also a refraction

. . . [and that] the identity of the 'we' does not extinguish the 'I'; the Spanish word for 'we' is '*nosotros*,' which literally means 'we others,' a community of *otros* [and *otras*], or others."[17]

It is true that Latina families are not perfect and that some of their character-istics are misguided and can cause damage to the family's members. We are not setting up Latina families and their relationships as the criteria for the biblical *shalom*. We are simply insisting on the need to change the metaphor tradition-ally used to refer to what Jesus' life and mission were all about. Kin-dom of God points to what many would say is the central institution of all societies. Kin-dom embraces understandings and values that are intrinsic to liberation-fullness of life. To create and sustain an institution where we can be ourselves in a safe way, where our well-being is of primordial importance, where a new order of relation-ships excludes all exploitation and abuse—this is indeed the kind of family all persons would welcome, and relate to goodness, to blessedness, to God.

To the question, "Who do you say that I am?" Latinas answer Jesus,

> You are my brother, my sister, my mother and my father, my grandmother, aunt, uncle, *comadre* and *compadre*, who stands with me and who struggles with me. You are amazingly special to me because I am amazingly special to you. You are my big brother protecting me, and you are my little sister whom I protect. You are my husband, my wife, my partner, my significant other for whom I am precious and who loves me unconditionally. You and I are family, Jesus. What more can you be for me? What more do you want me to be for you?

JESUCRISTO ME ACOMPAÑA SIEMPRE—
JESUS CHRIST AS FAITHFUL COMPANION

In the kin-dom of God, faith in *Jesucristo* rests squarely on the belief that, sup-ported and encouraged within *familia,* Latinas can begin to live in a different manner, in a just and loving way. Such a *familia* is open and welcoming of all, even though some may choose to exclude themselves. *Jesucristo* and the other Christs of the family are committed to live into the future reality: we are willing to work as hard as we can to establish a way of life that does not erase differences but considers them enrichments so that all can be part of the kin-dom of God. This preferred way of life is not a preconceived notion but rather a path that we create as we travel together. Cutting this path through the intricacies of life, both at the personal and at the sociopolitical level, struggling for justice and liberation in every aspect of our lives, so that everyone can live fully—that is what salvation is all about. What we learn from *Jesucristo,* our oldest sister and little brother, is that salvation is the responsibility of this whole family. Yes, if we truly believe that the purpose of Jesus' life and mission was to begin to create the kin-dom of God, then we can embrace the notion that salvation is not the exclusive task of *Jesucristo.* It is the task of all of us who have Christ as our last name. Allow me to give you an example from the world of Latinas' popular culture of what salvation looks like, of what belonging to and extending the kin-dom of God is all about.

One of the central characters of a soap opera called *Bendita Mentira* (Blessed Lie), televised here in the United States a few years ago, was Esperanza—the typical long-suffering mother who sacrifices everything for her children.[18] What is important to note was the interpretation Esperanza herself gave to her actions.[19] She never talked about sacrificing herself for her children but rather always saw what she was doing as loving her children. She saw sacrifice as a mere side effect of what she did, something indeed present but not necessarily valuable. She continually talked about love and allowed her children to live their lives, regardless of all the trouble they got into, standing with them through thick and thin. Two things about Esperanza started me thinking about her as a splash of paint that we can use in our understanding of what it means to embrace the mission for which Jesus died. First, Esperanza confessed to killing the lover of her daughter, a crime she did not actually commit, because she wanted to spare her daughter, whom she thought guilty of the crime. "Greater love has no man [*sic*] than this, that a man lay down his life for his friends."[20] A famous lawyer defended Esperanza at her trial. He said to the judge that Esperanza's love for her daughter "me reconcilió con la humanidad" (reconciled me with humanity.) Is this not what salvation is about, about being reconciled with humanity? Is it not "living with God"—and what else is the life of Christian faith? What else does it mean to be part of the *familia* of God? "Therefore, if any one is in Christ, he [*sic*] is a new creation; the old has passed away, behold, the new has come. All this is from God, who through Christ reconciled us to himself [*sic*] and gave us the ministry of reconciliation; that is, God was in Christ reconciling the world to himself, not counting their trespasses against them, and entrusting to us the message of reconciliation."[21]

In another episode of the *novela,* Esperanza's daughter was talking with a friend. This daughter, for whom Esperanza had sacrificed so much, used to "hate her mother" but later realized all that her mother had done for her and came to love her. The friend asks Esperanza's daughter what made her change her attitude toward her mother. The daughter answered, "Yo no sabía querer y ella me enseñó" (I did not know how to love and she taught me). The daughter then explained that Esperanza had taught her how to love by what she did, not by what she said. Is this not what salvation is about? Isn't salvation about loving neighbor, without measure, loving neighbor not in word but in deed? "Jesus . . . having loved his own who were in the world, he loved them to the end. . . . 'By this all men [*sic*] will know that you are my disciples, if you have love for one another.'"[22] Didn't Esperanza behave like a most worthy member of the Christ family?

Is it heretical to say that salvation is not exclusively the task of Jesus? I do not think so. This understanding of being co-redeemers with Jesus is what "the following of Jesus," or "discipleship," means. In the context of the kin-dom of God, what does it mean to be disciples of Jesus? First of all, in *mujerista* theology we try to take seriously the intrinsic link that exists between what has traditionally been called the "object" of our faith and the "act of faith." As Christian believers we do not create the "object" of our faith but believe that the object of our faith is a gratuitous "self-bestowal on us" made by God. This gift of self made by God, however, remains inoperative or ineffectual unless it occasions an act of faith. Therefore, the fact that we believe, which itself depends on God's self-bestowal, "testifies to a reality believed in and is an existential help to understanding what the concrete content of this reality [in which we believe] is."[23] To understand God we need to believe. To be able to know enough about ourselves as members of the *familia* of God, we need to be specific about what it means to believe.

Belonging to the *familia* of God, like belonging to any family, means being committed to the values and understandings specific to that family. This is why loyalty becomes such an important virtue in maintaining and enriching the links among family members. But family values are more than the mere transmission of what has been. Values exist principally as virtues; that is to say, values do not exist as abstractions but rather as practices. Without ignoring or denying totally what the values of the *familia* of God have been in the past and what these values are today, we believe that how they are effectively practiced is always in the process of being defined. This, of course, is rooted in our claim that all theology is histori-cal. But this claim that values are always in the process of being defined follows a central consideration of pastoral theology: the present situation has to be taken into account. The difference is that in *mujerista* theology we make concerns of the present operative not only at the level of pastoral care, at the level of implementa-tion, but also at the level of understanding who God is and what God is about, that is, at the level of theology. In other words, our understanding of the practice of discipleship—what it actually means to say we are followers of Christ—informs our theology. How we live our faith is intrinsic to our Christian faith.

When one talks about a Christology that emerges from the practice of faith and the personal experience of being a disciple of Jesus, one may be accused of embracing a free-for-all and an everything-goes attitude. This criticism sets relativity over against what is right. However, in *mujerista* theology we do not understand relativity as noncommitment to what is right but rather as recogniz-ing the centrality of struggling for liberation-fullness of life, in which faith and religion play a vital role, in the theological enterprise. The kind of relativity we have adopted is a "responsible relativity,"[24] a way of dealing with reality that takes seriously everyday experience. For us Latinas, being a disciple of Jesus means precisely to struggle to live each day in a way that promotes liberation-fullness of life and become worthy members of the *familia* of God. This is why we insist on the fact that Christology follows ethics, that what we believe about Jesus follows how we conduct our lives. This is why when it comes to being followers of Christ, what we have in mind above all is the right way of acting and being instead of right belief. Again, it is not that belief is not important; it is rather that what we believe about Christ follows our practice of discipleship.

Responsible relativity then allows us to free ourselves from objective uni-versals about the meaning of Christ that often have undergirded structures of oppression. It is precisely because responsible relativity recognizes the presence of subjectivity in all human thinking and knowing that we insist on the historicity of our christological understandings, unmasking so-called objective understandings as being mere subjective pronouncements of those who have the power to impose them as normative. Responsible relativity helps us to see that what we insist is "the" truth is only one of the possible explanations of reality and that the different explanations are not necessarily exclusive of each other but often, on the contrary, agree with each other, at least partially. This is why our christological understandings do not necessarily eradicate traditional ones or those elaborated by other communities. Responsible relativity also makes us be clear about the fact that endorsing a certain version of Christology demands accountability in specific and concrete ways for such a version and the consequences it brings. Lastly, when it comes to Christology, responsible relativity encourages the development of understandings and beliefs that are not offensive to other communities. This makes it possible to have a common point of reference that allows Latinas to join with other communities in the struggle for liberation. One thing is certain: our stance regarding responsible relativity in Christology insists on beliefs about Christ, salvation, the kin-dom of God, and discipleship that do not promote the liberation of some at the expense of others.

Discipleship for us Latinas is a practice of faith related to living as a worthy member of the kin-dom of God. Discipleship has to do with belonging, and belonging is not a static condition but rather an engagement in creating and sustaining relationships. Being family requires a certain way of being and doing. From a *mujerista* perspective, the "how" of this being and doing emerges from what it means to be a member of the family of God as well as from what we have to contribute to this family. In other words, it is in being family that we come to understand what family is. We cannot know the *familia de Dios* unless we throw ourselves wholeheartedly into being an active member of the kin-dom of God. Christology deals with what it means that *Jesucristo* is our sister and our brother; discipleship deals with what it means that I am a sister or a brother of *Jesucristo*. It is only in our efforts to be in a sisterly or brotherly relationship with *Jesucristo* that this meaning takes flesh. "In other words, it is in praxis, and not in the pure concept that the existence and reality" of the kin-dom of God appears and is known.[25]

What does discipleship consist of? What does being a member of the *familia de Dios* look like? It means being committed to liberation-fullness of life. It means insisting on nonobjectifying relationships. It means being adamant about including others instead of seeking to exclude them. It means being *familia* first and foremost with the poor and the oppressed. If you are oppressed, what does it mean to be part of the *familia* of God? It means keeping hope alive—hope in the possibility of justice, hope in being able to be agent of one's life, in being able to contribute to one's own fullness of life and the fullness of life of others in our *familia*.[26] But hope has to be grounded in actual possibilities or it becomes destructive illusion. Often the poor and the oppressed have no way of making hope operative in their lives, for there is no material reality on which to anchor it, no material reality that can sustain their hope and nourish it. For the poor and oppressed to be part of the *familia* of God means insisting at all times on their right to hope, to have others join with them in bringing about at least the most basic material conditions they need to be able to move from despair to hope. The poor and the oppressed contribute to making present the kin-dom of God in our world by insisting on the need to change radically oppressive structures instead of seeking to participate in them.

And for the oppressors? What do the oppressors (and here we do well to remember that the vast majority of us are oppressors in some way or other) need to do to become worthy members of the *familia* of God? Radical conversion is what is called for. Today another word for radical conversion is "solidarity" with the poor and the oppressed. To be *familia* of God, the oppressors have to come to understand that their privileges and well-being depend almost always on the misery and anguish of the vast majority of people in our world. To denounce such a stance and move away from it, oppressors have to realize the interconnections that exist among all human beings, and between human beings and the animal world and the biosphere that sustains us. Once this interconnection is understood, the hope of the poor and the oppressed becomes the hope of the oppressors: fullness of life for oppressors will not happen unless there is also fullness of life for the oppressed.

What role does *Jesucristo* play in all of this? *Jesucristo* together with the other members of the *familia* of God struggles to sustain the poor and the oppressed, to give them a reason to hope by working to create the material conditions they need to begin to move ahead in their lives. *Jesucristo* together with the other members of the familia of God struggles to make the oppressors among the family members and beyond understand that they are a threat to their own liberation—that no one will be able to experience fullness of life unless all are given what they need. *Jesucristo,* as other big sisters and little brothers do, cajoles, begs, encourages, demands, and cheers us on in our daily struggles for liberation. One of the most luminous understandings among Latinas about who *Jesucristo* is and what role he plays is that *Jesucristo* simply is with us in the midst of the ordinariness of life, that he simply walks with us. This is why among grassroots Latinas one rarely senses a crisis of faith despite all the suffering and ills present in their personal lives and in our communities. *Jesucristo* is not thought of as a magician who solves or should solve all the problems we face and free us from all of our troubles. Repeatedly we hear from our *abuelitas* and other older Latinas that what we need is not to be freed from the struggle, but to be given the strength to face the harsh reality of our world. As long as we have the strength to struggle, *Jesucristo* is with us. What is primordial about our Christology is the kind of following of *Jesucristo* that is nothing else but walking with him because he walks with us. *Jesucristo* always accompanies us, and that is why he is the Redeemer, the Savior, the Messiah, the Christ. And how do we know that he always accompanies us? Because we know he is *familia,* we are not alone. He is never alone.

JESÚS MÍO—PERSONAL RELATIONSHIP
WITH THE DIVINE

We were sitting in a big circle with grassroots Latinas discussing embodiment and sexuality. All of a sudden, Lola, one of the quiet ones in the group, spoke out of turn. In a hardly audible voice she told us a little about her intimate relations with the man who was her common-law husband for many years. With her face wrinkled by pain and folding her body as if to protect herself, she finished by saying, "Nunca tuvo para mí un gesto o una palabra de ternura" (he never had for me a tender gesture or a tender word). As she finished talking, she lowered her eyes and folded her arms over her chest as if signaling her unwillingness to let anyone else ever hurt her again. She had been wounded to the core of her being by being denied tenderness, that mode of love that can only happen at the most intimate levels of relationship.

Last December I arrived early at my small church, which sits in the midst of a housing project in East Harlem. Originally it was an almost exclusively Puerto Rican community, but more and more Mexicans have been moving into "El Barrio," as this area is called. The priest had agreed to celebrate the feast of Our Lady of Guadalupe, the invocation used in Mexico for Mary, the Mother of Jesus. Mexicans consider themselves daughters or sons of Guadalupe, so it is very important for the community here in New York City to celebrate her day. For Guadalupe's feast, the smell and sight of red roses filled the church. I sat where I could watch the people going up to the side altar where a picture of Our Lady of Guadalupe had been placed. A continuous procession of people made their way up to the altar, knelt, and lifted their eyes to the image of the Virgin. Anyone could see the love for Guadalupe that was reflected in their gestures, in the respect of their demeanor, in the tenderness with which they gazed at Guadalupe's picture. I closed my eyes and tried to understand why Guadalupe is so important in the lives of these people who approached her that day to renew their love for her, their commitment to her as her children. All of a sudden it came to me. Guadalupe is an image of the divine that looks like the Mexican people: her features are those of the Mexican indigenous population. That divinity resembles them means that the divine is not so far removed from them, yes? Gradually I came to understand something very important that I confirmed later on with my friends in the church. Women are used to loving others, to caring for others. So, in many ways, this side of the relationship with Guadalupe was not exceptional. But, as I looked at a middle-aged woman holding on to three little ones while lifting her eyes to Guadalupe, I realized that the difference in this relationship from other relationships is that the people believe that Guadalupe does care for them. She loves them back, with the tender love of a mother. These people might not be important to others, but they know they are important to her. In our Latina culture, personal relationships are at the center of our lives, at the center of the institutions and organizations—like *familia,* for example—that we create and use in our daily lives. No matter what problem we have and despite the fact that in our highly industrialized society benefits depend on the bureaucracy, Latinas believe that the best way to proceed always is by contacting someone who has personal connections and can vouch for them. Latinas depend on relationships and thirst for deep connections with others not only because we need them as intercessors but also because we need them to be fully ourselves.

It is unthinkable for us Latinas to conceive God in any other way than as a person with whom we have or can have a deep, intimate relationship. Thinking of God as a force of nature or as an energy or power in the universe is not understandable to us and certainly leaves us cold. The divine for us is personal; the divine is incarnated time and again in Jesus, in Mary his mother, in the holy people of past generations whom the church has proclaimed saints, in our ancestors, in the people of the community who during their lives have worked for the benefit of that community. The divine is not far from us in the churches where we worship. The divine is with us at all times. This is why we wear medals with images of the divine, why we have images of the divine hanging from the rearview mirrors in our cars, why we have home altars crowded with statues of Jesus, Mary, the saints, and pictures of all those who have done good and, therefore, are connected to the divine. When asked, Latinas answer that, "of course," their dead *abuelitas* are not God, Our Lady of Guadalupe is not God, St. Martin de Porres is not God, St. Barbara is not God. But Latinas know and say that all of these people have access to the divine, that they share in the divine as *alteri Christi*—other Christs.

A few stories illustrate how these *alteri Christi* function for us. In a workshop with a group of Mexican and Mexican American women in El Paso, I asked the women to whom they prayed in times of trouble. One of the *abuelitas* in the group blurted out, "To Guadalupe." When I asked her how come she did not pray to God, she said to me, "He is a man and he does not understand what happens to us women." Years later when I asked another group of women the same question in Bay City, Michigan, one of them assured the group that she prayed to God. Later that night she came to my room. "Earlier today I told you I prayed to God in times of trouble because I thought that was the right answer. But now I cannot fall asleep without coming to tell you that the truth is that I pray to Guadalupe." She proceeded to tell me that when her family had a car accident on a slippery highway, as the car was about to hit a cement wall on the side of the road, she screamed, "*Virgen de Guadalupe,* protect my children." Then I think about my own life of prayer. When I am in really difficult circumstances I pray to my *abuelita.* Knowing how much she loved me and cared for me when she lived with me on this earth, I have no doubt that she helps me in countless ways from wherever she is with God.

The divine is with us and among us, but it is so important to notice who is the divine for Latinas. The God whom the churches have proclaimed is an ominous God whose majesty and power confine him [*sic*] to a pedestal. He is a God to whom adoration is due but from whom one can expect nothing but what is due to us because of our sinfulness. He is a God that demands like a stern parent. This God is in many ways controlled by the church, for the church insists that it alone can tell us who God is and what God is like. In contrast to this far-removed God, Latinas find nothing but love and welcoming and help from our *abuelitas* and the saints. What about Jesus? Jesus is often seen only as God and, therefore, not too accessible to us. But then there is the very human *Jesucristo* suffering on the cross who touches our hearts and who understands our suffering because he too has suffered. And this is the *Jesucristo* we turn to, the *Jesucristo* who walks with us. Often theologians chide us Latinas—and our Latin American sisters and brothers—for concentrating so much on the Jesus hanging on the cross. Pointing to our lack of understanding of the importance of the resurrection of Jesus, these theologians fail to understand the importance of the personal in the lives of Latinas. They fail to see that for a true relationship with Jesus or with anyone there has to be mutuality, and mutuality needs commonality to exist. It is precisely the Jesus who suffers as we suffer—who is vulnerable as we are vulnerable—that is the *Jesucristo* to whom we can relate.

In my church, on the right-hand sidewall toward the front, there is a huge cross on which hangs a bloody body of Jesus crowned with thorns. I have noticed how some people always get on the right-hand-side line for Communion and simply stay there no matter how long that line is. I watch how each time they receive Communion, on the way back to their pews, they stop by the crucifix. Placing their hands on the nailed feet, they lift their faces to *Jesucristo*. "Lo trato de consolar" (I try to comfort him), one of the women said to me one day. She did not say much more, but I realized the importance for her of being able to do something for *Jesucristo*, the importance of being able to feel that she could take care of this *Jesucristo* who is her very own, her *Jesús mío.*

Can we humans have true relationship with God? To do so we have to be able to be much closer to God than common church practice and theological explanations allow. The divine has to be much more approachable, and we have to struggle to be real members of the *familia* of God if we want to come close to the divine. And here is where the work for justice comes into play, starting for us at home. Latinas struggle for their families, to make life possible for their children, to take care of the elderly in their communities, and to find at least a tiny space for themselves to flourish. They believe themselves to be good insofar as they do this; they are good precisely insofar as they take care of others.[27] This doing for others, being good, and being in a relationship with *Jesucristo* are very much intertwined. Though indeed the majority of Latinas would not express it this way, their relationship with *Jesucristo* and the other *alter Christi* ground their lives. Talking particularly to older Latinas, one senses this: how a profound relationship with the divine has transformed them, allowing them to see beyond what is observable, to counsel and comfort beyond their natural ability and expertise. Some of this has to do, undoubtedly, with the wisdom that experience brings, but I believe that much of this depends on their relationship with the divine. Often objectified by society, often considered by exploitative husbands as cogs in a machine used to produce care and satisfaction for them, often not appreciated by their children who demand from them the material goods so valued by society, Latinas long for deep personal relationships. Often they have nowhere to turn but to the various expressions of the divine that have become so important in their lives. This relationship with the divine, which in turn makes it possible for them to be in relationship with themselves, is what gives Latinas the strength to struggle for justice for themselves and others; it is what gives them the wisdom to survive.

Latinas are very emotional. We feel deeply, and in our culture we are not required to hide our feelings. We are taught, by example more than by anything else, to honor our feelings, for we grasp intuitively early in life that feelings are "a source of imaginative insight" and a motivation for our daily struggles.[28] Emoting, expressing how we feel, is indeed central to the way we relate, for it is in feeling and in allowing ourselves to feel that we come to know more deeply than is possible with only our minds.[29] But if feelings are to carry us beyond what we can grasp intellectually, they have to be intense and passionate; and for passion to exist, one's emotions have to have resonance. Mutuality is an absolutely essential element of a true relationship. Outside the mutuality of true relationships, passionate emotions can consume us and destroy us. Often, then, Latinas seek with the divine the passionate relationships they do not find with partners because we know that if we do not feel deeply, we are not living fully. In such relationships, mutuality is essential, so it is not surprising that we conceptualize the divine in a way that allows for true mutuality to exist. "*Jesucristo* needs me," we Latinas tell ourselves. "He needs me to comfort him in his sufferings, he needs me to help him bring people to the *familia de Dios*. God knows I need him! I need *Jesucristo,* for I know that I am precious for him."

This is Latinas' way of admitting and insisting on the centrality of relationships, on the need we have for mutuality. The divine has to be accessible to us, *Jesucristo* has to understand us, and we have to be able to contribute to the understanding of who *Jesucristo* is in our world today. We turn to *Jesucristo,* whom we love passionately for our salvation, to *Jesucristo* as "the source of creative, relational energy."[30] And frequently he is the only one with whom we can establish a true relationship, one in which we are not exploited but valued for who we are, a relationship that nourishes us, that saves us in a very personal and holistic way.

LIVING OUR CHRISTOLOGY

That many questions in life go unanswered is one of the most important things I have learned from grassroots Latinas. Many questions are nothing more than dilemmas, inexorable conundrums, and illogical realities. We can only accept them as part of our daily lives, for we do not have the means to deal effectively with them. For us Latinas, *Jesucristo* is not the one who gives us answers but the one who sustains us when there are no answers. Perhaps *Jesucristo* is actually more present to us in the questions, for they often keep us reaching further, stretching our understandings, enabling us to hope and to commit ourselves more and more to liberation-fullness of life for ourselves and for those for whom we are responsible.

As a consequence of this way of looking at life and because of what *Jesucristo* means for Latinas, *mujerista* theology does not seek to provide answers but rather to help us to go deeper in our questions about God and the divine presence in our lives. There is no single answer to Jesus' question, "Who do you say that I am?" What we Latinas have and, therefore, what *mujerista* theology can offer, is some hint of who *Jesucristo* is, some markers along the way for those who are open to seeing them, markers that show us where and how *Jesucristo* is present to us and with us in our daily lives. Sometimes the only way to understand who *Jesucristo* is for us and how he is present in our lives is through stories. Three stories come to mind.

The story of Helen Prejean, a Roman Catholic nun who has spent a large part of her life ministering in the United States to prisoners on death row, is told in the book *Dead Man Walking*. She describes the day she was accompanying Pat Sonnier, a man in Angola Prison, thirty-six hours away from being executed, hoping for a stay. After praying with him, Helen said to Pat, "If you die, I want to be with you." He answered, "No. I don't want you to see it." Then she said to Pat, "I can't bear the thought that you would die without seeing one loving face. I will be the face of Christ for you. Just look at me."

Ivone Gebara, a leading Latin American ecofeminist theologian, told me this story. One evening, when Ivone was returning to her house in a poor neighborhood in Brazil, a woman who lives near and whose son was very sick stopped her and excitedly told her, "God visited me today." Ivone was surprised and started talking to the woman trying to find out what had happened. A neighbor had turned over to the woman the money she had earned that day so she could buy medicine for her sick son. For Ivone's friend this neighbor had become God, had become Christ. This generous neighbor did not merely "represent" Christ but was indeed Christ made present in a poor neighborhood of Brazil in our own days.

Not long ago in New York City, where I live, a mother, helped by the grandmother, poisoned her daughter and simply disposed of the little body in a garbage can. They did it, they said, because the little girl was possessed by evil spirits. While the city authorities looked for the girl's body in the city's garbage dump, I was having a profound crisis of faith. "Where is *Jesucristo*?" I kept asking myself. "Why did God abandon this innocent little girl?" Then I realized it: that little girl was *Jesucristo* nailed on the cross. In her murder, as in the murder of Jesus of Nazareth, "There is salvation and there is light."[31] That little nameless girl was indeed *Jesucristo!*

NOTES

1. The Kyrie is part of the section of the Mass that deals with confession and forgiveness.
2. Carlos Mejía Godoy y el Taller de Sonido Popular, "Kirye," in *Misa Campesina*.
3. The words of the song are as follows: "Christ, Christ Jesus, identify yourself with us. Lord, Lord, my God, identify yourself with us. Christ, Christ Jesus, be in solidarity with us, not with the oppressive class that squelches and devours the community, but with the oppressed, with my people who thirst for peace."
4. Tom Driver, *Christ in a Changing World* (New York: Crossroad, 1981), 21–24.
5. Lisa Isherwood, *Liberating Christ* (Cleveland: Pilgrim Press, 1999), 133.
6. Ibid.
7. Ibid.
8. Ibid.
9. Gustavo Gutiérrez, *A Theology of Liberation*, 2nd ed. (Maryknoll, NY: Orbis Books, 1988), 99.
10. Ibid., 100–101.
11. Ibid., 101.
12. Jon Sobrino, "Systematic Christology: Jesus Christ, The Absolute Mediator," in *Mysterium Liberationis—Fundamental Concepts of Liberation Theology*, ed. Ignacio Ellacuría, S.J., and Jon Sobrino, S.J. (Maryknoll, NY: Orbis Books, 1993), 441.
13. Ibid., 442.
14. Antonio Gramsci, *Prison Notebooks*, ed. and trans. Quintin Hoare and Geoffrey Nowell Smith (New York: International Publishers, 1975), 9.
15. I am always apprehensive when any list is drawn, for lists are almost always read as if the elements in them could be isolated one from the other. I want to insist on the fact that the struggle for liberation is a holistic struggle, that we cannot be liberated socially, for example, without being liberated personally—within ourselves (psychologically) as well as socially (in our personal relationships). I want to insist especially in the fact that "spiritually" is not a category set apart—that spiritual is intrinsic to the category marked "personally." Here by "spiritual" I mean simply that the struggle for liberation also has to do with how we relate to God, a God that lives and moves and is among us, in us, a God that is in the social, in the political, as well as in the personal.
16. Roberto R. Álvarez Jr., "The Family," in *The Hispanic American Almanac*, ed. Nicolas Kanellas (Washington, DC: Gale Research, 1993), 155. The claims Latinas make regarding family are in no way unique, but that they are not unique does not mean that they are not specifically ours.
17. Roberto S. Goizueta, "*Nosotros*: Toward a U.S. Hispanic Anthropology," *Listening—Journal of Religion and Culture* 27, no. 1 (Winter 1992): 57.
18. "Soap opera" is the name given in the United States to theatrical plays televised in early afternoons on Monday through Friday. Women are the target audience for these *novelas*—novels—as they are called in Spanish. Because the target audience of the *novelas* in Spanish television are working-class Latinas—the most numerous group in the Latino/a population—Spanish *novelas* play at night instead of in the afternoon, when American soap operas, geared to middle-class women who work in their homes, can watch.

19. I hope the "religious" tone of the title of the *novela* and of the name of the mother—Esperanza means hope—is not lost on the reader.
20. John 15:13 (RSV).
21. 2 Cor. 5:17–19 (RSV).
22. John 13:1, 35 (RSV).
23. Sobrino, "Systematic Christology," 448.
24. What I call "responsible relativism" is an adaptation of the ideas of feminist philosopher Lorraine Code. She does not use this phrase, but the treatment of this term presented here is influenced by Code's work. See Lorraine Code, *Rhetorical Spaces—Essays on Gendered Locations* (New York: Routledge, 1995), 185–207.
25. Jon Sobrino, "Central Position of the Reign of God in Liberation Theology," in *Mysterium Liberationis,* 379.
26. See Sobrino, "Systematic Christology," 461 n. 10.
27. Ada María Isasi-Díaz and Yolanda Tarango, *Hispanic Women—Prophetic Voice in the Church,* 2nd ed. (Minneapolis: Fortress Press, 1992), 80–91.
28. Ibid., 79. See Dorothy Emmet, *The Moral Prism* (New York: St. Martin's Press, 1979), 11.
29. Mary Grey, *Redeeming the Dream* (London: SPCK, 1989), 87.
30. Ibid., 97.
31. Ibid., 375: "Then the poor can be theologized, posited as a *locus theologicus,* recognized as constituting a world in which the signs of the times occur. Now, one can even accept Isaiah's scandalous thesis: in the poor, in the crucified Servant, there is salvation and there is light."

Chapter 4

Constructing a
Cuban-Centric Christ

MIGUEL A. DE LA TORRE

Clement of Alexandria is reported as saying that "God saved the Jews in a Jewish way, the barbarians in a barbarian way." Likewise, God will save Euro-Americans in a Euro-American way and Hispanics in a Latino/a way. Nevertheless, there is an insistence by well-meaning progressive Euro-Americans to accept a Christ created in their image so that Hispanics can be saved in a Euro-American way. This is problematic. Why? Because any construction of Christ becomes the collective representation of any group of people, a symbolic expression that helps that group solidify as a Christian community, providing them with a sense of unity. Such a Christ transmits how their culture defines morality to the next generation, in effect providing divine sanction for how the culture organizes itself and determines which social behaviors to uphold. The question Latinos/as must ask themselves is if the Jesus of the dominant Euro-American culture is the same Christ who can provide Hispanics with a salvific gospel of liberation based on how he lived his life, by the actions he undertook, and by the words he preached as a reflection of those actions.

Unfortunately, the answer is no. The Euro-American Christ has historically been used (or muted) to divinely justify societal actions that have contributed to the marginalization of Hispanics. The Euro-American Jesus is the Christ of

President James K. Polk who, following the quasi-religious ideology of Manifest Destiny, led the United States in the military conquest of northern Mexico, preventing the future ability of that nation to build wealth and disenfranchising those the border crossed over. The Euro-American Jesus is the Christ of Theodore Roosevelt, who instigated a "gunboat" diplomacy that denied Latin American nations of their sovereignty and provided U.S. corporations the freedom and protection of extracting the cheap labor and natural resources of a people. These first imperialist steps resulted in the pauperization and U.S. migration of Spanish-speaking peoples from Central America and the Caribbean. The Euro-American Jesus is the Christ of present-day presidents and politicians whose main purpose is the maintenance of U.S. global hegemony. This domination of nonwhites abroad is mirrored domestically in the disproportionate disenfranchisement of Hispanics (and other nonwhites) from the economic and political benefits of society.

Versions of Christ presented to Hispanics by well-meaning Euro-American scholars and clergy have the ability to form major building blocks of the Latino/a identity. As such, these Euro-American Christs can be misconstrued as the intellectual or spiritual saviors of Hispanics. It should not be surprising that many Latinos/as look toward Eurocentric scholarship and doctrines in order to revitalize their study and understanding of Christ. But to do so causes Hispanics to envision Christ as a cultural extension of the Eurocentric mission. The necessary process of formulating their own Hispanic space from where Latinos/as can commune with a Christ indigenous to their own social location begins with the realization that Eurocentric thought has historically been hostile to the existential being of Latinos/as.

It really doesn't matter how progressive Euro-Americans construct Jesus or how liberally they attempt to interpret his words. As long as Latinos/as bow their knees to a Christ who is silent about what it means to live at the margins of Euro-American power and privilege; as long as this Christ refuses to motivate action among Euro-American churches to speak out about the marginalization faced throughout the barrios of this nation; as long as this Christ does not elicit Euro-Americans to stand in solidarity with the thousands who die in the Sonoran desert of Arizona because of unjust immigration laws; then those Hispanics insisting on worshiping the Christ who looks and acts like the dominant culture would in fact be worshiping the symbolic cause of their oppression. This is more than simply worshiping a Jesus who looks Hispanic (whatever "looking Hispanic" means). We are insisting on worshiping a Christ who understands what it means to be Hispanic and thus has something important to say to the marginalized, a message indecipherable to those accustomed to their power and privilege.

In order to sever the link between power and disenfranchisement, between privilege and marginality, Christ must be recognized as ontologically Hispanic. Just as Euro-Americans have for centuries worshiped a Christ in their own image, it becomes significant for Latinos/as to see the Divine as an ethnic Hispanic. Why? Because the white Christ of Euro-American history has been the

Christ who justified the historical reality of colonialism, slavery, racism, and oppression. It was in the name of this white Christ, the Christ who symbolized the protection of white Christian civilization from so-called Hispanic inferiority, that the marginalization of Hispanics became normalized and legitimized in the eyes of white America. The extent of the pervasiveness of the white Euro-American Christ can be noted in the colonialization of Hispanics' minds who have been taught to bow their knees not only to the image of this Euro-American Christ, but also to the social order it signifies—a social order detrimental to the Latino/a existence. Nevertheless, the Latino/a Christ is informed by the historical identification of Jesus with those who suffer under oppression. Christ's Latino-ness is not due to some simplistic attempt to be politically correct, nor to some psychological need existing among Latinos/as to see a Divine through their own cultural signs. Jesus is Hispanic because the biblical witness of God is of one who takes sides with the least among us against those who oppress them. In a white racist America, Hispanics (along with other communities of color) were the ones being oppressed, the ones who were hungry, thirsty, cast out, naked, afflicted, and incarcerated.

The white Eurocentric Christ is not only detrimental for Hispanics, but is also impotent in bringing salvation for Euro-Americans. In the famous biblical parable of the Sheep and the Goats as recorded in the Gospel of Matthew (25:31–46), Jesus divides those destined for glory (the sheep) from those destined for damnation (the goats). The salvation of those with power and privilege is contingent upon how they treated those who were starving, thirsty, aliens, unclothed, ill, and imprisoned. Usually, Hispanics occupy this space. The dominant culture finds its life (salvation) when it struggles along with those who are oppressed by attempting to alleviate, if not eliminate, the structures that cause death. Crucial to the understanding of this passage is the radical revelation made by Jesus. He ends the parable by stating (v. 45): "Then [the Lord] will answer [the condemned], 'Truly I tell you, just as you did not do it to one of the least of these, you did not do it to me.'" To "see" Jesus within U.S. history is to see him within God's crucified people, those oppressed by structural racism and ethnic discrimination.

Consequently, only a Latino/a Christ can liberate Hispanics. Why? Because Eurocentric Christs, no manner how benignly they are presented, will always be incongruent with the disenfranchised reality Latinos/as are forced to occupy. The question Latinos/as must ask themselves is: does the Euro-American Christ provide life and provide it abundantly for Hispanics (John 10:10)? If history is any guide, the Euro-American Christ has mostly provided disenfranchisement, despair, and death. In short, salvation for Hispanics will never be found in the divine symbols of the Euro-American culture. To commune with a Hispanic Christ is to incarnate the gospel message within the marginalized spaces of the barrios so that the actions and words of Jesus can infuse *la comunidad* (the community) with the hope of survival and liberation. For this reason, the Euro-American Christ that has served as the Hispanic anti-Christ needs to be rejected for a Christ constructed from within the Latino/a ethos.

Not only is the Latino/a Christ salvific for Hispanics, it is also salvific for Euro-Americans. As Euro-Americans attempt to base their theology and ethics on a "thick" Jesus, it is crucial to ask: who is this Jesus they want to thicken? If the answer is the same Eurocentric Christ of the dominant culture that is responsible for spiritually justifying much of the oppressive structures faced by Hispanics and other nonwhite groups, then Euro-Americans are at risk of worshiping a false messiah with no ability to save or redeem them, or anyone else for that matter. For the sake of their own salvation, Euro-Americans must put away their Euro-American Christ, whether he be "thin" or "thick," and learn to walk in solidarity with the Christ of the oppressed and the people with whom Christ identified in the parable of the Sheep and the Goats.

TOWARD A HISPANIC CHRIST

It is not enough to insist that a Euro-American Christ needs to be rejected. We must also envision how Christ is incarnated in the historical social location of Latinos/as. We begin by realizing that whatever Christ means to Hispanics, he must be understood within sociohistorical and ecopolitical contexts of the Latino/a community of faith that is responding to the biblical message of liberation. For Latinos/as, however, Christ is defined or understood foremost as a liberator. But Christ as liberator moves beyond narrow constricts of liberating Latinos/as from "personal sins." The Christ of Hispanics is just as concerned with the sins of the entire community, specifically those within the dominant culture whose sins wreak chaos and havoc upon the lives of those forced to reside on the margins. From the underside of U.S. culture, where Hispanics (along with other communities of color) are forced to suffer under the yoke of domination, a quest for a Hispanic Christ becomes a quest for liberation—liberation from racism and ethnic discrimination.

Hispanics are quick to point out that God has historically chosen the least among us to be agents of God's new creation. It is the stone rejected by the builders that becomes the keystone of God's created order (Matt. 21:42). The biblical story reminds us that it was not Rome, the most powerful city of the known world, where God chose to perform the miracle of the incarnation, nor was it Jerusalem, the center of Yahweh worship; rather, it was impoverished Galilee where God chose to first proclaim the message of the Gospels. From the margins of Galilee, the good news goes to the center of religious and political powers—a paradigm that places the white man's burden of Christianizing the margins of whiteness upon its head. Theological reflections from the perspective of Hispanics identify with a deity that habitually chooses a stone from the margins, rejected by the dominant culture, to carry out God's salvific plan.

The gospel message of liberation from oppressive societal structures resonates with Hispanics who discover that those marginalized in Jesus' time occupied the privileged position of being the first to hear the good news, not because they were holier, nor better people, but because God chooses sides. God makes a preferential option for those who exist under the weight of oppression. The radical nature of the incarnation is not that God became human, but that God assumed the condition of one of *los humildes* (the humbled). If God was to reincarnate today, God would come to us in the form of those most despised by the culture, those most humbled. I have no doubt that God would incarnate Godself as an undocumented immigrant, for they are the ones who are hungry, thirsty, naked, foreign, sick, and, if caught crossing the border without authorization, in prison. Why is it important to understand who Christ is through the lens of Hispanics? By making those humbled by the dominant culture of Christ's time the recipients of the good news, Jesus emphasized the political edge of his message. Any quest for understanding Christ within the United States requires making marginalized communities of color the starting point of all inquiries. This is not an attempt to romanticize Hispanic marginalization; rather, it is an attempt to understand Christ as a unifying symbol for Latinos/as.

TOWARD OPPRESSIVE CUBAN CHRISTS

If indeed God saves Euro-Americans in a Euro-American way and Hispanics in a Latino/a way, then God saves Mexicans in a Mexican way, Puerto Ricans in a Puerto Rican way, and Cubans in a Cuban way. What then is this Cuban way by which Cubans are saved? The movement of God within Cuban history transmits an understanding of Christ through cultural symbols understood by Cubans. Reevaluating these cultural symbols provides rich resources for understanding what Christ means to Cubans. But the question is, which Cuban Christ to follow toward salvation? Those Cubans who benefited from the power structures created on the island, like Euro-Americans, constructed a Christ to spiritually justify their political power and privilege. Therefore, it is not sufficient to simply look toward a Cuban Christ to be a salvific symbol for Cubans. The need exists to first debunk those Christs co-opted by political structures to benefit the few at the expense of the many. One such Christ requiring rejection is the first Christ presented to the island, the Conquistador Christ.

The essence of this Conquistador Christ was established during the centuries of the long campaign against the Muslim enemies of Spain. For seven hundred years, Christians battled to vanquish the crescent by way of the cross. Centuries of religious tension and conflict merged nationalism with Christianity (specifically Catholicism). Disciples of Christ were obliged to fight the enemies of the "true" faith. This crusading spirit was transplanted to the so-called New World. A Christ was worshiped under which avarice for riches and land merged with an evangelical spirit. The quest for glory and gold converged with a crusading fervor to rid Spain's dominions of Jews and Muslims on the mainland, and Native people on the margins of the emerging Spanish Empire. Spanish monarchs took the Great Commission to baptize literally all nations, spiritually legitimizing the conquistador's mission.

This Conquistador Christ became synonymous with the colonial enterprise. As such, it was unable to minister to or help the Native inhabitants of the island who were either being decimated or integrated into the Spaniards' economic project. This Christ was firmly established on the island partly due to an ecclesiological structure dependent on the Spanish Crown for the necessary funding to carry out its apostolic endeavors. The Conquistador Christ was so intertwined with the colonial system that it bore the stigmata of genocide and slavery. The presence of this Christ was safeguarded through complicity with and manipulation of the state's power. In return, the Conquistador Christ promoted the colonial venture.

Centuries of Spanish colonialism defined Cuban understanding of Christ as an extension of Spain. The influence of the Conquistador Christ on Cubans, due to four centuries of colonialism, is undeniable. During the wars for independence, the Catholic Church followed the lead of Pope Leo XIII, who supported Spain in its conflicts with the Cuban insurgents. The decision of the church to side with the Spanish Crown left freedom fighters no alternative but to also battle the church. On the eve of Spain's defeat, the bishop of La Habana, fearing a Protestant invasion, wrote a pastoral letter pleading "for civilization, against barbarism," in other words, for the Conquistador Christ of colonialism instead of independence. Unfortunately the Protestant alternative did not prove to be any more liberating than the Conquistador Christ. The oppressive understanding of Christ was further strengthened when the emerging U.S. empire defeated the declining Spanish empire during the Spanish-American War.[1]

Any hope on the part of the Cubans for obtaining independence from Spain was subverted by the rise of the U.S. empire. The imposition of U.S. hegemony within the hemisphere also had a religious counterpart, as the Euro-American Christ became part of the Cuban religious ethos. It is ominous that the first official Euro-American Protestant worship service in Cuba (excluding the brief English occupation in the 1700s) was held on a U.S. gunboat in 1871 in La Habana Harbor, officiated by Bishop Benjamin Whipple, an Episcopalian. This event characterizes the relationship that eventually developed between the United States and Cuba, a relationship that understood the political through the spiritual. The religious and political were again merged to create a Protestant Imperial Christ that was more concerned in establishing, justifying, and defending the imposed political reality in Cuba than spiritual piety.

Theodore Roosevelt is credited with "saving" Cuba from the Spanish empire. Likewise, U.S. Protestants attempted to "save" Cuba from Roman Catholicism. Protestantism at first appeared to be an attractive alternative to centuries of the Colonial Spanish Roman Catholic Church. The Protestantism of the American victors of the Spanish-American War implied modernity, prosperity, and progress. However, the Euro-American political rulers who came to the island perceived the Cubans as being morally deficient and intellectually backward—lacking basic cognizance for self-government. Protestant missionaries who accompanied them held similar views. Their propaganda of the time depicted their role as agents for civilization, charged by God to confront Cubans with their supposedly defective character and offer them redemption through a Protestant Imperial Christ. A typical comment expressed in church newsletters during the late 1890s would state, "The Churchmen of our [U.S.] land should be prepared to invade Cuba as soon as the army and navy open the way, to invade Cuba in a friendly, loving Christian spirit, with bread in one hand and the Bible in the other, and win the people to Christ by Christlike service."[2] But why send missionaries to a country where the vast majority claimed to worship Christ? Because Cubans were worshiping the "wrong" Christ. To be a "real" Christian meant acceptance of the Protestant Imperial Christ and everything this Christ signified, specifically the acceptance of U.S. political, economic, and cultural institutions and practices.

Rather than obtaining independence, Cuba experienced U.S. military occupation immediately following the Spanish-American War. With military occupation came the establishment of about fifty Protestant denominations on the island. In 1902 an interdenominational conference convened in Cienfuegos, Cuba, to literally divide the spoils of war. Northern Baptists were given Oriente and Camagüey, Southern Baptists acquired Las Villas, La Habana, and Pinar del Rio. Eastern Cuba was divided between Quakers and Methodists, while western zones were allotted to Presbyterians and Congregationalists. Episcopalians were awarded Matanzas and Santiago de Cuba. Cities in excess of six thousand inhabitants were declared open territory. No doubt some Cubans converted to Protestantism as a devout spiritual response to the missionaries' zeal, but probably as many converted because it seemed a prudent economical and social response to the presence in Cuba of the Protestant Imperial Christ.

This Protestant Imperial Christ was bonded to Euro-American capitalists who arrived in Cuba after the war as carpetbaggers. The Spanish-American War reduced Cuba to a wasteland, creating widespread indebtedness and providing cheap land and labor for Euro-American capitalists. Bankrupt properties were easily acquired by paying back taxes. By 1905 these Euro-American capitalists were able to acquire title to 60 percent of all rural property, thus economically replacing the bankrupt former Cuban ruling class. During military occupation, Military Governor Wood granted 218 tax-exempt mining concessions, mostly to U.S. firms.[3]

The economic takeover of the island had a religious component through the Protestant Imperial Christ. For example, the Methodist Candler School in La Habana was funded by and named after the founder of Coca-Cola. John D. Rockefeller established a boarding school for boys in El Cristo. The United Fruit Company in Banes and the Cuban-American Sugar Company in Puerto Padre subsidized the Quakers. The United Fruit Company provided three hundred rent-free acres to the Methodist Agricultural and Industrial School in Preston, Oriente, and Hershey funded a Presbyterian agricultural school in Aguacate.

Graduates of these schools usually took managerial jobs representing the interests of their Euro-American benefactors.[4] Mainline U.S. churches brought their liturgical, theological, and architectural styles to the island. Those who converted to Protestantism tended to be of modest social origins from the working and lower-middle class, living U.S. lifestyles and supporting Euro-American issues. They were presented with a Protestant Imperial Christ who was mainly concerned with conservative Euro-American individualism. The imposition of the Protestant Imperial Christ resulted in neutralizing Cuban spirituality, in the same way that imperialist policies emasculated the nation politically.

It would be a mistake to create a simple dichotomy between Euro-American oppressors and the Cuban oppressed. Not all Cubans opposed the U.S. hegemony. Many benefited from the relations, acquiring a taste for American goods, and willingly participated in maintaining the relationship. Handpicked financial advisors were needed to manage the assets of absent Euro-Americans. Those chosen were mostly white, educated in the States, and pro-United States. The success of the United States in Cuba may have begun as a function of political and military control, but eventually gave way to the creation of cultural conditions designed to construct Cuban identity via a Euro-American ethos.

Not surprisingly, the rise of Cuban nationalism during the 1920s was a direct challenge to U.S. economic and political domination. The political Cuban elite who benefited from the U.S. hegemony were reviled for willingly submitting to the United States. Consequently, any revolution conducted in Cuba would first and foremost be anticapitalist and anti–United States. The success of Castro's 1959 revolution did away with the Protestant Imperial Christ, replacing it with a Revolutionary Christ, but again, the Revolutionary Christ created its own structures of oppression.

Immediately after the success of the revolution, Castro was deified, becoming to many a Christ figure. On January 8, 1959, during his first national speech from Camp Columbia, at the moment Castro called for unity and peace, a white dove landed on his shoulder. For Christians, he assumed the role of Jesus, who underwent a similar experience during his baptism, as recorded in Matthew 3:16–17. By August of that year, the magazine *Bohemia* published a sketch by Luis Rey portraying Castro under a Christlike halo and with a heavenly countenance. An accompanying article by Mario Kuchilán wrote of the revolution's "miracle" and the "resurrection of (Fidel) faith." Fidel was more than just Fidel, he was "Jesus Christ incarnate, who came to put the affairs of Cuba, and other places, in order." During a speech to the coordinators of sugar cane cooperatives in La Habana a year later on August 11, 1960, Castro said, "Those who condemn this Revolution are condemning Christ, and they would be capable of crucifying Christ, because he did what we are doing." One Presbyterian minister preached, "Fidel Castro is an instrument in the hands of God for the establishment of his reign among men!"[5] In short, Castro embodied the Revolutionary Christ.

Many who professed a strong faith in Christ participated in the revolution as an expression of their commitment to Christ—a commitment understood to be grounded in their action against the socioeconomic injustices of Batista's regime. They saw the revolution and their participation in it as putting their faith into action to bring about justice. Catholic and Protestant believers actively cooperated with and served during the revolution. Two early martyrs were Frank and Josué Pais, Baptists killed by Batista's soldiers for leading an uprising in Santiago, and Esteban Hernandez, a Presbyterian, also tortured and killed by Batista's police. On the Catholic side, Father Sardiñas served as chaplain to the rebel army and was promoted to the rank of *comandante*. Father Madrigal was treasurer of the July 26 Movement, and Father Chabebe relayed coded messages to the rebel forces via his religious radio program. Although the church hierarchy remained silent during the insurgence, a significantly large percentage of Catholics, like the martyred Catholic student leader Echevarría, participated in the uprising.[6]

While there was early support for the revolution because of its initiatives to end gambling, prostitution, and political corruption, early support gave way to disillusion as the new regime took a more leftist tilt, specifically its closer relationship with the Soviet Union, the promoters of godless communism. Catholics and Protestants soon became engaged in counterrevolutionary activities. A showdown between the revolution and the church finally erupted. In a speech concerning the revolution's conflict with the Christians, Castro, on September 8, 1961, attempted to describe who this Revolutionary Christ was. He said,

> [The counterrevolutionaries] want to paint the Revolution as an enemy of religion, as if that had anything to do with the things that interest the Revolution. . . . The doctrine of Christ was a doctrine that found an echo among the slaves, among the humble people. It was persecuted by the aristocracy, by the dominant classes. These gentlemen, in contemporary times, completely abandoned the essence of the Christian doctrine, dedicated themselves to taking religion as an instrument to hide all the vices and all the defects of the present dominant classes, forgetting about the slaves of today, the workers, the peasants without land. These gentlemen separated themselves from the interests of the exploited masses, and from the humble masses, in order to carry religion on a silver platter to the great exploiters, to the dominant classes. They divorced themselves from the people, and they prostituted the essence of primitive Christianity.[7]

Additionally, in an article responding to church opposition, Castro went on to define Christianity as follows:

> A true Christian is one who loves his neighbor, who makes sacrifices for others, who obeys the doctrines of Christ and gives what he has in order to go serve his fellow human being. Let these "Christians" leave their temples and go to the fields to help the sick, plant trees, build houses, assist the Agrarian reform, sew smocks for children who have no clothes. That's what being Christian means. On the other hand, going to church to conspire against our fatherland is the action of a Pharisee—never a Christian.[8]

Eventually the church came to terms with the context in which it found itself.

On April 10, 1969, the Catholic Church broke with the past with the publication of the Cuban bishop's letter denouncing the U.S. embargo. Protestants also sought a rapprochement in 1977. The Confession of Faith of the Presbyterian-Reformed Church declared, "The Church lives joyfully in the midst of the socialist revolution." What developed was a revolution theology subjugated to a Revolutionary Christ and different from Latin America's liberation theology. For those who follow this Revolutionary Christ, liberation was already achieved and the people were already living in the promised land. The task, therefore, is not liberation, but constructing and building society within the revolution. This was achieved through a prophetic reading of Scripture that provided Cubans with the necessary praxis that was consistent with a revolutionary society. "Prophetic" does not mean the right to criticize the revolution. Rather, it was the revolution that is to be prophetic for the church. In response, the church was required to fall in step with the revolution. Still, when Christians reflect theologically on the revolution, it is not done for the benefit of revolutionaries, or to provide a service to the revolution. Reflection is done for Christians and the church so that they can render a service to both of them.

Many chose to leave the island since the revolution, finding themselves as refugees in the United States. Living in exile has become a recurring theme for Cubans. Historically, *el exilio* (the exile) has been a place for opposing whoever was in power on the island. Cuban communities in New Orleans (1850s), Tampa (1890s), New York (1930s), and presently Miami sought moral justification for the struggle to change the island's political reality. To signify the reality of exile, the development of the Exilic Christ occurred. This Exilic Christ was influenced by José Martí (national icon) who equated morality with nationality. The assumption developed that Cubans on the island desire to be rescued by those in exile—an assumption rooted in Martí's words and actions. He envisioned two Cubas—the real Cuba that is here, *aquí,* as opposed to the morally degraded Cuba there, *allá.* Cubans of *el exilio* were responsible for continuing *la lucha* (the struggle) to "save" *la Cuba de allá.*

Creating the memory of Cuba while in exile required a new understanding of Christ. The Exilic Christ provided psychological reassurance of legitimacy. Exilic Cubans can compare their success in exile with the less privileged Cubans who were left behind on the island. Regardless of the reality concerning the mythical golden exile, a success story was needed to construct exilic Cuban identity. It allows the Cubans in *el exilio* to visualize their success as the result of their own hard work and moral superiority. Equally, the economic misfortune of Cubans on the island became the direct consequence of their support for Castro or their incompetence in implementing Euro-American capitalist paradigms. Their failure proved their illegitimacy as real Cubans.

Religious faith takes the form of *la lucha* (the struggle), a counter-memory established as the starting point for their sacred space in exile. *La lucha,* also known as *la causa sagrada* (the sacred cause), ceased to be a struggle for liberation and became a religious crusade. It is understood as *la lucha* against Castro.

La lucha, as sacred space, represents the cosmic struggle between the "children of light" (exilic Cubans) and the "children of darkness" (resident Cubans), complete with a Christ (Martí), an anti-Christ (Castro), a promised land (Cuba), and martyrs (those who gloriously suffer in the holy war against the evil of Castro).

Cuban history, like the history of the United States, has constructed different Christs to justify the domination of one group by another. Yet where there is oppression, resistance exists. For those struggling to be recognized in the full dignity of humanity, a Christ who is rooted among *los humildes* of Cuba can provide an alternative. But who exactly is this Cuban Christ? I will call the liberative Christ for Cubans "the Ajiaco Christ," for such a Christ is capable of bringing together all the diverse ways of understanding Christ from the underside of Cuban history.

TOWARD A LIBERATIVE CUBAN CHRIST

Understanding a Cuban Christ that is liberative is basically an act of faith derived from two sources: the Cuban social existential location (reality) and the paradigm (ideal) derived by the community of faith, a model based on justice. This Cuban Christ avoids the Euro-American pitfall of a utilitarian individuality that relegates religion to the private sphere and transforms the public Christ into a personal savior. Conversion ceases to be simply a call to a new religion founded by Jesus, but becomes a radically subversive Cuban lifestyle. The faith called for is a special form of consciousness containing specific consequences for the will. Satisfaction of intellectual needs (the modernity project) is not the ultimate goal. Rather, the longing of the heart to answer the unanswerable questions of the Cuban alienated existence (from God, from nation, and from the fellow Cubans separated by ninety miles) becomes a religious quest for meaning. This quest for a Cuban Christ creates a sacred space where Cubans can grapple with their spiritual need to reconcile with their God and their psychological need to reconcile with their siblings on the other side of the Florida Straits. But as we have seen, past constructs of Cuban Christs merged political domination with spiritual justification for domination. These Constantinian Christs have proven to be false messiahs who moved away from any liberationist project.

How then do Cubans construct a Christ who can save? The construction of such a Christ requires Cuban symbols that can generate a unifying dialogue among Cubans. All people depict ultimate reality in a visible form native to their own culture. This is one of the main reasons that a Euro-American Christ is impotent for Cubans. Only a Christ who knows what it means to be Cuban can be salvific for Cubans. But how do we reconcile the diversity of Cubanness in one Christ? How can Cubans transcend their fragmentation as a people to create a genuine sense of cultural unity and integrity? Is it possible to come together as a people and see a synthesized Cuban Christ who can serve as a common symbol for all Cubans, black and white, rich and poor, male and female, islanders and exilic?

The consolidation of these vastly different expressions of the Cuban Christ can be found in what I will call an Ajiaco Christ. Fernando Ortiz was the first to use "ajiaco" to describe the Cuban diverse experience. Ajiaco is a Cuban consommé made from a variety of roots. As such, ajiaco becomes the collection of our indigenous roots—roots that symbolize the diverse ethnic backgrounds of Cubans and how they came together to form our *cubanidad,* our Cuban community. Ortiz used this term within the context of a Cuba composed of immigrants who, unlike those who came to the United States, reached the island on the way to someplace else. For him, ajiaco was a renewable Cuban stew where the Amerindians contributed the *maíz, papa, malanga, boniato, yuca,* and *ají.* The Spaniards added *calabaza* and *nabo,* while the Chinese added Oriental spices. Africans, contributing *ñame* and with their culinary foretaste, urged a meaning from this froth beyond mere creative cooking. Ortiz did not use "ajiaco" to mean that Cuban culture has achieved complete integration; rather, Cuba remains "a *mestizaje* [mixture] of kitchens, a *mestizaje* of races, a *mestizaje* of cultures, a dense broth of civilization that bubbles on the stove of the Caribbean."[9] Furthermore, Ortiz recognizes that Cuban culture is not a finished product. Like the ajiaco, the culture is a "vital concept of constant fluidity."[10] For Ortiz, *cubanidad* becomes a "condition of the soul, a complexity of sentiments, ideas and attitudes . . . a heterogeneous conglomerate of diverse races and cultures, which agitate, tremble, and disintegrate in the same social effervescence."[11] While none of the inhabitants (with the possible exception of the indigenous Taínos) representing the "ingredients" of the Cuban ajiaco originated from the island, all repopulated the space called Cuba as displaced people. While not belonging, they made a conscious decision to be rooted to this particular land. For this reason, ajiaco is and should be unapologetically the Cubans' authentic space from where they approach Christ and the wider world. It is a space that collapses the dichotomy existing between those who have historically been called the oppressors and those whom they have oppressed. We construct an Ajiaco Christ that honors and celebrates the diverse and contradictory elements of the stew, which come together in harmony to establish a new creation.

What then become the foundational symbols upon which we can base an Ajiaco Christ, a Christ that includes all the roots of our *cubanidad?* Several symbols indigenous to the Cuban ethos can serve us in construction of an Ajiaco Christ. Although an all-inclusive list does not exist, below are a few salient building blocks that should, at the very least, be included.

Building Block 1: Hatuey. The conquest of Cuba by the Conquistador Christ was met with resistance in the form of a *cacique* (a chieftain) named Hatuey. For three months he orchestrated a type of guerrilla warfare against the Spaniards. Eventually he was caught and condemned to death. As Hatuey was about to be burned at the stake, a Franciscan friar attempted to convert him to Christianity with the promise of heaven and the threat of hell. Hatuey is reported to have asked if there were Christians in heaven. The friar answered in the affirmative, to which the condemned Hatuey retorted that he did not want to go anywhere

where he would see such cruel people. Hatuey has become a historical symbol of Cuban resistance, specifically against foreign powers, such as Spain and later the United States. More importantly, Hatuey functions as a religious symbol, a proto-Christ who demonstrates Christ's mission for those residing on the underside of Cuban history. Hatuey, the so-called heathen, best depicted Christ to the so-called Christian Spaniards. Like Christ, Hatuey cast his lot with the persecuted and suffered death for the cause of justice at the hands of those desiring to enslave him and his people.

Building Block 2: Félix Varela. Varela was born in La Habana in 1788, ordained a priest, and elected as a delegate to the Cortes de España (Spanish parliament), where he distinguished himself by opposing colonialism. He earned a death sentence for proposing two bills, the first abolishing slavery and the second calling for an autonomous Cuba. Persecution forced him to seek political exile in the United States in 1823, where he worked with the poor and published *El Habanero,* a paper dedicated to science, literature, politics, and faith. The contribution of Varela to the creation of a Cuban-based theological thought comes in his active pursuit of consciousness raising. An exception to the clerical norm, Varela fought with those residing on the underside of colonial rule, raising awareness of widespread injustices, and holding those with power and privilege responsible for their abuses. Like the Brazilian educator Paulo Freire, who Varela predates by a century and a half, he saw the need to awaken *los humildes* from a traditional lethargy reinforced by colonialism. Spanish rule provided all Cubans with false consciousness, preventing them from seeing themselves as subjects with the ability to develop their own country. Through Varela's writings a version of what Freire would eventually term *conscientização* was introduced in Cuba. Varela wrote,

> Liberation and the religion have the same origin, and they are never in contradiction because there cannot be contradiction in its Author. The oppression of a people is not distinguished by injustice, and injustice cannot be the work of God. The people are truly liberated if they are truly religious, and I assure you that to be made a slave is precisely to begin by making one a fanatical. So distance is true religion from being the foundation of tyranny![12]

For Varela, liberation required the education of the people so that they could synthesize themes from liberalism (i.e., democracy) with transcendental divine truth. This enables a duty-based society to emerge, a society keen to ensure that opportunities are available for the people to perform.

Building Block 3: José Martí. José Martí was the leader of the revolutionary movement for Cuban independence, poet, journalist, professor, diplomat, and precursor of *modernismo* in Spanish letters. Born in La Habana on January 28, 1853, he was exiled to Spain, ending up in New York City, where he spent the last fourteen years of his life. He was responsible for organizing the armed invasion of the island, and successfully carried it out in 1895. Shortly afterward, he was killed during a skirmish with Spanish troops. Martí gave voice to the dream of the marginalized by calling for the construction of a liberated society based on democratic social justice, racial harmony, labor rights, and self-determination. The revolutionary figure of Martí, venerated as "the apostle of Cuba," serves as the primary symbol communicating the savor of Cuban theological thought. Like no other Cuban writer before or since, Martí skillfully blended religious, scientific, and artistic views to create an image of *patria* (fatherland) that can encompass the polycentric aspects of a complex and diverse Cuban people. Martí as a moral agent attempted to construct an idealized, secularized vision of Christian love, a love rooted in the figure and mission of Jesus Christ. Unfortunately, the romanticizing of Martí's life has led to his apotheosis in a way that ignores his words and works. He accused Christianity, when aligned with colonialist powers, of being a false religion. He attacked all structures that create poverty and believed in the ability of churches to address social problems. As an indigenous Cuban symbol, Martí serves us as a precursor to liberation theology. He can provide Cubans with their own cultural model of Christ the liberator. As a precursor to liberation theology, Martí advocated what later liberation theologians would term a "preferential option for the poor," which basically asserts that God is not neutral in the face of oppression. Martí, following the model of the historical Christ, makes the liberation of the oppressed central to his thoughts, whether the oppressors are Spaniards, North Americans, or fellow Cubans. For Martí, the disenfranchised possess the preferential option of God because they are closer to the truth of the gospel. He wrote, "As always, it is the humble, the shoeless, the needy, the fishermen who band together shoulder to shoulder to fight injustice and make the Gospel fly with its silver wings aflame! Truth is revealed more clearly to the poor and the sufferers! A piece of bread and a glass of water never deceives!"[13] To understand Jesus, one had to experience Christ's marginality. He further wrote, "To fully understand Jesus, it is necessary to have come into the world in a darkened manger with a pure and devout spirit, and to go through life touched by the scarcity of love, the flowering of cupidity, and the victory of hate. One must have sawed wood and kneaded bread amid the silence and transgressions of men."[14]

Building Block 4: Africans. An Ajiaco Christ must also be black so as to be a source of liberation from the sin of intra-Cuban racism. The abuse of black Cubans can be traced to slavery, where African slaves were forced to work eighteen-hour days, six days a week for the enrichment of white Cubans. Once enslaved Africans began working in sugar fields of Cuba, their life expectancy was about seven years. Although legal slavery ended in Cuba in 1886, abolition did not mean an end to racism or exploitation. Africans faced multiple so-called race riots, which provided cover for their decimation. Because the Cuban black experience closely resembles the lot of God's crucified people, their *lucha* (struggle) becomes central in the search for a Cuban Christ, even though a Christ who is black may appear heretical to those white Cubans who possess power and privilege. Another symbol that contributes to our understanding of the Ajiaco

Christ is the Afro-Cuban religion known as Santería. Even though Santería, due to racism, has historically been alien to white Cuban Christians, it is part, if not central, to Cuban identity as a whole. Santería developed into a pragmatic religion promising power for dealing with life's hardships. As a Cuban way of being and living, Santería is part of the Cuban ethos, an indigenous symbol of cultural resistance. To explain Santería theologically reduces the religion to a view of life, rather than a method of survival by way of cultural resistance. In this way, Santería meets the psychological need of accessing power within a powerless milieu. While the practitioner is impotent, *Olofi* (Christ), working through the *orishas* (quasi-deities), possesses the power to protect the humble and humble the powerful.

Building Block 5: Female Freedom Fighters. Accompanying Columbus on his second journey was an acquaintance named Miguel de Cuneo. As a reward for loyal service, Columbus "gave" him an indigenous woman. When Cuneo proceeded to "use" his new "possession," she resisted. Cuneo attempted to subjugate her through a whipping followed by rape.[15] The violation of this unnamed possession of Miguel de Cuneo illustrates the eventual conquest and rape of the entire island. Ironically, through the bruised and abused body of indigenous women like Cuneo's unnamed object, Cubans were birthed. What is important to note is that this unnamed possession of Miguel de Cuneo was neither willing nor passive. She resisted. She, along with numerous other anonymous Taino women, fought against the invading Spaniards. These dehumanized sexual possessions are among the first oppressed of the island. As such, they serve as prototypes for the first Cuban *mambisas* (female freedom fighters) during the wars for independence. If Christ is found in the locus of the conquered Other, then Christ must be feminine. If all forms of structural oppression that eventually developed in Cuba found their roots in oppressive male-female paradigms, then by seriously considering Cuban feminism, a process of liberation can occur. The experiences of these Cuban women as nonpersons become the subject of theology in the quest for the Ajiaco Christ, as their historical struggles become one of the sources that informs the understanding of who Christ is for Cubans.

Rejecting the Eurocentric Christ is never enough. A new way of understanding Christ, rooted within the Cuban ethos, is required. The five building blocks presented in this chapter are not exhaustive, but they do provide us with some Cuban symbols upon which to construct an Ajiaco Christ that can liberate and save Cubans in a Cuban way.

NOTES

1. It is important to note that Cuba's name (even though it was supposed to be their war for independence) is absent from the title given to the war. This was foremost a war between the empires of the Spanish and the Americans with Cuba as the prize.

2. Alice Hageman, "Introduction," in *Religion in Cuba Today,* ed. Alice Hageman and Philip E. Weaton (New York: Association Press, 1971), 21.

3. U.S. capital investment increased in Cuba by 700 percent between 1909 and 1929. As a result, 80 percent of Cuba's imports and 60 percent of her exports came from or went to the United States. During the 1920s, 95 percent of Cuba's main crop, sugar, was U.S.-bound. Forty percent of all raw sugar production was owned by Euro-Americans, and two-thirds of the entire output of sugar was processed in U.S.-owned mills, with the product leaving the island through the U.S.-owned Havana Dock Company. Additionally, 23 percent of nonsugar industry, 50 percent of public service railways, and 90 percent of telephone and electric services were owned by U.S. firms. Nickel deposits were mined and processed by Nicaro, a United States–built plant. Of the four oil refineries, two were owned by U.S. companies, a third by Royal Dutch Shell. All banks were in U.S. and British hands, with one-quarter of all deposits located in foreign branches. Approximately 90 percent of the export trade of Havana cigars went through the United States, which controlled half of the entire manufacturing process. See Hugh Thomas, *Cuba: The Pursuit of Freedom* (New York: Harper & Row, 1971), 466, and Philip C. Newman, *Cuba before Castro: An Economic Appraisal* (New Delhi, India: Prentice Hall, 1965).

4. Louis A. Pérez Jr., *Essays on Cuban History: Historiography and Research* (Gainesville: University Press of Florida, 1995), 63–71.

5. Carlos Moore, *Castro, the Blacks, and Africa* (Los Angeles: Center for Afro-American Studies, University of California, 1988), 63.

6. John M. Kirk, *Between God and the Party: Religion and Politics in Revolutionary Cuba* (Tampa: University Presses of Florida, 1988), 48–49.

7. Fidel Castro, "On Counterrevolutionary Activities of Priests," in Hageman and Weaton, *Religion in Cuba Today,* 130–32.

8. Kirk, *Between God and the Party,* 107.

9. Fernando Ortiz, *Los factores humanos de la cubanidad* (La Habana: Revista Bimestre Cubana, XLV, 1940), 165–69.

10. Fernando Ortiz, "La cubanidad y los negros," *Estudio Afrocubanos* 3 (1939): 3–15.

11. Ibid.

12. Félix Varela, "Estado Eclesiático en la Isla de Cuba," in *El Habanero, Félix Varela Morales* (Miami: Revista Ideal, 1974), 67.

13. José Martí, *Inside the Monster by José Martí: Writings on the United States and American Imperialism,* ed. Philip S. Foner, trans. Elinor Randall, Luis A. Baralt, Juan de Onís, and Roslyn Held Foner (New York: Monthly Review Press, 1975), 271–72.

14. José Marti, *Reader: Writings on the Americas,* ed. Deborah Shnookal and Mirta Muñiz (Chicago: Ocean Press, 1999), 78.

15. Tzvetan Todorov, *The Conquest of America: The Question of the Other,* trans. Richard Howard (New York: Harper & Row, 1984), 48–49.

Chapter 5

Encuentro con el Jesús Sato
An Evangélica Soter-*ology*

LOIDA I. MARTELL-OTERO

One of the earliest christological questions is recorded in the Gospel of Mark, chapter 8. Jesus approaches his disciples and asks them two questions: "Who do people say that I am?" and "Who do you say that I am?" (vv. 27–29). Answers have varied throughout the ages, but it continues to be *una pregunta vigente* (a critical question) for Christians. We can approach the question in a dispassionate and distant fashion—what do others say about Jesus? Or we can respond to it as a vitally important question that somehow affects us within our sociohistorical location, which impacts our community and our very positions of faith. In this essay, I take the latter position and articulate a Christology that is neither dispassionate nor objective, but rather arises from *una pregunta vigente* of belief and faith experience. I do not pretend to express a Christology that is representative of *la iglesia evangélicas* (Latino/a Protestant churches') faith statements.[1] Rather, I write as a bicoastal, and therefore bicultural, Puerto Rican woman who pastored, teaches, and worships among various *evangélica* faith communities, and continues to have the opportunity to share with some extraordinary women of faith along the way. For those unfamiliar with the term *evangélica,* I use it to denote the popular Protestantism that arose from the historic encounter of various Western Protestant groups with the *mestizo* popular Catholicism, which in turn is part of the fabric of Latin American culture and belief. *Evangélica* does not denote U.S. evangelicalism, with its attendant theological and political connotations, although some *evangélicos/as* find points of theological commonalities with it.[2]

In developing a Christology from the perspective of a Puerto Rican *evangélica*, I begin with some presuppositions: First, this is neither a Christology from above—although I assume Jesus' divinity—nor is it fully a Christology from below—though Jesus' full humanity is an integral part of his role as *soter*. This essay does not purport, therefore, to engage in the Chalcedonian arguments that I believe continue to plague christological conversations. Second, given my context, the biblical text is an essential source of Christology. Being raised in the church, my understanding of Jesus developed partly from reading Scripture and partly from its interpretations by women of faith who taught me to love the Gospel stories. This does not mean that as an *evangélica* I preclude the sources of tradition, critical reflection, praxis, sociohistorical location, and spirituality, but rather I seek to underscore that Scripture is a normative source which serves as a basis for judging any theological reflection. Thus I examine specific biblical narratives that I believe shed light about the Jesus Christ whom Puerto Rican *evangélicas* find to be saving. Third, as a result of personal growth as a constructive theologian I assume that Jesus Christ's person, life, mission, and soteriological importance cannot be severed from Trinitarian theology. Jesus Christ is not a "mediator" who has come to defend us against the wrath of God. Rather, he is *Dios hecho carne* (God made flesh), the incarnate One who has embodied in his very person and ministry God's love and salvific intent for humanity—indeed, for all of creation.

Given these presuppositions, my purpose is to develop a Christology through the lens of soteriology. In so doing, I seek to shed light not only on why Jesus is saving for *evangélicas,* but also in what way Jesus is saving. I seek to answer *la pregunta vigente,* "Who do you say that I am?" I do so by first establishing that Jesus is not an idealized or universalized everyman for the *evangélicas* who formed part of my theological formative community. Then, I describe the overall contours of Jesus' identity for them: Jesus the Christ is *encarnada* (incarnate) presence, who ultimately saves because he humanizes us in a world that erases us and casts us aside as surplus people. I examine two biblical paradigms—the stooped woman at the synagogue and the Samaritan woman at the well—to demonstrate this. I briefly discuss how *coritos* and *testimonios* are common vehicles of christological and soteriological expressions for *evangélicas.* I conclude by considering how an *evangélica* Christology contributes to the larger discourse of the Christian church.

JESUS CHRIST: SUPERSTAR

The Nicene and Chalcedonian creedal formulas evidence that Platonic, Aristotelian, and other philosophical thinking has influenced Christian theology and Christology.[3] The God of the exodus and prophets became the Unmoved

Mover, the First Cause—omniscient, omnipresent, omnipotent, dispassionate (*apatheia*), and unchanging. Jesus the Galilean, who was acknowledged as the Christ, became a Logos, mediator, sacrifice, and the paradigm for living a Christian life. Ironically, the early church's attempt to respond to the ontological questions about Christ resulted in losing sight of the very personhood of Jesus. While Christianity has rejected much of the philosophical assumptions about what constituted divinity and God's relations to humankind, nevertheless this heritage continues to influence christological dialogue and debates. Ultimately, who Jesus was as a true, incarnate historical person was marginalized from theological discourse. Even the so-called historical quests for Jesus served to underscore the loss of Jesus the person; indeed, "Questers" discovered a mysterious apocalyptic prophet—misunderstood by his own people and by modern society—a peasant cynic, or an exemplar of moral life.[4] In this ongoing conversation, Jesus became a cosmic ahistorical figure that transcends all times and all cultures. He became a type of Jesus Christ Superstar: an idealized human being and transcendent deity, *el hombre-Dios idóneo* to which all of us must aspire to be.[5] Classical Western Christianity espoused him as the sacrificial servant par excellence, the eschatological personification of self-giving love, and the ultimate social transformer. To be a true Christian, one is called to be a follower of this Christ. To be less than Jesus Christ is to somehow be less than human, less than Christian, a cosmic disappointment to a disapproving divine Parent.

Soteriology followed along the lines of christological reflections. Salvation has been associated with a number of paradigms. Jesus is the ransom for our sins, the atoning figure who satisfies our debt with God, or the substitute for a sinful humanity that deserves to die on the cross. Many contemporary Latin American theologians of liberation interpret Jesus' death on the cross as a paradigm for all those who die daily due to unjust social structures. Salvation thus images the achievement of an ideal. It is envisioned either as reaching a transcendent utopia—heaven—or an immanent one. Jesus' proclamation of the reign of God has been invariably interpreted as the overall framework for a predefined idealized society, an idealized transcendent eschatological reality, or both.

EL JESÚS SATO: THE INCARNATE SOTER

In the late 1970s, Orlando E. Costas and Virgilio Elizondo separately explored the theological implications of the Galilean motif that seemed to be emphasized in the Synoptic Gospel narratives, particularly in the Gospel of Mark.[6] From a Southwestern Mexican American perspective, Elizondo emphasized the theological importance of *mestizaje*. Costas, a Puerto Rican missiologist working in Latin America and in the Northeast, highlighted the missiological/evangelistic implications of "periphery." These two theological categories—*mestizaje* and periphery—point to Latino/a Christologies as holistically incarnational. They emphasize not just the what of Jesus (i.e., what he did for us), but also the who as important for salvation. Such a christological emphasis serves as a corrective for Anselmanian atonement soteriologies, with their almost exclusive focus on the cross as the sole means of salvation.[7] It echoes earlier Irenaean paradigms, reestablishing that the incarnation is as important for salvation as the cross and the resurrection.

As a Puerto Rican *evangélica*, I have summarized the conceptual intention of *mestizaje* and periphery under the rubric of *sato*. *Sato/a* is used in Puerto Rico idiomatically to refer to a mongrel dog or "mutt." Thus *satos/as* are not pure. Although initially referring to dogs, its use has broadened somewhat, and can refer to an act that is somehow of dubious moral character. "*¡Qué sato!*" is spit out almost like an epithet, just as today many in the dominant society spit out the word "illegal immigrant," or "Dominican," or "Puerto Rican," as if they were curse words. *Satos/as* are mixed breeds who are not perceived to be beautiful or of pleasing aspect. They are unwanted. They seem to lurk from the peripheral edges of polite society. People shoo them away. Stones are thrown at them. Shelters teem with them. *Satos/as* are the rejected ones in Puerto Rican society.

I believe that *sata* is an appropriate term because it is a specifically cultural term that aids in the articulation of a contextual Christology from a Puerto Rican perspective. I also believe it connotes the existential conjunction of *mestizaje* and periphery. It expresses the experience of being peripheralized—stereotyped, rejected, and insulted by the hegemonic centers of society. It underscores the experience of being relegated to the bottom rung of society precisely as one who is perceived to be nonhuman, impure, and of no intrinsic value—*sobraja*.[8] To use *sato/a* as a christological term is to raise the specter of the theological scandal of the incarnation. No one wants to be called a *sato/a*. No one wants to be reminded of his or her status of inferiority and rejection in this society. *Sato/a* connotes precisely those elements of pain, loss, and utter rejection from which so many seek to escape.

To speak of the *Jesús sato*, then, is to speak of Jesus' nonidealized, concretely historical, peripherally placed, *mestizo*, struggling, seeking, hoping human being-ness. It is to acknowledge that the One the tradition has identified as fully divine is fully carnal. Luís Pedraja refers to Jesus' "in-meatedness."[9] To identify him as *Jesús sato* also acknowledges that his social location as peripheral is always relative. One must be conscious of the fact that there lies the possibility of there being someone more peripheral relative to one's status. *Jesús sato* is the one who deliberately seeks the least of these, those who are more peripherally placed than he is precisely because he has experienced being a *sato*.[10] They include women, children, and others made disincarnate by kyriarchal structures of dominance. Kyriarchy (from *kyrios*, or "lord") refers to social structures that are complex pyramidal and interdependently multiplicative stratified levels of hierarchy and dominance.[11] In first-century Palestine, poor women and children were truly the *satos/as* of their society.

Jesus' *sato* status is not contingent solely on his being *mestizo*. His peripheral status as *sato* is not simply about biology, nor even about culture. His *sato* status is identified early in the gospel narrative as one whose very lineage is in dispute: "Who is his father?" His *sato* status denotes a marginalization not only due to his religious *mestizaje,* but also due to his questionable legality (*¿será bastardo?*)[12] and geographical location. This peripherally placed *sato* understands the status of being *sato/a,* of being considered *sobraja.* Thus *Jesús sato* is one who embodies/*encarna* the peripheral status of those to whom he is called to minister. In him, we discover that God is present at the periphery. This implies that God has deliberately chosen to become and be with those whom others reject as *sobraja,* and that God has embraced those whom religious folk have declared persona non grata. In Jesus' life and very being, the human value of all *satos/as* is underscored. Those made no-bodies by kyriarchal structures are humanized through the personhood and actions of this sacred *sato,* Jesus of Galilee. In him, we discover that salvation does not begin at the centers of power, but in the periphery, among the *satos/as,* who are made *santos/as* (holy)—called by God to witness and to embody God's salvation in the world.

This *Jesús sato* is faithful to his ministry among the peripheral *satos/as,* which leads him to confront the powers and principalities of his time—the societal structures that make people invisible. Such actions lead to a violent confrontation, and he is executed, *uno que sobra entre tanta sobraja.*[13] He dies "outside the gate" of humanization and justice, among abandoned *satos.*[14] The women who are the most peripheral in kyriarchal societies—*las satas hechas sobrajas*—are able to see God in *Jesús sato* in this place of humiliation, torture, and death, while his male disciples flee from such a peripheral place.[15] In this space filled with betrayal and horror, Jesus remained faithful to those who died outside the gate, and the women steadfastly remained as witnesses to Jesus. It is ironic that the cross, which is designed to strip one of one's full humanity, becomes the location where women became most visible. They stood by Jesus at the foot of the cross and were the first at the tomb. Consequently, they were the first to acknowledge the miracle of the resurrection. They are the first purveyors of the good news of salvation: *las satas son llamadas a ser santas*[16]—witnesses to God's faithfulness and grace, amid realities of destruction and death. Among them and with them God promises to bring life, transformation, and hope.

BIBLICAL PARADIGMS: *JESÚS* AS *SOTER*

Various biblical narratives can serve as paradigms to represent how *evangélicas* perceive *Jesús sato* to be *soter.* In this section I analyze two in particular because they underscore the themes I have discussed thus far: Jesus as healer and his ability to humanize those who have been dehumanized by kyriarchal social structures. Luke 13:10–17 recounts the story about the bent-over woman whom Jesus encounters in a synagogue as he is teaching. Jesus' encounter with the Samaritan woman at the well is described in John 4:4–42.

Woman Bent Over: Healing Presence

Healing is integral to an *evangélica* soteriology and Christology. It is also a powerful motif in Jesus' preaching. It is invariably linked with his proclamation of the reign of God. While some of the Gospel writers sought to downplay the christological title of Jesus as *theos aner,* the link between reign and healing is too powerful to interpret as simply an act of a miracle worker.[17] The term *soter* is a recurring one for Luke, and his healing narratives are generally associated with this term.[18] Thus healing is more than just the removal of an illness. It is *shalom*—communal as well as personal, historically concrete, holistic well-being. It is a healing of the fractures of society that damage people on a daily basis.[19] It is integrally related to the actual realization of God's reign.

Jesus encounter with the bent-over woman demonstrates this well. According to the Gospel of Luke, Jesus is teaching in the synagogue on a Sabbath day when he calls to the woman. The woman is never named. She seems to be alone. Latinas who read this passage can identify readily with this woman. They too are nameless. They are dismissed. They are *sobraja,* too often bereft of social networks. They bear the brunt of *las luchas diarias* (daily struggles) leaving them bent over in their struggle to survive. They are required to provide for their families, but the means to do so is often beyond their reach. They are lacking in "vital connections" that others take for granted.[20] Even health care often is inaccessible to them.

Commentators have noted the importance of the setting: Jesus calls to her in the synagogue, a sacred space. Interestingly, it is a space normally apportioned to men; one does not usually associate women with synagogues in first-century Palestine. Furthermore, he calls to her on the Sabbath day. Traditionally Sabbath is associated with rest (Exod. 20:8–11). Yet Sabbath has a deeper significance: it is God's self-gifting to humankind. In this space, one shares in the divine life. It is an *imitatio Dei*—God rested on the seventh day. Thus, Sabbath is a celebration of God's intent for wholeness for all of creation and the historical anticipation of the fullness of the eschatological reign.

It is ironic, then, that in this doubly sacred place, the woman's affliction had been ignored for eighteen years. She was not provided with rest; she was stooped. The fullness of her humanity was unacknowledged. The depth of her pain was discounted. As a pastor, I have accompanied Latinas to doctors who have laughed at them, ignored their afflictions, and even mistreated them. While the church has often been a place of sanctuary for Latinas, it has also been a place that has added to their burdens due to sexist and cultural expectations. Very few *evangélica* churches create spaces where Latinas can sit and rest.

It is no wonder then that the text refers somewhat ambiguously to a "spirit of weakness" (*astheneia*) in describing the woman's malady. Contemporary scholarship has sought to determine if the text is referring to a demonic spirit that has bound her or institutional forces that dehumanize women. I suggest that the latter interpretation is supported by the context of the text.[21] With no apparent male figure to intercede on her behalf, she is vulnerable. She is treated as *sobraja*. Certainly, Latinas know about the social, cultural, economic, and political spirits that inhabit their world, draining them of *fuerza vital* (strength and hope). Neither is the response of the synagogue leader foreign to Latinas. They too have encountered those who would reinscribe their marginal status, ignore their cries, and resent their attempts to bring justice to their cause. Jesus alone defended this woman's right to wholeness—he insists that it is "necessary" (*dei*) that she be healed. Latinas trust this Jesus because he understands their pain and recognizes that they are daughters of Abraham, and not *sobraja*. As *hijas* they are part of God's family with equal rights to partake of God's promises and blessings.[22] Just as the pericope ends with the woman straightened and praising God, so Latinas lift up their heads and give witness to the power of God's saving presence in their lives. This is not just a healing of physical ailments, as necessary as that is, but also *katartismos*—a healing of the social fractures that tear communities and churches apart.[23]

The Samaritan Woman: *Una Sata Llamada a Ser Santa* (A *Sata* Called to Be a Saint)

The biblical passage of the encounter between Jesus and the Samaritan woman also serves as a paradigm for an *evangélica* Christology. Samaritans were the *satos/as* of their time, perceived as illegitimate inhabitants by Jews. Thus they were considered strangers in the very land in which they were born and where they had lived all their lives. Considered biologically, religiously, and ritually impure, these *satos/as* lived at the margins of a colonized Israel. This parallels the particular experience of U.S.-born Latinas, who are perceived as cultural *satas,* belonging neither in the space where they are born nor to the home of their cultural/biological forebears.[24] Always perceived as foreigners, this sense of alterity is an integral component of their existential and epistemological reality.

The passage points not only to the sense of alterity with regard to the centers of power, but also to the tensions that exist within the liminal space of periphery. Peripheral groups are often in conflict among themselves in a bid to survive within kyriarchal structures. This enables centers of power to retain their hegemonic status. This particular pericope in the Gospel of John references the long-simmering debate between Jews and Samaritans to determine who was more faithful to Scripture, and who truly worshiped "in spirit and truth." It is no coincidence that this debate takes place between a Galilean *sato* and Samaritan *sata*. The passage is a reminder that one needs to be attentive to the sin of periphery: that marginalized groups can be and are oppressive to each other as a result of the sin of kyriarchy. While Jesus is a peripheral Galilean Jew, he is still a Jew and male. He thus has power and privilege over a Samaritan woman. The passage thus exemplifies the nuances of sin, influenced by culture, color, class, gender, and religion. Latinas often experience these nuanced levels of oppression as they come into conflict with other oppressed groups in their struggle for survival. They are subject to the oppression of sexism leveled against them in their communities and churches by Latinos and non-Latinos. They can encounter conflict with other women, including other Latinas. The sin of periphery is as destructive as the sin of hegemony that spawns it. It is an internalized oppression that renders Latinas powerless and voiceless.

The text about the Samaritan woman is also relevant to the reality of Latinas because she has been punitively objectified and victimized by kyriarchy. Specifically as a woman, she was subject to the rules of levirate marriage of her day. Her conversation with Jesus reveals the extent to which she was exploited by this system: she has had five husbands, and her present consort offered her no legal protection. Levirate marriages take place due to economic and social necessity. This predicament placed her in a vulnerable relationship that denied her the security of a marriage contract.[25] Her *sata* status is compounded: she is not only an other as a Samaritan, but also as one who resides outside the gate of legal protection. She is nothing more than *un estorbo*.[26] Her peripheral otherness is highlighted by the fact that she has no name in the narrative. She is simply identified by her *sata* status.

Traditional scholarship has often mistakenly stereotyped the Samaritan woman as immoral. Such interpretations underscore her otherness. It is easier to impose one's views upon the other when that other is faceless, nameless, and powerless. This again mirrors the experience of Latinas in the United States. As surplus *satas,* they reside in peripheral neighborhoods, segregated because they are not perceived to be full, valuable members of U.S. society. They are stereotyped as shifty, irresponsible, ignorant, and even criminal. Given the social and economic pressures, they often are forced into what Luise Schottroff has called "consecutive, or levirate, marriages" with men who refuse to avail them of socially acceptable or legal status.[27] Sometimes, that status is denied them by the reality of governmental regulations, which would lead to a cessation of much-needed support if they married. The result of these incongruent circumstances is that Latinas also are perceived to be immoral.

Jesús sato encounters this Samaritan *sata*. Perhaps because of his own location and experience, he seems to empathize with her plight. He engages her, thus acknowledging her full humanity. In the process of their conversation, she is able to "call her situation by name and free herself from it."[28] This encounter between a *sato* and even more peripheral *sata* allows Jesus to insert "himself into the conditions of her life," and in so doing bring about change: to allow her to realize that to be a source of living water, she must first be free from the dependence on a man who thus far has only used her.[29] She can rest! To do so is to "worship in spirit and in truth." Thus *Jesús sato* is *soter* and is as much a source of liberation for her as he was for the bent-over woman. It is important to note that their dialogue is not about philosophical conundrums. There is no talk about an idealized transcendental heaven. It does not entail a debate on metaphysics. *Jesús* is *soter* because he is instrumental in liberating her from a concrete situation caused by the integral multiplicative sins of sexism, racism, cultural discrimination, and classism. *Jesús* is *soter* because in him the Samaritan woman encounters God's faithful presence. As with the woman in the synagogue, the Samaritan *sata* did not have to go searching for God. God has come for her. In this *Jesús sato,* God has called to her.

The Samaritan *sata*'s encounter with the Galilean *sato* empowers her. She finds her authentic voice in speaking with him. She discovers that doors cannot be closed to her because, contrary to kyriarchal claims, God is not the exclusive property of any one culture, religion, gender, or class. She can access God's salvation because God is open to those who seek to worship in spirit and in truth. Spirit is *ruach, pneuma,* and therefore intimately related to life. To seek in spirit and in truth is to recognize God as the source of life itself. Such grace cannot be exclusive, but rather is related to the very purpose of God's salvific intent from creation. In discovering this good news *(euangelion)* the Samaritan woman goes forward to share it with her community. The Samaritan *sata,* once considered no better than *sobraja,* is called precisely because she is *sata* and *sobraja.* She comes into her own and, as such, she becomes a conduit of life and good news: she speaks in spirit and in truth. Thus *la sata es ahora llamada santa* (the *sata* is now called a saint)—the *sata* becomes a holy agent of the Lord. Through her, others come to Jesus.

Through Jesus as a fully human *sato* person of his context and time, God makes a profound statement: that God is to be found within the confines of human history, in the ambiguities of life, embodied in One who did not transcend his culture and limitations. Perhaps this is what Paul meant when he quoted the hymn in Philippians 2:6–7: that Jesus did not claim to be more than he was, but emptied himself *(kenosis)* of glory. This very human who is God present among us provides the Samaritan *sata* with a salvific moment. That this takes place in human history underscores its momentary nature for the woman; indeed, Jesus' role as *soter* is ambiguous, for as soon as the woman returns to her village, she is erased again. The men acknowledge that they came because of her *testimonio* (witness). Nevertheless, from that point on, the conversation takes place directly between them and Jesus. She is no longer acknowledged. She is no longer named. She is *sobraja* once again. The salvific moment that takes place gives us hope that a greater transformation will take place. It is hope in an eschatological future. History is filled with the ambiguity of promise not fulfilled. This is not an idealized Jesus, nor is salvation an idealized utopia. It is promise. It is hope. The eschatological proviso is that what takes place now impels us forward to a promised possibility. It allows us to dream. It gives us a foretaste of what it can be fully and therefore gives us courage and strength to struggle. It acknowledges our right to self-care and rest. The passage ends on an ambiguous note for *satas* and yet it provides a sign of hope: her presence cannot be fully eradicated. She has left behind an empty jug—no longer to be exploited—and a town transformed by her witness.

CÁNTICO DE ESPERANZA: SINGING A SONG
IN FOREIGN LANDS

This is the Jesus that Latinas know. This is the salvation that they have experienced. *Evangélicas* are often the conduits of evangelism and agents of sacrificial service in their churches, among their family members, and in the larger community.[30] Few are known by name, and even fewer are recorded in historical annals. In the larger community, they face discrimination for being poor, brown, non-English-speaking women. There is no need here to repeat the statistics that represent the often grim social realities of the Latino/a community.[31] They are among the poorest and most marginalized of this nation. They often face social, cultural, religious, and linguistic discrimination.

Latinas face the quadruple oppression of color, class, culture, and gender. They are dehumanized and dismissed as *sobrajas* and *estorbos*—a problem that needs to be eradicated. They lack access to the vital connections that would allow them to care for their families, for whom they largely are responsible.[32] They lack access to quality housing, health care, education, and even such basics as fresh food.[33] They face discrimination in the church, where often they are marginalized in spite of the fact that *evangélicas* make up 60–70 percent of churches' memberships.[34] What is ironic is the fact that the church is often a place of sanctuary for them. It is the one place where they can be themselves, understood, and find some relief from the incessant social pressures they face on a daily basis *en el mundo*.[35] Finding little to no grace wherever they turn, they call upon Jesus.

Subsequently, they discover that he has encountered them *en el camino* (along the journey), along the journey. Jesus is found to be *en lo cotidiano* or (in the everyday spaces) of their lives. The importance of *lo cotidiano*—literally "the every day"—as an epistemological and theological category has been explored by Ada María Isasi-Díaz, María Pilar Aquino, and others.[36] Daniel H. Levine defines it as "the structured patterns of action, discourse, norms, and established social roles that appear when religious and cultural exchange is considered 'from below.'" It is therefore a space where powerless and "peripheric" people seek meaning for, and control of, their lives.[37] *Lo cotidiano* is where *satos/as* live, where the impact of structural sin is most evident, and conversely, where *evangélicas* feel the closest to God.

Encountering Jesus in the spaces of the everyday allows one to perceive who he is for Latinas. In spite of their expressions about *la sangre de Cristo* (the blood of Christ), or that salvation is *la vida eterna* (eternal life), their praxis reveals a more nuanced Christology and soteriology. Thus, for *evangélicas* Jesus' identity cannot be separated from his *soter*-ology. The Christology-soteriology dialectic is the response to *la pregunta vigente*—"Who do you say that I am?"—within their context, articulated concretely in the prayers, *testimonios,* and *coritos* of *evangélicas*. He is *el Jesús sato*: a real human being who reveals God's saving presence in the midst of the ambiguities of life. This is the Jesus to whom they pray, the one who sends the Spirit to empower them, defend them, heal them, speak to them, and fulfill their lives with *ruach*/life. They know him as intimately as he knows them. He knows their struggles and their pain because he has experienced them. He is flesh as they are flesh. He knows hunger, poverty, abandonment, loss, suffering, humiliation, and even death. *Jesús, el sato Galileo* (the *sato* Galilean), is the ever-present one. He listens. He seeks. He responds. He understands. He is flesh as they are flesh, and yet he is unlike them. He is God who has embraced their very humanity. Therefore they cease to be *sobraja satas* and discover that they are sacred daughters of God. *Las satas son santas* (the *satas* are saints). *Jesucristo el sato* has overcome the sinful structures that oppress them. In his resurrection, *evangélicas* perceive an affirmation of God's promise that death and destruction do not hold the last word. In his life, they see that God is truly and fully present to them. Because he lived, they now have new life. Because God did not allow him to remain dead, they have a promise that they, too, will overcome the vicissitudes of life. The resurrection reveals that God sought them and embraced them as they are and where they are. They are no longer discounted or excluded but welcomed into the full presence of the Triune God where they can rest from *la lucha diaria*. Being anointed by the Spirit is both a consequence and a confirmation of the validity of their encounter with the *Jesús sato*. They are thus empowered to walk with Jesus. The intimacy of the relationship gives them the confidence to call upon him no matter how large or small the petition might be. So they pray: for food, rent, healing, their family's safety, and the transformation of their neighborhoods. They pray for justice and cry out against whatever demeans or diminishes their lives. They pray in faith because the Jesus that they seek is neither dead nor absent. He is *Chuito, el Jesús sato* (*sato* Jesus), the faithful one who died outside the gate and remains in the peripheral spaces that they inhabit to save, heal, and restore.

They also sing. My memories of church are always of extraordinary women singing their hearts out. Many of their songs were from familiar biblical texts, but given a nuanced and richly textured meaning that told their stories. They sang songs of thanksgiving and praise, as well as laments and prayers for help. When these women of faith experienced their lives as continuous struggles, they would lift their voices and sing:

> Aunque un ejército acampe contra mi, no temerá mi corazón
> Aunque contra mi se levante guerra yo estaré confiada en mi Jesús.[38]

I pastored a church in New York when a woman's eighteen-year-old son was shot in the head as he sat on a stoop next to his older sister. The young man—a former member of my youth group—died instantly, an innocent victim of the senseless violence that affects so many of our communities. As much as she had tried to keep her family safe, this woman of deep faith was now facing an unspeakable tragedy. Overwhelmed by a profound sense of loss and grief, one Sunday morning, she came to the altar and sang with all her heart and soul:

Oye oh Dios mi clamor
A mi oración atiende
Desde el cabo de la tierra clamaré a ti cuando mi corazón desmaye.
Llévame a la roca que es más alta que yo
Porque tú has sido mi refugio, Señor.[39]

Her hands and face raised to the heavens, tears streaming down her face, this heartbroken mother cried out to *Jesús soter* to save her by taking her only son into his arms and sustaining her with his abiding presence during her darkest hour. Regardless of the original meaning of the psalm, *evangélicas* like this mother sing it to affirm that Jesus is their rock and foundation, a stronghold against the powers and principalities of death. Jesus will sustain them, protect them, and lift them up from the depths of despair when they face circumstances over which they are powerless.

This Jesus who is of their flesh—*de carne y hueso* (flesh and blood)[40]—is accessible to them, unlike so many social structures that exclude and silence them. He is not "Jesus Superstar"—a docetic ideal. Belief in him does not eliminate the tragedies and struggles they face. Nevertheless, *Jesús sato* is more than just flesh; he is also "God made present." He sees their pain.

Venid a mi todos los que estáis trabajados, todo el que esté cansado
Y os haré descansar, os haré descansar, os haré os haré descansar.
Llevad mi yugo sobre vosotros y aprended di mi que soy manso.
Porque mi yugo es fácil y ligera mi carga
Y hallaréis, hallaréis, hallaréis, descanso para vuestras almas.[41]

In him they can rest because the Lord is their rock, their strength, their life, and their salvation. They experience profound moments of grace and of joy, even in the midst of tragedy and death. *Jesús sato* is the faithful one who provides for their needs. He is the God of justice who acts a *justo tiempo y en el momento preciso*—in the precise moment.

Que bueno es alabarte, o Señor, y cantad salmos a tu Nombre.
Anunciar por las mañanas tu misericordia y tu fidelidad cada noche.[42]

This is the Jesus who inhabits the spaces of every day and every night.

Sata women give honor and praise to this *Jesús sato* in their churches not just through song but also through *testimonios*. *Testimonios* are salvific moments because they are the vehicles whereby the voiceless speak with power and authority. They are sacramental moments that embody an affirmation of God's incarnate presence in the spaces of their everyday lives. *Testimonios* negate the sexist assumptions that deny women their rightful places in the sacralized spaces of the church. Women stand in the pulpit to tell the world that their God is present, that *Jesús sato* has responded to their cry, and that the Spirit of the Lord has anointed them. *Testimonios* allow them to be conduits of wisdom. They teach, exhort, and give voice to the tragedies that are woven into *la vida cotidiana*. As the Samaritan left behind a jug of water to mark an affirmation of her full worth and humanity, so *evangélicas* leave their stories, reminding a community that God continues to do powerful things in their midst.[43]

CONCLUSION: A *SOTER*-OLOGY OF *EL JESÚS SATO*

The issue of Jesus' identity is a critical question, *una pregunta vigente,* in our day not just for Christian Latino/a communities, but for the wider Christian church. It has been under the name of Jesus that nations have been invaded and people have been murdered en masse. It is also true that Jesus has inspired acts of generosity and social transformation that have transcended borders. We do well to remember Albert Schweitzer's warning that too often the Jesus we see is a reflection of the prevalent trends of the time.[44] We can too easily turn Jesus into an excuse for our sin and greed. Thus it is imperative to remember that Jesus is not simply the object of historical curiosity, the paradigm for theological reflection, nor the idealized imagery that counters all that we are not. Jesus was a human being who lived in a particular time and in a particular place. Christianity claims that in this person God was present to us in a distinctive way. It claims that to know Jesus is to know something about God, and that to know Jesus we also know something about humanity.

I believe that an *evangélica* Christology contributes important insights to *la pregunta vigente* about Jesus' identity. First, an *evangélica* Christology underscores that salvation does not begin at the centers of power. Rather, salvation is mediated from the periphery through the *Jesús sato.* Therefore, God is found primarily amid the most invisible, most marginalized people. Jesus lived and died outside the gate, where the *satos/as* of society reside. Jesus' identity as a *sato* living in the most peripheral places of the world serves to place in relief the sin of kyriarchy. Those at the centers of power are not able to mediate salvation because by their very hegemonic nature they are the cause of sin and injustice. They make others invisible and voiceless—no-bodies who are treated as *sobraja.* *Jesús sato* embodies that invisibility, but subverts it by calling the *satos/as* of the world to be the evangelists of good news: that God is in the midst of them, overturning structures of injustice and transforming the no-bodies to be some-bodies. In Jesus, the *satos/as son hechos santos/as.* Those rejected as *sobraja* are children of God. Those who would maintain sinful kyriarchal structures in turn are challenged to hear the scandal of the good news: that Jesus stands outside the gate calling to them to the peripheric places of salvation.

Second, *evangélica* Christology reminds us that to explore who Jesus is cannot be divorced from what Jesus does in our midst. That is to say, Jesus' identity is *una pregunta vigente* because through him we discover God's saving presence in the midst of the most peripheric people, those treated as *satas, estorbos, y sobrajas;* but at the same time, it is in his saving ministry that we discover him to be a real historical being. Jesus is human! He is *Jesús sato.* This is an incarnational Christology *de calle* that is willing to embrace ambiguity as a historical reality. Yet to acknowledge its *carne* and ambiguity does not diminish the soteriological power of the incarnation. Jesus is saving not because he died, but emphatically because he lived. Such an incarnational Christology serves as a corrective to the abundance of atonement soteriologies that reduce Jesus to a suffering cipher on a cross, a disembodied paradigm that too often has been reduced to an annual Easter ritual. An incarnational Christology *de la calle* is a desire to remind the church that God's active and salvific presence is already at work in this *sato,* who encounters women bent over and bleeding, women seeking rest and affirmation of their full worth. In his very being as *sato,* Jesus is already saving because he makes visible, *encarna,* that which the world has sought to erase. In him, through him, and with him, *las satas son hechas santas.* His death is not to be discounted. He died outside the gate of hope, help, or humanity. There he remained faithful to his ministry and to the *satos/as* who die daily. He died an unspeakable death that exposed the evil of kyriarchy. His death is not paradigmatic, nor poetry, nor a means of mystical ecstasy. Death and suffering are never ennobling. Therefore, the resurrection is critically important, for through that singular act God reminds us that God does not abandon the *satos/as* of the world. We receive a promise that marginality, disembodiment, and death are not the last word; that the hegemonic powers are no powers at all; and that God is the power that overcomes all powers and principalities. Thus Jesus' life and ministry are crucial to any balanced Christian soteriology.

Third, an *evangélica* Christology balances the emphasis of Jesus as a model for sacrificial service with one that calls us into a vocation of self-care and rest. In 1980, Judith Plaskow objected to the preponderance of male-centered theologies to define sin almost exclusively as hubris.[45] Feminist, womanist, and other theologies have since developed understandings of sin that encompass injustice, internalized oppression, and low self-esteem. Nevertheless, too many theologies from the center continue to interpret salvation as the transformation of people for loving service to the other. For *la Samaritana* and the bent-over woman, the issue is not about loving "the other," or serving the community; rather, it is freedom from exploitation and an inability to be cared for. Salvation is rest: from illness, from exploitative relationships, and from *la lucha diaria.* *Evangélicas* with whom I have shared resonate with these stories. In addition to the continued injunctions in Exodus and Leviticus to honor God's Sabbath, there are First Testament texts that point to rest as an important eschatological/salvific motif.[46] An *evangélica* Christology underscores that rest and restoration are profoundly salvific moments that point to a truth about the reign of God. Rest is not just about doing nothing, but about participating in a divine event. Rest is something God does. Rest is not a human invention but a truly Spirit-led grace wherein we enter into a "holy dance" with God.[47] As one who perennially dances with God, *Jesús sato* has come to invite us to join. As we do, let us remember Jesus' words:

> Y si supieses qué significa: "Misericordia quiero, y no sacrificio," no condenarías a los inocentes. Porque el Hijo del Hombre es Señor del día de reposo. (Matt. 12:7–8, VRV)[48]

May the Lord of *satos/as* grant us the grace and wisdom to know when to rest, when to dance, and when to sow.

NOTES

1. I use the term "Latino/a" to denote a gender-inclusive form of a word that has come to be indicative of the varied communities of people who descend from sundry Spanish-speaking countries and now reside within the contiguous United States. The limitations and problems of this terminology have been amply discussed in other forums. See Fernando F. Segovia, "Hispanic American Theology and the Bible: Effective Weapon and Faithful Ally," in *We Are a People! Initiatives in Hispanic American Theologies,* ed. Roberto S. Goizueta (Minneapolis: Fortress Press, 1992), 26–27. Also Zaida Maldonado Pérez, "U.S. Hispanic/Latino Identity and Protestant Experience: A Brief Introduction for the Seminarian," *Perspectivas* 7 (Fall 2003): 96–97.
2. Cf. George Marsden, ed., *Evangelicalism and Modern America* (Grand Rapids: William B. Eerdmans Publishing Company, 1984), ix–xii.
3. Plato's conceptualization of the cosmos as a projection of idealized Forms has contributed to a worldview that seems to create hope for a utopia that is never obtained but always sought. For more on Plato's articulation on Forms, see Constantin Ritter, *The Essence of Plato's Philosophy,* trans. Adam Alles (New York: Dial Press, 1933), and Dewey J. Hoitenga Jr., *Faith and Reason from Plato to Plantinga: An Introduction to Reformed Epistemology* (Albany: State University of New York Press, 1991).
4. Albert Schweitzer, *The Quest of the Historical Jesus: A Critical Study of Its Progress from Reimarus to Wrede* (Baltimore: Johns Hopkins University Press, 1998); John Dominic Crossan, *The Historical Jesus: The Life of a Mediterranean Jewish Peasant* (San Francisco: Harper Collins, 1991); John P. Meier, *The Marginal Jew: Rethinking the Historical Jesus,* vol. 1, *The Roots of the Problem and the Person* (New York: Doubleday, 1991).
5. Translation: "ideal man-God." "Man" is used intentionally to underscore gender bias.
6. Orlando E. Costas, *Liberating News: A Theology of Contextual Evangelization* (Grand Rapids: William B. Eerdmans Publishing Company, 1989). Virgilio Elizondo, *Galilean Journey: Mexican-American Promise,* rev. ed. (Maryknoll, NY: Orbis Books, 2000). For further analysis of the soteriological implication of *mestizaje* and periphery, see Loida I. Martell-Otero, "Liberating News: Towards a U.S. Hispanic/Latina Soteriology of the Crossroads," PhD diss., Fordham University, December 2004.
7. For recent critiques see Marit Trelstad, ed., *Cross Examinations: Readings of the Meaning of the Cross Today* (Minneapolis: Fortress Press, 2007). Also J. Denny Weaver, *Nonviolent Atonement* (Grand Rapids: William B. Eerdmans Publishing Company, 2001). Earlier critiques include Joanne Carlson Brown and Carole R. Bohn, eds., *Christianity, Patriarchy, and Abuse: A Feminist Critique* (Cleveland: Pilgrim Press, 1989), and Rita Nakashima Brock, *Journeys by Heart: A Christology of Erotic Power* (New York: Crossroad, 1995).
8. *Sobraja* literally means "leftovers." Ada María Isasi-Díaz uses the term "surplus" to denote a similar concept—that of society's penchant to discount people as if they have no intrinsic value; see "Un Poquito de Justicia—A Little Bit of Justice: A Mujerista Account of Justice," in *Hispanic/Latino Theology:*

Challenge and Promise, ed. Ada María Isasi-Díaz and Fernando F. Segovia (Minneapolis: Fortress Press, 1996), 329.

9. Luís Pedraja, *Jesus Is My Uncle: Christology from a Hispanic Perspective* (Nashville: Abingdon Press, 1999), 76.

10. See Costas's discussion of the three layers of periphery in *Liberating News,* 49–50.

11. Elisabeth Schüssler Fiorenza, *But She Said: Feminist Practices of Biblical Interpretation* (Boston: Beacon Press, 1992), 115.

12. Translation: "Is he a bastard?" or "Is he illegitimate?" Cf. Luke 4:22.

13. Translation: "A leftover among so many leftovers."

14. Heb. 13:12–13. Cf. Orlando E. Costas, *Christ Outside the Gate: Mission beyond Christendom* (Maryknoll, NY: Orbis Books, 1982), 188–94.

15. Victoria Phillips argues that some of the women were as much disciples as the men, while others were "believers." See "Full Disclosure Towards a Complete Characterization of the Women Who Followed Jesus According to Mark," in *Transformative Encounters: Jesus and Women Re-viewed,* ed. Ingrid Rosa Kitzberger, Biblical Interpretation Series 43 (Leiden: Brill, 2000), 14–19.

16. Translation: "The *satas* are called to be saints."

17. Cf. Edward Schillebeeckx, *Jesus: An Experiment in Christology,* trans. Hubert Hoskins (New York: Crossroad, 1995), 424–26.

18. See Joseph Fitzmeyer, *The Gospel According to Luke I–IX,* Anchor Bible 28 (New York: Doubleday, 1981), 20.

19. Martell-Otero, "Liberating News," 376–78.

20. David T. Abalos, *Latinos in the United States: The Sacred and the Political,* 2nd ed. (Notre Dame, IN: University of Notre Dame, 2007), 118.

21. See R. Alan Culpepper, "Stooped Woman," in *New Interpreter's Bible,* vol. 9, *Luke, John* (Nashville: Abingdon Press, 1995), 274; Hisako Kinukawa, "The Miracle Story of the Bent-over Woman (Luke 13:10–17): An Interaction-Centred Interpretation," in Kitzberger, *Transformative Encounters,* 297.

22. Blanqui Otaño, "Nueva Identidad de la Mujer Encorvada: Exégesis de Lucas 13.10–17," in *Teología Desde la Mujer en Centroamérica,* ed. Irene Foulkes (San José, Costa Rica: Sebila, 1989), 129–30.

23. Loida I. Martell-Otero, "Of Satos and Saints: Salvation from the Periphery," *Perspectivas* 4 (Summer 2001): 16–17.

24. Approximately 60 percent of the total Latino/a population is U.S.-born. See Roberto R. Ramírez, "We the People: Hispanics in the United States," Census 2000 Special Reports CENSR–18 (Washington, DC: U.S. Census Bureau, 2004), 8. Also, Pew Hispanic Center, "Statistical Portrait of Hispanics in the United States, 2006," http://pewhispanic.org/files/factsheets/hispanics2006/hispanics.pdf.

25. Luise Schottroff, "The Samaritan Woman and the Notion of Sexuality in the Fourth Gospel," trans. Linda M. Maloney, in *What Is John,* vol. 2, *Literary and Social Readings of the Fourth Gospel,* ed. Fernando F. Segovia (Atlanta: Scholars Press, 1998), 162–64.

26. Translation: "a bother; a problem that disturbs the status quo."

27. Schottroff, "Samaritan Woman," 162–64.

28. Ibid., 164.

29. Ibid., 168–69.

30. For example, see Virginia Sanchez Korrol's documentation of the Rev. Leoncia Rosado (Mama Leo) in "In Search of Unconventional Women: Histories of Puerto Rican Women in Religious Vocations Before Mid-Century," *Oral History Review* 16, no. 2 (Fall 1988): 47–63. Also see Elizabeth Conde

Frazier and Loida I. Martell-Otero, "U.S. Latina Evangélicas," in *Encyclopedia of Women and Religion in North America,* ed. Rosemary Radford Ruether and Rosemary Skinner Keller (Bloomington: Indiana University Press, 2006).

31. These have been documented throughout the years by various authors. For recent statistics, see "Hispanic Heritage Month 2008: Sept. 15–Oct. 15," Facts for Features CB08-FF.15, U.S. Census Bureau News (Washington, DC: U.S. Department of Commerce, 2008), http://www.census.gov/Press-Release/www/releases/archives/facts_for_features_special_editions/012245 .html. Also, Martell-Otero, "Liberating News," 113–23.

32. Abalos, *Latinos in the United States,* 109–16. For current statistics on Latinas in the United States, see Felisa Gonzales, "Hispanic Women in the United States, 2007," rev. May 14, 2008, Pew Hispanic Center (Washington, DC: Pew Research Center, 2008), http://pewhispanic.org/factsheets/factsheet .php?FactsheetID=42.

33. See Clara E. Rodríguez, *Puerto Ricans: Born in the U.S.A.* (Boulder, CO: Westview Press, 1991), 109–10.

34. Rev. Rafael Martell, pastor of the Iglesia Bautista Cristiana de Soundview in New York, once commented that if all the women would leave his church, he would be forced to shut it down immediately (personal communication, New York City, 1995).

35. Translation: "in the world."

36. Ada María Isasi-Díaz, *Mujerista Theology: A Theology for the Twenty-First Century* (Maryknoll, NY: Orbis Books, 1996). Maria Pilar Aquino, "Theological Method in U.S. Latina Theology: Toward an Intercultural Theology for the Third Millennium," in *From the Heart of Our People: Explorations in Catholic Systematic Theology,* ed. Orlando O. Espín and Miguel H. Díaz (Maryknoll, NY: Orbis Books, 1999). See also Loida I. Martell-Otero, "Lo Cotidiano: God in the Spaces of the Everyday," *Witness* 83, no. 12 (December 2000): 21–22.

37. Daniel H. Levine, *Popular Voices in Latin American Catholicism* (Princeton, NJ: Princeton University Press, 1992), 317, 320.

38. Translation: "Even though an army encompasses against me, I will not fear. Even though war is waged, I will trust in my Jesus" (based on Ps. 27). Unless otherwise specified, all *coritos* are based on the Reina Valera (VRV) revision of 1960, and all translations are mine. It is interesting that this particular rendition has added "in my Jesus," even though those words are not part of the original psalm.

39. Ps. 61: "Hear, O God, my cry, and to my prayer be attentive. From the ends of the earth I will cry out to you when my heart is faint. Take me to the rock that is higher than me because you are my refuge, O Lord."

40. Literally, "of meat and bones."

41. "Come to me all who are overworked, all who are tired and I will give you [literally, make you] rest. Take my yoke upon you [trans. note: "you" is in the plural, which means that the yoke is carried as a communal enterprise] and learn from me [because] I am meek, and you will find rest for your souls. Because my yoke is easy and my burden is light" (based on Matt. 11:28–29).

42. "How good it is to praise you, O Lord, and to sing psalms to your name. Proclaiming your mercies each morning, and your faithfulness every night."

43. For more on *testimonios,* see Loida Martell-Otero, "Women Doing Theology: Una Perspectiva Evangélica," *Apuntes* 14, no. 3 (Fall 1994): 81–82; Elizabeth Conde-Frazier, "Latina Women and Immigration," *Journal of Latin American Theology: Christian Reflections from the Latino South* 3, no. 2 (2008): 54–75.

44. Schweitzer, *Quest of the Historical Jesus,* 4, 398–403.
45. Judith Plaskow, *Sex, Sin and Grace: Women's Experience and the Theologies of Reinhold Niebuhr and Paul Tillich* (Lanham, MD: United Press of America, 1980).
46. Cf. Matt. 11:28–29; 12:22–31; 25:14–21; Luke 10:38–39; John 6:1–12.
47. Cf. Molly T. Marshall, *Joining the Dance: A Theology of the Spirit* (Valley Forge, PA: Judson Press, 2003), 6–9.
48. "And if you knew what this means, 'Mercy I desire, and not sacrifice,' you would not condemn the innocent. For the Son of Man is lord of the day of rest" (my translation of the Spanish text).

Chapter 6

Christology from a Latino/a Perspective

Pentecostalism

ARLENE M. SÁNCHEZ-WALSH

One of the first things you know when you seemingly recover your wits after speaking in tongues for the first time is that something has happened to you that you could not envision happening to you in the Catholic church of your youth. Aside from the fear and trembling that must be a part of the whole exhilaration package, you know that you have moved beyond something, and that a spiritual part of you that will have to be reconciled with the rest of you will require some educating to get it right. Pentecostalism and Latinos/as have been engaged in a century-old relationship of mutual education. A once, and still, predominantly Catholic community that does not see the Pauline Christology as the only filter with which to see Jesus has now found itself affixed to an evangelical/pentecostal community that rarely, if ever, viewed Jesus in anything other than Pauline-colored glasses. As such, Jesus becomes the central figure in the faith; the Holy Spirit is important, but more as a spiritual agitator, burnishing and washing away all of our lives' collective stains. God is synonymous with Jesus, so there is no real difference and not really an emphasis on uncovering any difference. Mary, banished to the metaphorical closet with all the other *santitos,* candles, rosaries, icons, and questionable clothing, has nothing else to say, or else, if she does, we are not supposed to listen to her. Jesus is it. Jesus as Baptizer in the

Holy Spirit (Doctrinal Jesus), Jesus as Healer (Liberator Jesus), Jesus as Coming King (Political Jesus): all are part of the Latino/a pentecostal experience, and they serve as appropriate touchstones to discuss how Christology in our community may have one common stream emanating from a pentecostal experience and faith, but manifests itself in many different varieties.

In order to accomplish this task, it will be well worth it to borrow some tools from the sociology of religion and create some typologies that fit the existing categories of Jesus as described above. Despite the desire to never speak in generalities, the chances that scholars will do so is pretty high, since stating in any way that we speak for everyone and we can categorize everyone somehow is not satisfactory. There is a way to group people so that some baseline characteristics can be said about most people in that grouping—not a perfect way to talk about Latino/a Pentecostals, just one of the more satisfactory methods I have found since the diversity of theology and life experience does not lend itself to easy definitions or narratives.

The Doctrinal Jesus becomes the first Jesus that Latino/a Pentecostals encounter. Within this Jesus lies the seeds of a faith to be passed on to both the next generation and the new convert. This Jesus shows you the way, the truth, and the life, literally and symbolically. The Doctrinal Jesus is thoroughly evangelical (limited salvation to those who confess Jesus as Lord), a demarcation of truth (only what is written about Jesus in the Bible counts), and a mirror that we all stand before every day (the apex of piety, morality, and Spirit-filled living). This Doctrinal Jesus also represents the boundaries of the pentecostal faith that, in at least the classical traditions, require the Holy Spirit to work in certain prescribed ways for someone to be considered truly pentecostal. For someone to come into the initiation ritual that makes one pentecostal—speaking in tongues—one needs to know why this is important. What difference does it make? The Doctrinal Jesus is there to make sure that the spiritual hierarchy of Pentecostalism remains intact. Now, whether or not this Doctrinal Jesus ever maintains this hierarchy, whether most of global Pentecostalism meets these demands today (current evidence suggests they don't),[1] for many, is irrelevant. What is relevant is maintaining the standard; it is what defines people's faith, and for people entering into a new faith, or passing on an old one, retaining control of your identity is the most important thing, superseding actual practice. We return later to the role of Doctrinal Jesus in shaping a Hispanic pentecostal identity.

If current surveys on the subject are to be believed, globally, Pentecostals no longer identify themselves solely with the practice of speaking in tongues;[2] in fact, most of them identify more with divine healing. Latino/a Pentecostals, since Azusa Street through to today, also seem to adhere to that cohort. The next picture of Jesus that seems to be the most characteristic of Pentecostals is Jesus as Healer (Liberator Jesus). Within this portrait are two views that often go toward opposite ends of the Protestant spectrum. Pentecostals view divine healing as the imprimatur of a God who is active, concerned, and involved in every aspect of created order; from headaches to terminal illness, God heals everything. For many Pentecostals, this is the ultimate liberation. There need be no other since to be free of chronic illness, cured of terminal diseases, means that one can live one's life fully, liberated from the shackles of ill health. Beyond physical illness, divine healing encompasses just about everything else that can afflict a person and alter their optimum lifestyle of good health, prosperity, and worry-free living.

Of course, this version of Liberator Jesus exists in large part only in the pentecostal community. A Liberator Jesus who is not concerned with larger systemic ills, communal solidarity, and political and social transformation—that is not much of a liberator. Who gets to define liberation in this case largely depends on what use that definition is to the group. Latino/a Pentecostals don't need to call Jesus a liberator to believe that Jesus heals; their belief is rooted in experience and the power of narratives. Latino/a Christians outside this circle may need to define liberation in political terms because it is the life of ideas, of politics to which they wish to affix their label. Healing at the hands of Jesus is compartmentalized to their privatized times where they can be spiritually engaged. We take up this tension and further examine the role of Jesus the Healer later in this essay.

The final Jesus that Pentecostals makes use of to form their religious identity is Jesus as Coming King (Political Jesus). Assuming that many Latino/a Pentecostals come to the faith as converts, not as generational adherents, a crucial theological treatise that must become part of their lexicon and their worldview is the eschatological view of most American evangelicals since the early twentieth century—premillenial dispensationalism, a unique reading of certain biblical texts (the prophetic book of the Hebrew Bible, especially Daniel, Ezekiel, and Isaiah; and the New Testament book of Revelation, and passages from 1 Thessalonians in particular). The kingdom of God, the perfection of humanity, the end to suffering is not possible in this life; there must be certain events that lead to an end-time scenario that culminates with a battle that will finally cast all evil out into the proverbial lake of annihilation (fire). As such, Latino/a Pentecostals have, until recently, been so enthralled with this particular aspect of their theological identity that rarely, if ever, have they engaged in any overt political agenda. In fact, this Jesus, the Coming King, and its attendant eschatology of the last days has mitigated against the entrance of a vibrant social justice agenda into many Latino/a Pentecostal churches. While one could argue (as I do) that this view is still the dominant view of most Latino/a Pentecostals, this view has its detractors, its modifiers, and its revisionists, all of whom we discuss later. What is important to note is that arguments over who gets to define words like "liberator" and "healer" have similar arguments over the Coming King and Political Jesus as well.

DOCTRINAL JESUS: JESUS AS BAPTIZER WITH THE HOLY SPIRIT

Suggesting that Latino/a Pentecostals are encountering Jesus for the first time within their pentecostal context sounds terribly insulting, especially if we are talking about former Catholics. But that is often the expectation: converts are expected to enter into a lifelong process of learning about Jesus. This is a not-so-subtle response to what many Latino/a Pentecostals view as incorrect views about Jesus taught by the Catholic Church. However theologically suspect those claims may be, the Jesus taught in many pentecostal churches, seminaries, and Bible institutes is different. Doctrinal Jesus within the Latino/a pentecostal community emphasizes an evangelical conviction that there is no salvation outside of confessing that Jesus is Lord. It also emphasizes a literalist interpretation of the life of Jesus in that only what is recorded in the New Testament is fair game for teaching and instruction, which is expected since the normative Protestant reading of Jesus is much the same. By far the most prominent secondary role that Jesus plays for Pentecostals is "baptizer with the Holy Spirit."

That Jesus baptizes you with the Holy Spirit and the evidence of that act is the ability to speak to God in a language you did not previously know would be enough to convince people of the necessity of this spiritual event. What may also be happening here, with regard to Latino/a Pentecostals, is placing the preeminence of Jesus on display, in that the place that was once reserved for the Father, Son, Holy Spirit, Mary, and the saints is now solely the purview of Jesus. Supernatural activity, which, according to Orlando Espín, Latinos/as are predisposed to[3] (if they come to Pentecostalism from Catholicism) is no longer under the control of anyone else but Jesus. The only other comparable person who is capable of such actions is the Holy Spirit.

Doctrinal Jesus' centrality to the core spiritual activity of Pentecostals cannot be overstated. The initial argument that Jesus plays this central role as the one who offers this experience in the first place makes it all the more essential. Indeed, this viewpoint makes it hard to see through the many layers of linguistic games that Pentecostals and charismatics play when trying to explain the difference between the baptism of the Holy Spirit, being filled with the Spirit, the indwelling of the Spirit, and at least three or four other modes of saying basically the same thing, theological hairsplitting aside.

Another powerful role that the Doctrinal Jesus plays in the life of many Latino/a Pentecostals is that he is the one who now becomes central to faith; for many, there is no other reason for faith, in that there are no more multiple mediators and there is only one way to salvation. Accepting this Doctrinal Jesus introduces Latino/a Pentecostals into the evangelical emphasis on the exclusivity of the work of Christ. This is important because it gives converts a new language that they can use to discuss Jesus, one that differs from Catholic understandings as Jesus being the savior of the world, and that salvation is a sacramental process.

Doctrinal Jesus also serves the purpose of being the standard of piety, which, along with generous portions of Pauline teachings, helps place Latino/a Pentecostals fairly securely in the Holiness branch of contemporary evangelicalism. Though they do not talk like Holiness folks—I have never heard a Latino/a Pentecostal talk about being sanctified—they certainly have internalized these teachings, and for many, this quest for a perfected piety becomes the prism by which one's belief, practice, and action are read. Thus, when discussing the final section of this paper on eschatology and the Political Jesus, it should come as no surprise that eschatology matters. There should not be a presumption of a fixation with things eschatological, but rather, historically, that accepting the Holiness-inspired view of piety is presumed to be the surest way to know you are living correctly for Jesus.

JESUS AS HEALER: LATINO/A PENTECOSTALISM AND THE LIBERATOR JESUS

In speaking with a Latino/a pentecostal pastor of the Word of Faith persuasion about his views of Jesus, healing, and the certitude the pastor displayed with regard to God always healing, I heard Jesus referred to for the first time as a liberator, and as the ultimate manifestation of liberation theology.[4] This alternative reading of liberation theology by this avowed "orthodox" Word of Faith pastor struck me not so much as a misreading of the term, but a reappropriating of a term for a congregational setting that would normally not be comfortable with the political nature of liberation theology. Pastor Marco's reappropriation can and should be debated, but that is not my task here. My task instead is to try to understand the multiple roles that the Liberator Jesus plays in the lives of Latino/a Pentecostals, first by looking at the traditional notions of Jesus as a healer, then taking Pastor Marco's definition and placing it against what liberation means to the lives of most Latino/a Pentecostals. First, Jesus as Healer.

If Latinos/as, like other Pew survey respondents, no longer view speaking in tongues as the mark of being pentecostal, then they, along with other Pentecostals worldwide, adhere to the idea that healing is a better marker for who is pentecostal and who is not. Viewing God as active, concerned, and involved in every aspect of the created order, Latino/a Pentecostals view Jesus as key to their liberation from a whole host of physical, emotional, and spiritual ills. For many, this is also viewed as true liberation. There needs to be no other liberation, since to be free of illnesses, worry, and anxiety means that one can live one's life fully and victoriously, and, in that, reach the height that one's pentecostal spirituality offers.

Defining "liberation" in overly political terms—in theological terms that privilege Catholic teaching rather than evangelical belief—has not generally been a part of the pentecostal overview of who Jesus is. This may be difficult for some to comprehend, but if one allows for an alternative reading of Jesus as Liberator/Healer, then it is not as difficult. For some, however, appropriating "liberation" without affixing "theology" next to it tends to ruin categories that are invested with as much theological currency as political currency. For Pastor Marco, the Word of Faith minister from Southern California, the idea that God does not call people to remain in their imperfected states of illness, but decidedly wants to heal everyone, is a promise that not enough people really internalize. They receive it as a doctrinal statement of the Word of Faith movement, but they really don't believe that it is possible for God to heal everyone, chiefly because it has not empirically been proven to be true. From that conversation with that pastor, I did begin to explore the idea that though the Word of Faith theology may not be accepted by every Latino/a Pentecostal, the idea that healing equals liberation, especially when broadening out the categories to include emotional and psychological healing, makes a lot of sense. For a population with less access to health care than the general population, and even less access to mental and behavioral health care than the general population (due to cost as well as due to cultural taboos), that one finds ultimate liberation from pain and suffering through Jesus makes Pentecostalism all that more attractive.[5]

At this same Word of Faith church, I visited one Sunday morning when the normal altar call for healing was not particularly long, but it was interesting for another reason. An elderly woman walked up for prayer and was turned away by the pastor, who quietly asked her if she had been up for prayer for that same illness. She answered "yes" and was asked to sit back down. One could view this as pastoral malpractice, or one could (as I did) view it as a dispassionate ethnographer, noting that this pastor fit neatly into my newly created typology of Orthodox Haginite.[6] For the purposes of this chapter, it serves us well to note that the pastor was, in his orthodox way, supporting the doctrine espoused by Kenneth Hagin (a key Word of Faith teacher),[7] that once you have prayed for healing, you cannot pray for the same healing again since that displays a lack of faith in God. A lack of faith will cause a lack of healing; therefore, Pastor Marco was only doing what he had been taught, and this would ultimately lead to victory for this woman, strengthening her faith by supporting her apparent lack of faith.

I never found out whether the woman received her healing, and as a practical matter, it almost never matters whether it is empirically provable.[8] What matters, as many researchers have told us, is that the adherents believe that they have been healed, that they believe that they have been liberated. It is this sense that if they did not receive their healing now, they will receive their healing sometime, or they will be healed emotionally, psychologically, or in another nonphysical way that will demonstrate to the person—and equally as important, to the congregation—the efficacy of prayer, trust, and faith that Jesus heals.

Writing about Latino/a Pentecostals for the last fifteen years—and knowing that the way much of the material is gathered for any meaningful analysis begins with capturing the narratives of the adherents and capturing their history—is essentially a very large, very unwieldy oral history project. What I have also learned is that what Latino/a Pentecostals think about Jesus is also transmitted orally. Therefore, analyzing the power of narratives in relation to viewing Jesus the Liberator is crucial to understanding how this definition has come to pass.

When asking people about healing, whether in a survey or in an interview, they invariably mention themselves as a case subject, or they know of someone who has been healed. I have had minimal accounts of working with Pentecostals who claim never to have known of healing or of being healed themselves. This is the power of narratives: "I may not have experienced anything, I may even have doubts, but I hear from others that this is possible." Evangelical Christianity places a premium on faith. People have faith that these narratives cannot all be false, that there is some truth to them, first because they mimic scriptural accounts, and second, because that is what a loving God would do. That is what a personal savior does, and these narratives add to that belief. These stories therefore become canonized as the proof one needs to secure one's own belief in healing. Since healing has been expanded to include emotions and the psyche, nearly everyone I have ever interviewed has relayed some kind of knowledge of healing, whether personal or otherwise. These stories demonstrate staying power.[9]

Latino/a Pentecostals build and rebuild their faith lives through pain, disappointment, and disempowerment not through the cognitive acceptance of liberation theology but through the existential reality of God's power and the stories that flow from that experience. Most Latino/a Pentecostals are not unaware of the plight of their community, but since they largely view their faith in wholly individualistic terms, they, like Pastor Marco, are not malevolently ignoring their brethren so much as they are trying to demonstrate the efficacy of their own faith, if not triumphalistically shouting it out to anyone who will listen. Jesus heals, he saves, he does all the things we need to make it through life, and so to view Jesus as an ultimate liberator is theologically exactly what conclusions we are left with when pentecostal Christology is weaved throughout the fabric of Latino/a religious life.

POLITICAL JESUS: JESUS AS COMING KING

Few things baffle progressive Latino/a Christians more than the resistance Latino/a Pentecostals seem to have toward social justice. Why wouldn't this group, a large and active segment of Latino/a religious life, not be fully engaged in repairing the tattered fragments of a historically marginalized community? I don't have the answer to that question, but I believe there are some reasons that have not been adequately explored. First, there tends not to be a contextualized examination of the eschatological profile that Latino/a Pentecostals have largely accepted to be the most biblically correct way to examine the end times. An in-house disagreement also exists among Latino/a Christians. Some believe that if the faith does not systematically question the structural evils of society and attempt to right this off-course ship, then these churches are not effectively doing social justice ministry. Pentecostals, for their part, are very good at informal networks that indeed do provide services, but these focus solely on the betterment of the individual. They do not view their work in compassion ministries as insufficient; rather, they simply are doing the ministry they believe Jesus encouraged. For many of these Pentecostals, Political Jesus, Doctrinal Jesus, and Jesus the Healer are one and the same, and to value one over the other is problematic and deters the church from its overarching goal of conversion first, service later. In order to flesh out these points, this section tries to place this

Political Jesus within the evangelical historical/theological context and create helpful typologies in an attempt to understand the varied ways that Latino/a Pentecostals view the Political Jesus.

Because numbers are tricky to work with, I hazard that even the most conservative estimate of the Latino/a Catholic/Protestant breakdown is about a 70/30 split.[10] That being the case, it is safe to assume that most of that Protestant growth occurs through conversion. Conversion being the primary mode of transmission, the reeducation of Latino/a Pentecostals then necessarily must include the addition of premillennialism as the answer to how the world will end. Latino/a Pentecostals generally remain disengaged from social justice faith work because of the premillennial eschatology that many adopt upon conversion.

The Pentecostalism that attracts Latinos/as is firmly rooted in the evangelical tradition. Premillennialism holds that there will be a physical second coming of Jesus, where he will reign on earth for one thousand years before finally culminating the drama that is world history with a final apocalyptic battle that ends the story once and for all, with evil finally defeated. It may be worthwhile to note briefly that American evangelicalism did not start with its premillennial theology. It has vacillated between premillennial and postmillennial ideas, where working for the kingdom of God on earth would be an assured way to gain the favor of God and usher in the millennial reign. Evangelicals retracted to the safe harbor of premillennialism in the late nineteenth and early twentieth centuries. When faced with the loss of revamping the American empire in their own image, evangelicals seemed to abandon the idea that this society and, by extension, the world could be perfected (war, immigration, perceived moral decay, and evolution all contributed to this disappointment). A casualty of this retrenchment was the loss of the impulse for social reform, which was then (and remarkably still today is) demonized as a slippery slope that leads from well-meaning social action to theological relativism. Within this broad argument are the seeds of how many Latino/a Pentecostals have been socialized to accept the outlines of premillennialism, where the perfectibility of humanity is impossible and therefore should not even be attempted.

Part of this socialization process is produced by two unrelated but ultimately critically important theological and sociological impulses working together. Catholic eschatology that Latinos/as may or may not have been exposed to is amillennial (denying the thousand year reign), and there is also an overall focus on not looking for the end times as a safeguard against suppressing apocalyptic fervor. This is in tandem with the reality that most Latino/a Catholics live their faith lives in the realm of popular Catholicism rather than doctrinal propositions; any millennial ideas that may have captured the Latino/a religious imagination did so by leaving that to *La Virgen*. In nearly twenty years of exposure to Latino/a Catholic churches, I never saw or heard expositions on Augustine's take on millennial theology (which, with some modifications, is where the church's position is today), but I heard about and saw lots of brochures about Fatima. There is little doubt that one reason why any residual apocalyptic theology had to be cast aside upon entry into Pentecostalism was its "unbiblical" origins. With that, Latino/a Pentecostals are then freed to and indeed asked to become serious Bible readers, and if interpreted correctly (literally), then they too should come to the conclusion that premillennialist views are correct.

If sociological studies are correct, most people who convert are those who are loosely affiliated with their faith and do not have a strong sense of identification with that religion.[11] I think it is safe to say that a portion of Latino/a converts, attenuated to Catholic eschatology, were and are ready to adopt American evangelical premillennial ideas regardless of what that means for the broader context of social action. Why? Because as an evangelical, the new cultural, social, and theological currency is biblical literacy, piety, and evangelism. Placed in this context, evangelical eschatology mitigates against the entrance of a vibrant social justice agenda in Latino/a pentecostal churches, because it is a dominant theological construct in a world filled with constructs. For evangelicals/Pentecostals, these constructs are not made out of metaphorical straw (we know how that house ends up), but rather they are built brick by scriptural brick.

Perhaps borrowing this useful tool from sociology will help explain what this eschatological glue is and why its ungluing is a process of generational shifts. Traditionalists, modifiers, and revisionists can, with some certainty, be found in various stages of passive reception or active engagement with the Political Jesus that takes issue with systemic social ills that affect many Latino/a communities.

Latino/a pentecostal traditionalists tend to be from immigrant and first-generation churches.[12] Their view of Political Jesus is informed by the acceptance that Jesus does speak quite a bit about poverty, taking care of widows and orphans, but their response is usually within the context of compassion ministries. What takes up much more of their time and their passion are things such as evangelism, Bible studies, and missions work. I have not in fifteen years of working in and studying Latino/a pentecostal churches ever found a church in this category that had a ministry in place to counter the systemic social ills that often befall immigrant communities. First-generation ethnic churches have traditionally seen themselves as bulwarks against liberalism in their denominations.[13] This idea that one is contributing to maintaining theological orthodoxy in the face of overwhelming capitulation to modernity strengthens their theological and ethnic identity. Because these churches tend to be more literalist, more charismatic, and more politically conservative, there is no room for social justice agendas. Even though they may represent what churches should do, social justice is too closely associated with Marxism to offer any comfort. Nevertheless, because they are literalists and do try to exemplify Christian teachings on hospitality, caring for the poor, and watching out for their neighbors, what many of these traditionalist churches have aside from compassion ministries are many informal networks that serve their communities through activities like food giveaways, job offers, counseling, baby sitting, and countless other services. Still, these networks are usually not tied to a larger social justice mandate. The question might be asked here, so what? If this type of activity is replicated literally thousands of times in hundreds of Latino/a pentecostal churches, why is that not an expression of a Political Jesus? For many progressive Christians, this narrow definition doesn't fit with the larger ideas of what Jesus' political face should look like. The reality might be that the political face of Jesus looks very different depending on where one forged their definitions of Jesus and faith.

Modifiers are generally second- and third-generation Latino/a Pentecostals who tend to want to bridge the gap between the traditionalist and revisionist groups. What drives many of these modifiers is that they have expressed a disappointment with the Latino/a church at large, the failure to hold onto the successive generation of children raised in traditionalist churches. Modifiers are trying to reincorporate the Political Jesus into their churches by talking more about overt manifestations of injustice: immigration, education, and a myriad of social pathologies. Modifiers tend to be leaders, mostly pastors; they are better educated, bilingual, and have often sought to be better educated theologically, specifically because they found the lack of social justice in their churches to be troubling. As leaders, they may infuse their compassion ministries with more pointed references to systemic ills, because their congregations tend to be mixed generations. It is often difficult to incorporate something that many view as extraneous and not part of one's gospel work.

Revisionists are usually third- or fourth-generation Latino/a Pentecostals who may or may not still be in the Pentecostal Church, and more often than not, they act on their impulses to incorporate social justice as a part of a parachurch ministry. Revisionists have often found that there is simply no room for their political and theological difference within a traditionalist Latino/a pentecostal church. Anecdotally, many of these revisionists whom I have interviewed view their life in the church to be broader than their local church. Since they feel that their responsibility is to a larger community and not to a specific church, revisionists tend to work through parachurch organizations.[14] Often, revisionists have outgrown their home church's legalism and lack of social witness and seek out other churches or organizations to fill that theological vacuum. As such, organizations like the Latino Leadership Circle arise as responses to a lack of a social justice agenda in pentecostal churches, while maintaining the spiritually active commitments they have to charismatic practices.

There is simply no way to adequately address all of the varied ways that Political Jesus is represented in Latino/a pentecostal churches, from the informal networks that make up most of the day-to-day ministerial encounters of one Latino/a Pentecostal to another to the formalized links to social justice agendas that tackle issues as varied as immigration, education, prison reform, poverty, sexism, and so on. One way to see this is that as this christological view is interpreted through many different lenses, one can view political motives as worldly instruments that the church should not use to accomplish any of its goals, to politics being one of the main instruments in bringing forth the kingdom of God on earth. This premillennial-to-postmillennial switch is perhaps the most significant contribution to Latino/a pentecostalism by the revisionists, who are trying to reignite the postmillennial fervor for social mission that was evident in the nineteenth-century evangelical church.

CONCLUSION

On one of his many trips back and forth from Mexico, American pentecostal missionary Henry C. Ball mentioned that he received his certificate of fumigation. Fumigation was a typical procedure that people crossing the U.S.-Mexico border in the early to mid-twentieth century had to endure, only this procedure was usually reserved for Mexicans. Ball, one of the pioneers of pentecostal missions to Latinos/as, does not tell us whether he had to endure the humiliation that hundreds of Mexicans endured. One doubts that Ball was sprayed with pesticides on his many trips back and forth to Mexico. Ball's recounting of this episode was an aside; it did not offer any insight into the procedure, it was not critical of the overall program, and it did not cause Ball to be introspective about the plight of Mexican border crossers. Without comment, we are left to fill in the blank with our own assumptions that such procedures were acceptable. Ball, as emblematic of early pentecostal—specifically, Assemblies of God—missions, seemed not to be able to articulate any theological response to this program, or indeed any injustice that befell Mexican immigrants. More so, most if not all pentecostal missionaries viewed such injustices (and they knew of and wrote of others) as secondary to salvation.

This view, it should be noted, is not unusual, but it is quite remarkable for what it says about several facets of the borderlands pentecostalism that Latinos/as became enamored of at the beginning of the twentieth century and still turn to today as an exemplary representative of who Jesus is and what our response should be. This borderlands pentecostalism is very much a product of its southern and midwestern roots, thoroughly evangelical and conservative in theology and practice. There are few if any theological tools that H. C. Ball availed himself of in order to make sense of injustice, aside from the eschatological hope that this injustice too shall pass. This borderlands pentecostalism had little if any tolerance for the contemporary notion of acculturation, but rather saw its duty to assimilate masses of Latinos/as into this very American faith as quickly as possible, thereby speeding up the rate at which converts sloughed off erroneous Catholicism. Catholicism, after all, was not simply wrong. It was the gateway for all sorts of social pathologies, many of which ironically had much to do with being Mexican; sloth, disease, and poverty were all marks of deficient faith and character.[15] Because maintaining one's ethnic identity had little if anything to do with becoming pentecostal, denominations simply did not put any emphasis on issues related to how being ethnically different affected your station in life. Whatever it was, God was going to make it better. When the Mexicana workers complained to Ball about not getting enough money for their piece work as pecan shellers in San Antonio, his response was that their reward would be in heaven, and to persevere.

The Jesus that Latino/a Pentecostals have been introduced to, have accepted, and have shared with others is a fluid figure, fully human so he can be related to and talked about, fully divine so that we can attribute all things supernatural to him, the one who baptizes, heals, saves, and is coming again. How Latinos/as interact with these aspects of Jesus depends largely on their cultural context and their social location, though this very thought would horrify some. If we came to Pentecostalism from Catholicism—where there were mediators and miraculous events attributed to saints and Mary—we found that these supernatural events, placed in the strict context of *sola scriptura*, were now filtered through the lens of Jesus and placed solely under his power. How that happens, how one comes to that conclusion, is outside the purview of this chapter, but it does serve to note the fluidity with which Latinos/as engage in and make the critical engagement with their faith. The serious study of these varied communities becomes all the more crucial if we are ever to understand the profundity of "that they may all be one," and why that goal remains elusive.

NOTES

1. http://pewforum.org/surveys/pentecostal (October 2006).
2. Ibid.
3. Orlando Espín, *The Faith of the People: Theological Reflections on Popular Catholicism* (Maryknoll, NY: Orbis Books, 1997), 142–43.
4. Rev. Greg Marquez, "Interview," Imperial Valley Christian Center, El Centro, California, March 15, 2007.
5. According to a joint report by the Pew Hispanic Center and the Robert Wood Johnson Foundation, 42 percent of Latinos/as are uninsured (the largest uninsured group of all racial/ethnic groups). Also, according to a study conducted in 2005 by the Institute for Hispanic Health (a part of the National Council of La Raza), Latinos/as were less likely to receive care for depression (the most common form of mental illness among Latinos/as), and were less likely to receive quality mental health care as compared to other multiracial groups. The study notes that Latinos/as seemed reluctant to utilize mental health services mostly because they did not believe in airing their *ropa suicia* (dirty laundry) in front of people who were not part of their families. See *Hispanics and Health Care in the United States: Access, Information, and Knowledge* (Washington, DC: National Council of La Raza, 2008), 4; *Critical Disparities in Latino Mental Health: Transforming Research into Action* (Washington, DC: National Council of La Raza, 2005), 6–7.
6. Kenneth E. Hagin was the founder of Rhema Ministries and considered the founder of the modern Word of Faith movement. Among Word of Faith ministers, there is a broad spectrum of theological belief that encompasses their adherence to strict Word of Faith teachers. In my typology, Orthodox Haginites would be those who advocate literalist readings of Hagin's writings and sermons, resist modifications to some of Hagin's more controversial ideas (good health is always a provision that God provides for those who have faith), and furthermore view many of the attacks on Hagin's theology (even those accusations, some of which proved true, such as a plagiarism charge) as demonic assaults on the Word of Faith that demonstrate the truth of the

doctrine. Within the Word of Faith movements, then, there are the Orthodox Haginites. There are also moderates, characterized by a desire to keep the spirit of Hagin's teachings consistent while moving away from the more extreme ideas, and in turn, adding their own ideas as central to the faith. Reformists seem to want to claim a Word of Faith heritage, without specifically making Hagin the apex of prosperity teachings; they would also try to make Word of Faith teachings more acceptable to the larger Christian body.

7. "Believers Blog": hindfeet/christianblogsites.com/blog/, accessed December 11, 2008. This Web site is dedicated to Hagin's teachings. In the "Faith for Living" section, Hagin makes it clear that it is not only God's intention to always heal, but that divine healing is intertwined with salvation. This is one of dozens of comments, sermons, and remarks that Hagin made over his lifetime which suggested that healing was always God's desire.

8. David Chidester, *Authentic Fakes* (Berkeley: University of California Press, 2005). Chidester's premise for his book, and my inclusion of his work, ever so briefly can be summed up from the preface: "They do authentic religious work by negotiating what it means to be a human person in relation to transcendence, the sacred, or ultimate human concerns. As a kind of religious activity in American popular culture, these are all authentic fakes, doing real religious work in forging a community, focusing desire, and facilitating exchange in ways that look just like religion" (viii).

9. Arlene Sánchez-Walsh, *Latino Pentecostal Identity: Evangelical Faith, Society and the Self* (New York: Columbia University Press, 2003). For further discussion on the creating of narratives and their power, see chap. 3, "Normal Church Can't Take Us."

10. http://pewforum.org/surveys/pentecostal (October 2006).

11. Rodney Stark, "Why Religious Movements Succeed or Fail: A Revised General Model," *Journal of Contemporary Religion* 11, no. 2 (May 1996): 134–35.

12. This typology is my own, derived from ethnographic research covering the last fifteen years. Synthesizing scholarship on the subject is not a difficult task; since my book was published in 2003, there have been no major monographs on the subject of Latino/a Pentecostal identity. Normally, this would be a point of academic pride for an author; in actuality, it is a troubling development that two major disciplines—history and sociology—and subfields—religious history and sociology of religion—have not done much with the topic.

13. "Religious institutions are generally recognized as conservative and notoriously slow in making adaptations to changes in the social environment. The problem of adaptation is accentuated in ethnic churches because of the extraordinary character and degree of the generational changes with which they must cope" (Mark Mullins, "The Life-Cycle of Ethnic Churches in Sociological Perspective," *Japanese Journal of Religious Studies* 14, no. 4 (1987): 325.

14. David Ramos, phone interview, April 14, 2008. Ramos explained the demographic and religious makeup of the membership of his organization, thus adding to my typological definitions.

15. Gilbert G. González, *Culture of Empire: American Writers, Mexico, and Mexican Immigrants 1880–1930* (Austin: University of Texas Press, 2004), 169.

Chapter 7

"Who do you say that I am," *Jesús* or Jesse?

A Reflection on Christology and Christian Identity

HUGO MAGALLANES

The question "Who am I?" is a common question that most of us, at some point in our lives, begin to ponder and reflect upon to define our identity, the meaning of life, our purpose in society, and other relevant aspects related to our personal goals and our place in the world. Reflecting on identity elements and aspects that define it is not a recent task. For many years philosophers and theologians alike[1] have sought to provide parameters and frameworks of reference to help us understand who we are. More recently, psychologists and counselors[2] also have provided means and tools for us to discover our identity. In following these parameters, most authors lead us to find our identity in our history and background as reliable sources to determine who we are and how our identity is shaped. But when it comes to the identity of marginalized social groups, this search is quite elusive, because it is difficult to trace one common historical background for a social group that has been defined by others and not by the group itself.

This process is not any different for particular individuals who are members of these groups. As James A. Banks points out,

> Each individual has a total picture of self that is largely a product of the individual's interactions within his or her social environment. How a person views himself or herself is cogently influenced by significant persons within his or her social world. Often individuals who exercise power over a person's life, such as parents and teachers, are important influences on the development of an individual's self-concept.[3]

In the case of marginalized individuals and groups, those who exercise "power over" them in many instances define them as inferior. Marginalized social groups do share a common identity and background that pattern their identity and experiences of oppression. Generally, the social location of marginality and the identity that issues forth from it is typically one that has been given and imposed; of course, it is different from one that is self-determined. Furthermore, marginalized social groups may share some common elements, but not all the members of the group will have identical experiences; thus, they may or may not fit the given and determined parameters ascribed to them. For example, in the United States, for many the category of "Hispanics" encompasses all Spanish speakers; however, within the so-called Hispanic group, there are many diverse backgrounds and historical traditions based on countries of origin and their time in the United States—that is, first-, second-, or third-generation.

Often, the identity of marginalized groups and their understanding of their history is at odds with the way groups in power conceptualize them. In other words, the way that one group constructs its identity may be completely different and in clear opposition from the way that other or dominant power groups view them, perceive them, and define them. Those in power appear to always have a favorable and self-legitimating reading of historical events that they claim is correct, objective, and right, while the social understanding and historical interpretation of marginalized groups are too often seen as deviant, subjective, and biased. In his book *Mañana,* Justo L. González refers to this peculiarity: "Even the name 'America' raises the question: What preposterous conceit allows the inhabitants of a single country to take for themselves the name of an entire hemisphere? What does this say about the country's view of those nations who share the hemisphere with it?"[4] According to González, members of the dominant culture in the States have appropriated for themselves the name "America," which by so doing dismisses the claim of all the other countries in the Western Hemisphere. In fact, on occasion I introduce myself to members of dominant groups in the United States saying I was born in North America, which inspires them to quickly try to correct me. Typically, they proceed to inform me that Mexico is not part of North America. In their mind, there is only one America—the United States of America. Although some of the members of the dominant U.S. society include Canada among its definition of America, in my experience Mexico is almost always excluded from that geographic definition. It seems to me that a superior or exceptional narrative is part of the interpretive frame of reference for many members of the dominant U.S. society. And, of course, some of these dynamics are not much different from personal narratives and the way we construct our personal and social identity.

In addition to these general social categories and dynamics, we can easily observe that members of marginalized groups see themselves as members of other subgroups as well, and often they see themselves as affiliated with other identifying factors that may not be considered predominant in their own group. Yet the dominant group would insist in placing all persons under the same label. For example, the way the term "minorities" is employed to describe all persons who are nonwhite (that is, not part of the dominant group) demonstrates how the defining discourse of a powerful majority becomes a standard view in society; indeed, those outside this standard gaze are typically lumped together as "minorities." In other words, the binaries are the powerful versus the powerless, majority versus minority, white versus people of color, and so forth.

For the above reasons, the dominant group (those in power who may or may not be the majority), intentionally and unintentionally, fails to see and understand the richness of backgrounds and important contributions that others, different from them, make to society and culture. For example, first-generation immigrants from Mexico are often viewed with a common lens by members of the dominant culture in the United States—the one-size-fits-all approach to understanding their culture and background. Although many first-generation Mexican immigrants have many identity elements in common, multiple factors also diversify them. For example, the great majority of them identify themselves as Christians, but under this category there is great diversity in their denominational affiliation, such as Catholic, Charismatic Catholic, mainline Protestant, evangelical, pentecostal, and so forth. Because the defining discourse of dominant culture imposes labels, homogenizes strangers, and determines the standards of identity for marginalized groups, the voices, rich traditions, and valuable contributions of cultural and linguistic minority groups are overlooked.

Thus, I want to consider and explore the notion of Christian identity as defined by the dominant culture and its impact for developing an inclusive understanding of Christology, one that invites and affirms other groups, as opposed to one that imposes and delineates. In what follows, I look at the Christian narrative and the way the dominant culture uses aspects of it to promote an agenda that favors and sanctions the ideas and practices of the dominant culture.

JESUS ACCORDING TO PETER:
A CHRIST-LESS DEFINITION?

Before I explore the sociological, historical, and political practices of the dominant culture, I want to begin my analysis and exploration with Jesus' self-identity. Although I believe that the identity of Jesus presented in the Gospels is not free from the cultural and sociological interpretation of its time, the Gospel narratives give us an understanding of the identity of Jesus by discussing the character of his ministry. I focus here on the conversation Jesus initiates by asking his followers who they think he really is. In the Gospel of Mark, Jesus inquires about the nature and determining factors of his identity, simply by posing a direct question to his disciples: "Who do people say that I am?"[5] I believe this inquiry is extremely important since Jesus himself is calling into question his identity and wants to know how he is perceived by his disciples and the community at large. We should be asking this very question, while trying to understand the meaning of Christian identity. I believe that by looking at the Markan concern to determine the identity of Jesus, a space opens up for understanding the meaning of Christian self-identity and discipleship, which may even challenge the established views of a static, exclusive, and stagnant Christ.

In the Gospel of Mark, when Jesus asks his disciples, "Who do people say that I am?" they reply by sharing what they have heard and by telling him what people are saying about him. The collective answer was an association of Jesus with a great prophet Elijah and with John the Baptist. Although Jesus was a popular figure and people knew of him and his teachings, their perception of Jesus did not match what Jesus wanted to communicate to them in teachings and sermons. After hearing what the public said of him, the Markan Jesus turns to his closest friends, to those who have shared meals with him, those who have been with him during his teachings and preaching, those who have experienced miracles and have seen firsthand his authority and power. Certainly, the close friends of Jesus would be able to provide an accurate depiction of his identity. So, Jesus asked his disciples, "Who do you say that I am?"[6] In the Gospel account, Peter replies, almost instantly, "You are the Christ!" For some readers, those who are quick to move to theological assumptions that favor their social location, Peter's response represents an affirmation of faith, a theological declaration, and objective claim. Readers who follow this approach can easily imagine Jesus' face with a big smile and a grin of satisfaction since one of his friends knows and has identified him as the Christ, which is a proper theological label. For them, his close friend Peter knows, understands, and firmly states the identity of Jesus.

In fact, Peter's statement seems to be a long-awaited response to Jesus; surely Jesus was pleased by the declaration. After all, this was his mission, to reveal his identity to his disciples, to his followers, and to the whole world. However, Jesus' response to Peter's declaration is puzzling to say the least. There seems to be a problem with Peter's answer, which up to this point seemed to be the correct theological statement. After Peter's reply, according to the Gospel of Mark, Jesus warned Peter and the rest of the disciples not to share this message regarding his identity with anyone.[7] Again, this is quite a surprise, why does Jesus want to conceal his identity? Why is he trying to prevent the dissemination of his identity? Is Jesus not the Christ? Is the identity of Jesus not attached to the prophetic and royal aspects of the messianic title? Was Peter wrong in his declaration? If Jesus is not the Christ, then who and how do we define his identity?

In attempting to respond to these questions I would like to suggest taking a close look at Peter's answer and what he may have had in mind when he declared that Jesus was the Messiah. From Jesus' response in the text, one can imagine that Peter's literal answer was correct—that is, using the term "messiah" to describe Jesus—but maybe the social and political implications of the term were not the same ones that Jesus had in mind.[8] If this was the case, perhaps Peter's own aspirations and personal agenda got in the way. Maybe Peter was defining Jesus according to his satisfaction, imposing on him a notion that, although it may have been popular and widely recognized during his time, carried a heavy dose of Peter's self-promoting purposes. If Peter, like many others during his time, thought of the Messiah as a liberating figure and as a political power broker who would bring prosperity and change to current oppressive structures, then one would easily think that those closely associated with this liberating political figure would receive special favors and would get to enjoy the benefits of a new order under a renewed leadership. Perhaps this is what Peter had in mind as he quickly responded to Jesus affirming that Jesus was indeed the Messiah.

Peter, a close friend who had shared many important events with Jesus, seems to miss the point by his reply to the question posed by Jesus concerning the issue of his teacher's identity. Peter projects his own set of values on Jesus in a way that could arguably be intended to seek self-promotion, power, and authority. In a way, Peter's answer is one that represents a selfish way of thinking and an egocentric worldview. Perhaps this is why Jesus demands that Peter and the rest of the disciples not share this "good" news with others. What the textual issues, interpretations, and explanations suggest is that we construct our Christian identity too often in a similar self-serving manner. We selectively construct our identity, we look for ways to affirm our history and promote our agenda, and we look for self-validating practices and for ideologies that protect our personal interests. But this self-centered approach in constructing identity is exacerbated when the person doing it claims membership in the dominant culture, which includes an interpretation that enjoys the kind of collective affirmation that promotes and insists that one's personal interpretation is valid, correct, and objective. Without a doubt, self-centeredness is a human problem, but in the conversation between Jesus and Peter, the story continues to assist us in developing our personal and Christian identity.

As the story develops, Jesus begins to disclose his future sufferings and rejection. He describes to Peter and the disciples, with strong conviction, his final destiny. And Jesus' description is distant and strikingly different from what Peter, the rest of the disciples, and the community as a whole believed the Messiah was supposed to do. Jesus discloses his self-identity as one that embraces suffering and sacrifice as essential aspects of his personhood and mission. Jesus chooses a path of self-denying and endures suffering as a way to demonstrate who he is. Harold Recinos provides a helpful insight in understanding the implications of Jesus embracing suffering:

> Jesus' suffering directs us to question the meaning of the stories of women, the poor, and all people in desperate need. A Jesus who reveals God is with the lowly utters good news of change to hurting people. What is certain is that those who find solace in the image of a suffering Jesus are summoned to discover Christ's presence in the anguish of the poor and oppressed.[9]

According to Mark, the Messiah is not one seeking earthly power and popular fame, but One who gives himself for the sake of others, One who embraces a life of self-denial by placing others first, One who takes an unpopular road with all the wrong people, and One who rejects glamour, fame, and prestige. If this is Jesus, maybe this is precisely the reason that Jesus prevented Peter and the disciples from spreading Peter's definition of his identity as Messiah. In other words, Peter, the apostles, and the crowds all failed to see and understand Jesus' identity; they, like us, were looking after their own interests and self-promoting agenda.

Furthermore, after Jesus reveals his identity and shares with the disciples what it entails, Peter, with the same quickness and boldness with which he responded to Jesus' first question, immediately interjects and tries to prevent Jesus from taking the road that leads to Jerusalem—to his suffering, rejection, and death. Peter tries to persuade Jesus not to go to Jerusalem. Now, it is Jesus who quickly responds and rebukes Peter in a not-so-kind way: "Get behind me, Satan!" which seems to corroborate my interpretation of Peter's motivation. It is clear to see that Peter's agenda and the recently revealed identity of Jesus are at odds. Peter was looking for something for himself. Perhaps following Jesus was a way to receive political favors. His definition of Jesus as the Messiah had little to do with Jesus, and it was filled with egocentric and power-seeking benefits. No wonder Jesus rejects this type of thinking as one that comes from Satan, one that has human motivations as a priority rather than placing the "things of God" first.[10]

JESUS IS JESSE ACCORDING TO THE DOMINANT GROUP IN THE UNITED STATES: A CHRIST-LESS SOCIETY?

Now, if we take this interesting narrative in which Jesus discloses his identity by correcting Peter's confession and the crowd's perception; if we take this narrative and use it as the grounds to build the foundation of our Christian identity and faith, then we would be required to leave our assumptions and self-serving definitions aside to meet Jesus and to learn who he is. Obviously, this is quite an impossible task since Jesus (physically) is no longer with us; however, Jesus in the Gospel narratives provided guidelines of his self-identification. He not only revealed himself to his disciples and followers but Jesus also disclosed himself to others; perhaps those of us who never had the opportunity to meet Jesus in the flesh will someday encounter him spiritually and also know where to find him in the world. One narrative that helps us clearly identify Jesus is found in Matthew 25. In this text Jesus clearly identifies himself with those who thirst or are hungry, in prison, sick, naked, and strangers. In this crucial passage and many others,[11] Jesus clearly identifies himself with marginalized groups, strangers, outsiders, those on the wrong side of social norms, those considered by the civil society as inferiors, and those who have no means to repay favors. This Jesus identifies with marginalized and oppressed persons, the least of society who are defined by dominant social groups in unfavorable ways, those persons who seldom have the chance to express themselves with their own voices.

What does it mean that Jesus identified himself with the marginalized? What does it mean that Jesus rejected Peter's answer? Why did Jesus prevent Peter's self-centered definition from spreading? What does it mean to be identified with Jesus Christ in a nation where many citizens consider themselves Christian and whose civil religious tradition images nationhood in divine election language? What is the role of Christians who are members of a society that sees itself the most powerful nation in the world? How should Christians in this nation construct their identity? Is it possible to reconcile the claim of Christian identity with a history of ethnic cleansing, slavery, segregation, wars of conquest, racism, and racist nationalism? We could frame these questions by suggesting a simple point: it would appear that the history of American exceptionalism would have one think that the country, like Peter, declares Jesus is the Messiah in a way that legitimates its power, purpose, and asymmetrical relations in the world, while ignoring the way Jesus claims an identity with marginality.

Many historical events, approved laws, and common practices seem to indicate that mainstream Christianity in the United States stands closer to Peter and far from the focus of Jesus' rebuttal of Peter's answer than to the question of Jesus' identity. For example, the near annihilation of Native Americans done with the approval (and often willing participation) of Christian Pietists, who had fled the British Empire in search of religious freedom, and the enslavement of Africans for centuries with the use of Scripture to maintain and justify the oppressive slave system bespeak a denial of Jesus' identity as the Messiah of good news. Although the U.S. Constitution sought to promote freedom and liberty at the time it was written, it first predicated citizenship on the exclusion of race, class, and gender. The very Constitution of the United States, said to reflect religious principles and promote individual freedom and liberty, assured a state of voicelessness for black slaves thought in early America to be not quite human—lacking humanity and equality by two-fifths!

Without a doubt, the ideology and practices of Manifest Destiny further reveal an egocentric, imperialistic, and power-seeking identity that favors dominant culture groups and is justified by their interpretations of the Christian narrative. The conquest of the West in the name of Christian evangelization and progress turned strangers encountered in the new lands into inhuman, inferior groups deserving all that came their way. Strangers were not complete, because they needed true religion, legitimate culture, Western education, and submission to the purposes of social progress as defined by dominant conquest. And of course, since the dominant group believed its way of cultural life and religion was superior to that of cultural others, encountered strangers were not only forced to submit to the imposed vision of life. Defeated strangers had to relinquish their identity, and if they wanted to be counted, they were required to allow the dominant group to define them, label them, and locate them in inferior positions in the newly ordered society. Briefly stated, dominant groups have historically defined other groups according to their terms and without their participation;[12] they have created categories and labels that empower them to set social rules, while defining others as outsiders. Dominant classes have created and promoted laws, rules, and traditions designed to protect themselves, while leaving marginal and vulnerable people to survive on the goodwill and charity of that same dominant group.

I believe this tendency is the one that Jesus clearly refused to accept as part of his identity. In fact, it is this type of power-seeking attitude and trait that Jesus denounced as coming from Satan. Indeed, it is ironic that the dominant group in the United States claims a Christian narrative as an important and instrumental element in its identity, yet its practices, history, and interaction with marginalized groups show that its identity according to Jesus is more in tune with the practices of injustice, inequality, and the denial of life—all elements easily associated with the symbolism of Satan. Since power elites place and continue to make a power-seeking agenda and egocentric desires their ultimate concern, they continue to neglect and oppress strangers and marginalized people in society.

In the previous pages, I have attempted to provide an alternative understanding of Christian identity by connecting the history and practices of the dominant group with issues of marginality in the United States. Now I want to mention an interesting fact. Many boys from Mexico and other Latin American countries are often named "Jesús." When these men and boys find themselves in the United States, their name becomes the center of an interesting controversy. Their name, "Jesús," just like the main character of the Gospel narrative, is considered irreverent by the dominant group. The collision of these two cultural and religious naming practices results in the name "Jesús" being replaced by "Jesse"! The dominant group once again finds a way to impose the objectivity of its interpretation and erases the cultural and religious value of the name "Jesús" to maintain its sacredness. At schools and at work, many young boys and men are asked to change their identity to fit in and to adjust to their new reality, which is defined by dominant cultural values that disregard Latino/a cultural, religious, and family values. Although more deserves to be said about the social and psychological implications of changing one's name to fit in and about the conflict that the name-changing practice creates among the extended family, instead I focus on what it says about the Christian identity of the dominant group in the United States and its Christology.

When "Jesús" becomes "Jesse," it is not simply a matter of pronunciation, but is a sign of theological domination. The ideology of the dominant group behind this name-changing practice is rather easy to see: How could a Hispanic be Jesus to us, the "official" members of the one and only Christian nation? In short, it is impossible for a Hispanic to know who Jesus is; in fact, Hispanics need to be educated in the way of the proper Christology and the orthodoxy that is only produced by the dominant group in the United States. I suspect that for many, this chapter, and perhaps this whole book, would be considered not as a Christology but rather as an exploration of sociological and cultural practices among Hispanics. But why is this work not considered as integral in the development of Christology? Because "Jesús" has been forced to become Jesse! Because for many in the dominant group there is only one definition of Jesus, one Christology, and one Christian identity, and all others are considered deviant. Precisely for this reason, it is extremely important to consider the way that Jesus identifies himself and the way Jesus reacts to Peter when his definition of Jesus carried Peter's own interest and agenda.

Has the dominant group, by claiming to have an exclusive right to define "Jesús," missed Christ altogether? Can a nation that prints "in God we trust" on its currency claim to know Jesus, while building a wall to keep so-called illegal aliens out? If the dominant group trusts in God, why doesn't it ask God how to treat strangers? If its trust is in God and its Christian identity defined by Jesus, why does the dominant group trust its own agenda of political advancement and imposition of identity? I believe self-centered Christians and the many members of the dominant group have for years produced a theology that affirms the norm, the standard of power, and for this reason the group's positions neglect and deny other voices. The interpretations of the dominant group did not (and do not today) allow other interpretive perspectives, due to their imposing ways of promoting their cultural/theological interpretations on all communities as right teaching or orthodox understanding. Those who claim to have the right theology and the proper interpretation of Christology, like Peter, may have arrived at the proper terms and nomenclature, but according to Jesus they have missed his true identity. Their words may be right, but their practices are Christ-less.

A CALL TO CONVERSION (CHRISTIAN IDENTITY): FROM A STATIC TO A DYNAMIC/FLUID CHRISTOLOGY

I began describing aspects that form and shape identity. Now I pause to reflect on my personal cultural identity and experiences. I grew up in a town bordering Mexico and the United States; hence, my formative years were shaped by the clash of cultures occurring on a daily basis along the border. Once on vacation with my parents visiting southern states in Mexico, I realized that many of the things I considered part of my Mexican cultural heritage were not considered Mexican for persons who lived in the southern regions of Mexico. Similarly, when I traveled north into the territory of the United States, what I believed were American identity traits were not viewed as truly American. I gradually realized that my identity was a product of two cultures; moreover, I became aware that both in Mexico and the United States a dominant discourse defined authentic cultural identity, while any deviation from this pure identity was rejected. Later, thinking about these experiences and reflecting on them theo-logically, I realized that social groups develop cultural rules for conserving their history and traditions, even at the expense of others. The need for security and stability leads groups to define themselves, and often the process of developing this definition comes by the *via negativa*—by asserting that the group is not like others. In other words, groups create an us-versus-them dichotomy. And of course, when two or more groups collide (cultural wars), the definition of the group in power, the dominant group, always prevails. This dynamic is described by Zygmunt Bauman as follows:

> With the *pluralism* of rules (and our times are the times of pluralism) the moral choices (and the moral conscience left in their wake) appear to us intrinsically and irreparably *ambivalent*. Ours are the times of *strongly felt ambiguity*. These times offer us freedom of choice never before enjoyed, but also cast us into the state of uncertainty never before so agonizing. We yearn for guidance we can trust and rely upon, so that some of the haunting responsibility for our choices could be lifted from our shoulders. But the authorities we may entrust are all contested, and none seems to be powerful enough to give us the degree of reassurance we seek. In the end we trust no authority, at least, we trust none fully, and none for long; we cannot help being suspicious about the claim to infallibility. This is the most acute and prominent practical aspect of what is justly described as the "postmodern moral crisis."[13]

Bauman acknowledges the ambivalence between groups, in our case cultural, that claim that their reality and expressions are objective. He also notes that by such acknowledgment, groups in power create the conditions of suspicion the moment they impose their definition of a legitimate structured reality. Bauman offers a tentative solution to this social dynamic, which requires a new moral understanding for social relationship. He argues,

> Reciprocity is the vital attribute morality does not possess—but should possess if one wished it to be universalizable. The duty of one partner is not the other partner's right; neither does the duty of one partner demand an equivalent duty on the side of the other. A stance does not wait to become moral until it has been reciprocated and thus turned into an ingredient of dual or multiple *relationship*. Nor is it the expectation, however vague, of being reciprocated that makes it moral. The contrary, rather, is the case: it is equanimity with which the subject views the question of repayment, reward, or equal standard that renders him or her, for as long as such equa-nimity lasts, a moral subject.[14]

What Bauman is describing is an equal relationship between groups and individ-uals who embrace conflicting claims. Bauman is calling for a reciprocal relation-ship among equals in which the exchange of ideas and cultural assumptions are dealt with within a framework of "equanimity." In light of Bauman's discussion and the concern to understand Christian identity and Christology, let us exam-ine the idea of conversion, which assumes a shift in religious identity.

The word "conversion" comes from the Latin word *conversio,* which employs the same Latin root for the Spanish word *conversación* (and the English word "conversation"). These two words—"conversion" and "conversation"—seem to be at odds; the first one denotes a change in one's identity, a change in one's worldview, while the second one denotes an exchange of ideas and words in a social interaction setting. Rather than focusing on semantic differences, I want to suggest that the word "conversion" be understood by the idea of conversation. In other words, conversion can be understood as a social interaction, an exchange of ideas, but in an environment of "reciprocity" and "equanimity" that insists that the interlocutors are dialogue partners capable of changing each other.

Conversion as dialogue assumes that a conversation is under way among equals; hence a dominant group is required to admit and recognize its history, social location, and privileged position, while the nondominant groups engage in dialogue predicated on their equality of status with the dominant group. In conversation of this kind, all voices have value and are heard, and all persons' view of social reality is acknowledged for its validity and contribution to social understanding. Ada María Isasi-Díaz describes this dynamic in reference to theological work:

> A multiplicity of theologies calls for true dialogue, what I call engagement. Engagement requires a relationship of empathy as well as commitment to a joint search. Of course this means that there can be no real dialogue, no real engagement between Latino/Hispanic Theologians and others, unless they take time to know us and the struggle of Latinas and Latinos and we take time to know them and the struggles of their people. In a way this kind of engagement would change radically the face of theology and theological studies since the point of reference and what everyone is expected to know and to espouse would no longer be "mainline" theology or official theology. Real engagement among theologies and theologians would mean that a multiplicity of methods would be examined, and that theological praxis of different communities of struggle would become intrinsic to theological education. Engagement among different theologies would prevent us from falling into total relativity and individualism since all engagement is, in a sense, a calling to accountability.[15]

According to Isasi-Díaz, engagement or conversion as a conversation among equals requires the kind of empathetic intentionality that is conducive to mutual understanding. In terms of Christian identity and Christology, the dominant group has a tendency to define Jesus and develop a Christology that reflects an ethnocentric and self-centered perspective, which seems to be contrary to Jesus' self-identification with the poor, the least of these, the marginalized, and the stranger. Thus, based on my biblical interpretation, in the United States, the dominant group (primarily among mainline denominations) looks at Hispanics from their self-centered perspective, preventing Latinos/as from expressing themselves and imposing on them their values as part of the "true" Christian faith. By doing so, like Peter, the dominant group misses completely the identity of Jesus and rejects the essence of who Christ is.

Latino/a interpretations of Jesus promise to transform members of the dominant society by way of conversation on the meaning of Christian identity. Indeed, the dialogue that may develop between the Latino/a margins and members of the dominant society can be transformative. Those who control power in church and society may find themselves more inclined to rethink Christology from the perspective of the margins, rather than self-centeredness. In other words, the ongoing conversion of Christian identity I would argue is found in reciprocal and equal relationships with the stranger, the alien, and the poor (many of whom are Hispanics in the United States) and by entering in a personal and social engagement with them. Conversion as conversation leads us away from the static Christology established by the powerful. By engaging in conversation with those at the margins, dominant culture groups may discover that Christ is already present in strangers, aliens, and foreigners, inviting all to create a new condition for living.

NOTES

1. See Richard Lints, Michael S. Horton, and Mark Talbot, *Personal Identity in Theological Perspective* (Grand Rapids: Eerdmans, 2003).
2. See Rupert Brown and Dora Capozza, eds., *Social Identity Processes: Trends in Theory and Research* (Thousand Oaks, CA: Sage, 2002).
3. James A. Banks, *Teaching Strategies for Ethnic Studies* (Boston: Allyn and Bacon, 1991), 78.
4. Justo L. González, *Mañana: Christian Theology from a Hispanic Perspective* (Nashville: Abingdon Press, 1990), 37.
5. Mark 8:27.
6. Mark 8:29.
7. Several New Testament scholars and Markan scholars in particular have provided different interpretations of Jesus' demand for silence after Peter's declaration of Jesus as Messiah. "Peter called Jesus the Christ, and Mark introduces Jesus in the same terms but the word never appears on Jesus' lips. In fact, he responded to Peter's confession by telling his followers not to tell anyone about this conversation. It is a surprising command that has been explained in various ways. For Wrede it was the church's rather clumsy apology for its proclamation of a messiah who never claimed to be the Messiah (1971: 218–21). The Jesus Seminar, which casts Jesus as a wandering Jewish cynic, finds corroboration in the word Messiah not appearing on Jesus' lips (Funk et al. 1993: 75). Aune, on the other hand, identifies a sound reason for Jesus' silence on the subject. In the first century eschatological movements it was considered God's right to designate who the Messiah would be, rather than a title that someone might claim (1969: 31). . . . The language of Mark 8:30 places Jesus' messianic identity among the various secrecy motives in the Gospel" (Ronald J. Kernaghan, *Mark* [Downers Grove, IL: InterVarsity Press, 2007], 158).
8. Marie Noonan Sabin explains that the term "messiah" had many variant meanings, but "[t]he one constant in all these variations was that a 'messiah,' as God's agent, was always imagined as victorious in his work. When Mark shows Peter rebuking Jesus for telling them he would die, he is showing Peter reacting on the basis of this assumption of victory and triumph. By the same

token, when Mark shows Jesus rebuking Peter, he is indicating that Jesus was rebuking him for this assumption" (Marie Noonan, Sabin, *The Gospel According to Mark,* New Collegeville Bible Commentary [Collegeville, MN: Liturgical Press, 2005], 75).

9. Harold J. Recinos, *Who Comes in the Name of the Lord: Jesus at the Margins* (Nashville: Abingdon, 1997), 49.

10. Mark 8:33.

11. See, for example, Mark 9:30–35; 10:32–37; and 10:42–45.

12. James A. Banks, addressing these concerns, writes, "The social, cultural, and ethnic variables that influence how historians perceive their data result in historical bias. A historian's view of the past is influenced by his or her culture, personal biases, purposes for writing, availability of data, and the times in which he or she lives and writes. Because the historian can never totally reconstruct past events and is unable to report all the data he or she uncovers about particular events, he or she must use some criteria to determine what aspects of an event to report. The historian must also interpret historical events. History cannot be written without presenting interpretations and points of view" (*Teaching Strategies for Ethnic Studies,* 80–81).

13. Zygmunt Bauman, *Postmodern Ethics* (Cambridge: Blackwell, 1993), 4–5.

14. Ibid., 56.

15. Ada María Isasi-Díaz, "Strangers No Longer," in *Hispanic/Latino Theology: Challenge and Promise,* ed. Ada María Isasi-Díaz and Fernando F. Segovia (Minneapolis: Fortress, 1996), 373.

Chapter 8

Exploring Latino/a Titles for Christ

ZAIDA MALDONADO PÉREZ

As a Latina, I cannot talk about Christology without some reference to the role of race in U.S. social relations. Nevertheless, I must confess that the topic of race wears me out: it is physically and emotionally exhausting. To me, talk about race is a bit like peeling a *guineo verde* (green banana): when you are done trying to pry the skin off the *guineo,* not only are your nails broken and stained from the *guineo*'s sap, the skin beneath your nails burns and stings. Talking about race means objectifying myself. It means becoming an "it" so that others can put me in a petri dish and move me around, one arm here, one leg there, so that they can get a better look, feel, hypothesis. It's like getting my skin and all my *Tainoness* ripped out to be examined, somewhat like a soothsayer examining the entrails of a goat. Even my *mancha de plátano,* a brown spot that colors a section of my otherwise white arm, seems to hurt and wants to yell out, "Soy boricua pa' que tu lo sepas!"[1] and leave it at that.

I'm a whopping fifty-two years old, and I can't remember a time when the issue and question of race didn't glare at me like a flashing neon sign. But the difference in this venture is that the *Jesucristo* to whom I refer below and whom I have known and knows me, bears the pain of this scrutiny with me. And this is what Christology is about for me. It is more than a systematic rendering of my understanding of the person (and work) of Jesus. It is about my experience with this *Jesucristo* who has opted to enter time and history to turn my world—our world—upside down and inside out. In the beginning, in the middle, and in the end, the Christology I present is also my *testimonio* (witness). It is a very personal rendering of an experience of the *Jesucristo* given to me through my community of *hermanas/os* and nurtured through the many faces of God I have experienced in my denomination, my seminary experience, and my theological studies. You will find here a reflective piece that seeks not only to acknowledge and celebrate my Latino/a/U.S. context, but to express something of the encounter between this Christ of (and beyond) the text, something of the God who sent him, and something of the Holy Spirit who makes the Trinity or the *Santa Familia* real to me.

I learned early on that titles are important. I am not referring to "Doctor" or "Reverend" or such honorific titles. I have in mind titles that have social consequences that transcend these vocational references. These titles, often disguised as "categories," are "Hispanic" (also called "Spic" or "alien"), "white" (often synonymous with the "real" American), and "black" (or African American, used, I thought for a time, to differentiate certain people from the "real" Americans who did not need an adjective before their name). More so than "Mr." and "Mrs.," "Dr." or "garbage collector," we use these particular titles to assign sociopolitical worth, entitlement, privilege, and honor.

Just as titles reflect a society's values, an important window on Christology is the lens implied by the designation Latina/o, which mediates an understanding of Jesus. I explore here aspects of Scripture and tradition, especially centering attention on the role and impact of our experience as Latinos/as in the United States in shaping and informing our christological preferences.[2] The reader should know that my experience includes a pentecostal upbringing (my father was a pentecostal pastor) and a mainline experience through my seminary training and my choice of denominations.[3] These experiences and traditions ineluctably color my view and my U.S. Latino/a evangelical Christology.[4]

WHAT'S IN A TITLE?

Titles say a lot about a society's expectations of the individuals to whom they are assigned. They are a society or community's way of ordering existence and safeguarding their values—usually those of the status quo. A person can have several titles, some of which can be earned through extensive study in a particular field or vocation, and others are given to us by virtue of cultural and social determinants that include our place in a family and our adherence to social norms (e.g., mother, sister, stepsister). Titles mediate cultural perceptions and serve as keys to understanding a community's interpretation of ranked social roles. As we think about a society's rules of social interaction, paying attention to the labels attached to its members then provides insight into a community's culture and values.

Many titles were associated with Jesus, which evangelicals say express something about early Israel's expectations of him as well as serving to reveal Jesus' character and ministry. In other words, for Latino/a evangelicals, Jesus is not a "metaphorical idea," a peg in a metaphysical system created to explain the early church's notion of the Trinity. For evangelical Latinos/as, Jesus is truly the Son of God. He is not just someone who was especially loved by God (as the Deists would say) or adopted by God (as the Arians said). He was not self-delusional and not just a teacher of morality, as G. W. F. Hegel and I. Kant suggest. Latino/a evangelicals understand that *Jesucristo* (Jesus Christ) is the subject and author of our faith, "the Christ," God's Anointed One, our Savior (Acts 4:12).[5]

Latino/a evangelicals affirm that Jesus did more than fulfill expectations connected with these titles; he also subverted them by filling them with new meaning. By doing so, Christ claimed his Lordship over the titles, thereby also revealing anew the divine will and order called the reign of God. For instance, Jesus, interpreted by faith communities as the expected Messiah, the King of Kings, chose not to live with the comforts and adulations of a sovereign. Rather, this King had "nowhere to lay his head" (Matt. 8:20). The ministry of Jesus reflects how he subverted social rules by engaging with those categorized as untouchables, outcasts, and impure; indeed, he invites these rejects to follow him and makes them special advocates and bearers of good news. Jesus violated and redefined the religious and social rules of exclusion, thus alienating the religious authorities. Finally, Jesus, the "Lord of Lords," served everyone and invited into his community the ridiculed, scorned, and battered; crucifixion hence awaited such a troublemaker in society. For Latino/a evangelicals, what is especially noted is that Jesus' subversive action is to be imitated in the world as a way to live out of the reign of God, the witness that is holy and pleasing to God (Matt. 25:31–46).

The titles given to the one who became incarnate have not been forgotten. Indeed, we repeat them Sunday by Sunday in our preaching, hymn singing, and prayers. Yet we neglect and compromise the subversive character of the cultural mores that Jesus seeks to dethrone, and we neglect their implications for daily living and witness to God's reign. Jesus is often made to fit the cultural norms of the status quo. By emphasizing a rereading of scriptural titles for Jesus and their implications for practical living, Latinos/as play an important role in keeping the subversive memory of Jesus alive.[6] In what follows, I discuss a number of the titles Latinos/as use to express an understanding of the person and work of Jesus Christ. They may be scriptural titles or extrabiblical, culturally determined ways of thinking about Jesus that are only "scriptural" in the sense of being based on an understanding of Jesus in the revealed scriptural tradition.[7] As titles do, they also reflect our understanding and expectations of those who seek to follow the one who claims to be Lord of the titles, the subversive One, Jesus the Christ. Thus, they aim not only to describe, but, true to the Christ, they seek to convict, challenge and, yes, incite holy subversion.[8]

El Cristo Roto (the Broken Christ) and the "Fork-Christ"

In my office you will find an array of crosses of varying sizes. Some are made of wood, glass, and various kinds of metal.[9] One favorite image in my office includes a picture of a tomb made in the form of a cross, which includes a *Jesús* figure made of plaster protruding from a tombstone. As I view this picture, I am aware of an image of a maimed, broken Christ, a *Cristo roto*, arms and lower legs missing, bones protruding, porous face looking down from the cross, mouth open almost conveying words, eyes expressing deep concern, and in terrible agony gasping for what seems like air. This *Cristo roto* (broken Christ) makes me think about my *abuelito* (grandfather) who had his legs amputated a few years before dying. I imagine him identifying with this mutilated Christ. I think, too, how this Christ can serve as a metaphor for a dismembered spirituality—one that, caved in on itself, disengages from directing ministry in the struggle (*luchas*) that bears witness to the new sociopolitical order modeled for us by Christ.

Indeed, this *Cristo roto* seems to be speaking to, convicting, and challenging whoever happens to cast a look his way. It is a powerful picture that will capture your gaze every time you look at it.

Another cross in my office is from Uruguay. Jesus is made out of a fork, hence I call this religious symbol my *Cristo Tenedor* (Fork-Christ). I love this one, not only for its craftsmanship, but for what it can imply. The Fork-Christ reminds me that Jesus' food is both spiritual and real, like rice and beans, chicken tacos, mangú, collard greens, egg noodles, and mashed potatoes; forks are for eating. When I look at this cross made from an eating utensil, I am reminded of the hunger felt daily by Latinos/as and too many people around the world. These crosses, however, are not only reminders of the suffering of Christ and the suffering of the many for whom he gave his arms, his legs, his very being. They represent the *Jesús* who knows the pains of the children who beg for food on the streets and of the woman who sits with her baby pleading for mercy at the gates of the cathedral. Christ imaged as fork means he meets us in our struggle for daily bread. Meanwhile, the *Cristo roto* wants to reach our hearts, and the Fork-Christ our stomachs with real food that gives life. As I think of the images of Jesus on these crosses, I know he knows the pain of those who have been physically, psychologically, or economically broken—those who feel helpless enough to have to cry out, "Dios mío, Dios mío, ¿por qué me has desamparado?" ("My God, my God, why have you forsaken me?") (Mark 15:34).

"Ponle por nombre Jesús pa' ver si te sale bueno"
("Name Him Jesus to See Whether or Not He Turns Out Good")

Schoolteachers in predominantly Latino/a districts know that *Jesús* is a popular name in our communities. A mostly Roman Catholic practice, parents who name their sons *Jesús* believe they are honoring the Son of God, Jesus Christ. But a well-known Christmas song that calls for naming your son *Jesús "pa' ver si te sale bueno,"* that is, in hopes that the boy "will turn out to be good," seems to suggest that the custom has a spiritual basis. Instead of a superstitious practice, this naming custom reflects a familiarity with the earthly Jesus, a desire to gift a son to One they love, a sense that the name itself provides protection and brings good fortune to the one who bears it (daughters are often named Maria for similar reasons).[10] In short, naming one's son Jesus offers power to the individual and suggests the permanent availability of Jesus, rather than a distant or transcendent Christ. The naming practices found in Latino/a communities suggest that an emphasis on the humanity of Jesus makes this title especially important for Latinos/as.[11]

In Latino/a communities, the name "Jesus" given to a son also is a reminder of the cross. The cross of Christ is a stark symbol of many who have nowhere else to run for succor and no one else who truly understands their desperation. The crucified Lord knows the pain of crucified people. Roman Catholic Latinos/as especially portray their understanding of the cross by wearing crucifixes and engaging in passion plays and processions, while evangelicals express their theology of the cross through their preaching, the liturgical importance of the *Siete Palabras* (the Seven Last Words) services during Lent, and dramas depicting Jesus' death and resurrection.[12] I am reminded, for instance, of a song from his Roman Catholic roots that my father, a pentecostal minister, introduced to the congregation years ago. The song appeals to God's mercy through the pain, blood, and even bile shed by Jesus on the cross. "Por tu preciosa sangre," we implored, "piedad, Señor piedad. Si grande son mis culpas, mayor es tu bondad!"[13] In the words of Roman Catholic Sixto García, this crucified *Jesús* accompanies us "in sorrow and oppression, and we can touch him, mourn with him, die with him, and yes, also hope with him."[14]

Growing up pentecostal, I also remember this *Jesús* being preached as *Emanuel,* God with us in the barrio, in the factory, in the welfare office, in the dark when the electricity got shut off because of an unpaid bill. Concentrating solely on the cross as the center of our faith meant focusing on the pain and prejudice that kept many parents earning low-income wages, and the prejudicial barriers that kept their children from aspiring beyond what they were taught was their lot in society. The cross was all too familiar and unbearable. Our missionaries gave us a God who loved us enough to suffer and die on a cross for us; we also needed a God who loved us enough to show us how to live and thrive. Certainly, I am not claiming Jesus' suffering to be a restricted representation of Latino/a suffering. I do believe there is an "infinite qualitative difference" between the incarnate God and ourselves.[15] Rather, in the broken body of Jesus on the cross, Latino/a Christians see their own experience of brokenness. In our communities, the boy named Jesus can rest assured that God-in-Christ understands the Latino/a struggle and yearning for abundant and real life. In our communities, we are certain that *Jesús* is our *Redentor* (Redeemer), our *Libertador* (Liberator).

Jesucristo: Divino-Humano

The early church debate over the divine and human natures in Christ did more than address the question of the nature of our salvation. By arguing for Christ's full humanity and full divinity, they countered the underlying flesh-spirit dichotomy present in a Christianity influenced by Greek philosophy. Subsequently, the dualistic thinking that emerges in early Christianity elevated the spirit over the flesh and the mind over the body, leading to a hierarchical ontology; indeed, the docetic Christology held that Christ had only the appearance of flesh, which denied among other things the value of creation. Against this, Niceno-Constantinopolitan Christianity affirmed the full redemption of spirit *and* body, thereby also affirming a more Hebrew notion of person as a nondualistic, organic whole.

The Word becoming flesh, the union of the divine and human, has redemptive qualities that reach beyond otherworldly expectations. When God enters history in Christ, the divine worth and salvific purpose of human beings is disclosed; thus, experiencing life as a Jew, a Samaritan, a Puerto Rican, Honduran, Ecuadorian, Filipino, or African American is given meaning and purpose. For Latinos/as, the Word made flesh has deep meaning, especially when growing up in a white dominant society.[16] As a young girl, there were many times when I wondered what was wrong with me and why I was often compelled to change my ways when an "americano/a" (white person from the United States) was around. This constant and exhausting putting off and putting on of my *latinidad* tacitly taught me that, like an otherwise comfortable pair of jeans, it was not good enough for all occasions, especially those that mattered the most.

Rereading the Scriptures from my Latina experience empowered me to see that Christ's incarnation overcomes these divisions in society. From the beginning, God breathes unity into the created order, God seeks to unite humanity with God's self through Christ, and to use history through which to reveal the divine will and purpose. Christ the Jew calls us within particular cultures to become followers of him, because all cultures "have sinned and fall[en] short of the glory of God" (Rom. 3:23). As I read the Scriptures in light of my cultural experience, I became aware that *Jesucristo* calls us to follow him by bringing with us the gift of culture, even as we are also called to critique and challenge it. The incarnate Word reveals the truth of humanity and the meaning of the divine.

El Jesucristo Mulato and the *Mulato* Body of Christ[17]

The term *mulato* means of mixed breeds or mixed blood or ancestry. It is thought to be derived from the word "mule," the offspring of a male donkey and a female horse or mare. More than an anthropological term, this was a political category used to differentiate between the "pure-bred" or "pure" race and those who carried the mixed blood of slave and owner, conqueror and conquered. To be mulatto was to be a *sato,* a mongrel, a nonperson.[18] Those who equate purity of blood and race with perfection will find this title for Christ offensive.[19] This should not be more offensive, however, than depicting Jesus as being white with blue eyes! Below I discuss Christ as *mulato.*[20]

In my view, to speak of Christ as a *mulato* is a way to build on the very mystery of the incarnation. The *mulato* Christ sacralizes what was otherwise considered offensive existence in the world. To serve the *mulato Jesucristo* is to see ourselves through the eyes and very being of the one who Himself knows what *mulatez* means. As Luis Pedraja argues, Christ, the incarnation, that is, the joining together of the human and the divine, is "the ultimate act of *mestizaje* and *mulatez.*"[21] Because we are members of a mixed body of Christ, we are *ourselves mulato/a* or *mestizo/a* members of the body of Christ in history. By virtue of the one named Holy One (Luke 1:35; 4:34; Acts 3:14), we become a holy hybridity; a *familia* in Christ, sisters and brothers of one another, sons and daughters of the One God, all united through the infusion of the Spirit of love that bonds the Trinity.[22]

As a Latina, I understand what it is to have Spanish, Taino, and African blood running through my veins. My own Moorish name "Zaida" has its roots in yet another prior conquest—that of Spain by the Arabs. Thus, like others, I am a community of worlds, events, and heritages that make me who I am. But, for those of us who often define ourselves in opposition to those-other-than-who-we-are, the idea of being part of a *mulato* body of Christ may come as somewhat of an uneasy surprise. After all, when was the last time you thought of yourself as *mulato* or *mestizo* or *sato?* (In many ways, Latinos/as and other persons of color are always reminded that we are "other-than-white.") Yet, to speak of a *mulato* Christ means to focus on the scandal of difference as something divinely ordained. And, if divinely ordained, then this "mulatto" body whose head is the Christ ought to become a critical part of our self-understanding and self-identity.

My *mulatez* becomes the arm or the head or the toe which the body cannot do without (1 Cor. 12:12–14ff.). Paul reminds us that these gifts, as well as our joys and sorrows, should be welcomed and acknowledged by the one body, God's church. It is only as this body, through the power of the Holy Spirit, strives to value each other and function together as the one *mulato* body of Christ that we witness and bring glory to its head, Jesus, the *mulato* Christ. As your sister, my *puertorriqueñidad* (Puertoricanness) becomes part of your "body" makeup, and your own racial/ethnic background becomes part of mine. We are unity of difference conjoined in, by, and through Christ, who is himself part of a tri-unity, a *comunidad,* a *familia.*[23] By uniting with creation, the *mulato Jesucristo* invites us, his *mulato* church, to become partakers of the divine nature (2 Pet. 1:3, 4) through the power of the Holy Spirit.[24]

El Jesucristo Profeta ("Christ the Prophet")

By virtue of our relationship and rebirth in Christ, Latino/a evangelicals claim sanctification as a condition of their identity. We are called to bear witness to this gift by pursuing sanctified lives (Lev. 19:2; 11:45; see also Exod. 15:11; 1 Sam. 6:20; Ps. 99:9; Isa. 6; 1 Pet. 1:15–16ff.; 2 Cor. 7:1; Heb. 12:14, et al.). Scripture admonishes us to "pursue peace with all, and the sanctification without which no one will see the Lord" (Heb. 12:14 NAB; I have removed "men").

Prophetic living is intimately tied to the meaning of sanctification. The term "holy," or "to sanctify" in the Old and New Testaments (*kadesh* or *kodesh* in the Hebrew and *hagios* in the Greek), refers to the act of separating, consecrating, or preserving something or someone for God.[25] Like the vessels that were set apart for use in God's temple, we are also set apart (made holy, sanctified) as vessels for God. Paradoxically, we are sanctified or separated in order that we may become integrated and engaged in the messy task of speaking/living forth the good news of reconciliation and the promise of a new order of justice, peace, and mercy for a world that is sorely in need of it.

For Latinos/as, sanctification or being made holy does not mean separating ourselves from this-worldly struggles. This only makes us complicit participants in the violence against the neighbor and the creation we are called to love. The prophetic Jesus calls us to fully engage the world in order to help transform it. This inevitably becomes a call to prophetic ministry: a ministry informed by God's prophetic utterances in the Hebrew Scriptures and embodied in the person and work of *el Jesucristo Profeta* (Acts 3:22). For me, to be prophetic means speaking truth to power with the understanding that this must be a "speaking" best expressed with our actions.

POLITICS AND ECONOMICS

In 2007, Bill Moyers spoke at the Fiftieth Anniversary Celebration of the United Church of Christ, and he shared statistics of the ever-widening gap between the haves and have-nots in the United States. "For years now, our political and economic system has been fixed to favor people at the top."[26] The numbers that followed were daunting. In 1960, the income gap between the top 20 percent and the bottom 20 percent was thirty-fold. Now, he continued, there is a seventy-five-fold difference. The share of the wealth to the top is up 7 percent, representing a 7 percent drop to those in the lower half. Eighty percent of all income gains are benefiting the top 1 percent of our people. His illustration of a pie unequally divided among one hundred guests vividly helped to drive the meaning of these statistics home. It is "like inviting a hundred people over for some pie, cutting the pie into 5 slices, giving 4 of the slices to just one person, and leaving one slice for the remaining 99."[27] Not surprisingly, Bill Moyers reminded us that the "remaining 99" will end up fighting each other for the one slice.[28]

Referring to an article in *The Economist,* Moyers stated, "The United States risks calcifying into a European style class-based society."[29] In contrast, however, "the typical child starting out in poverty in Europe or Canada has a better chance of climbing out of it than a child born in poverty in the United States."[30] In fact, statistics show that 34.4 percent of all Latino/a children in the United States are now living below the poverty line. Non-Hispanic children under the poverty line make up 10.6 percent of the total. Among these, Puerto Rican children are reported to have the highest rate of poverty of any Latino/a group.[31] But, Latino/a or non-Latino/a, no child should grow up poor in the richest nation in the world. Indeed, it is a sad paradox that in one of the wealthiest and most powerful empires of the world, we would still have 37 million poor and 45 million without health insurance.[32]

RACIALIZATION AND SEGREGATION

By racialization, I mean the construction and imposition "of a specific image based on a set of assumptions or stereotypes . . . to a certain race," which is fueled by xenophobic attitudes or unfounded prejudice.[33] The result is a typecasting that, undergirded by the powers that be, serves racist ends. A look at the data on American public opinion on immigration can help illustrate the process of racialization. A study conducted by Thomas Espenshade and Maryann Belanger, both Princeton University sociologists, looked at twenty organizations over the span of more than thirty years and found that "Latin American and Caribbean immigrants in general, and Mexican immigrants in particular, rank somewhere near the bottom in terms of how Americans view immigrants from different parts of the world. European immigrants are most favored, and Asians fall in the middle."[34] In contrast with Asians, Latin Americans are viewed as more likely to "commit crimes and take advantage of welfare, and less likely to work hard, do well in school, and have strong family values."[35] In fact, Latinos/as, according to the Sentencing Project Report, are the "fastest growing group being imprisoned" among all state and federal inmates.[36] Along with being the majority of those arrested for immigration violations, Hispanics "experience discrimination during arrest, prosecution and sentencing, and are more likely to be incarcerated than whites charged with the same offenses."[37] The National Council of La Raza got it right when it said that this amounts to "losing a whole generation of people"—what ought to be seen as a "national tragedy." They see crime and justice issues as "the new civil rights issues of the 21st century." [38]

The politics of race and xenophobia result in segregation. This is also connected to white flight and to a concentration of Latinos/as in cities and states where low-skilled, service-centered jobs are most available. According to the Harvard Civil Rights Project, Latino/a children attending U.S. schools "are now facing the most intense segregation (by race and poverty) of any ethnic and racial group in the United States."[39] According to the same study, this trend will increase rather than decrease, creating further inequalities in educational opportunities and other benefits. Their plight is further exacerbated by a daunting dropout rate.[40] Although they only comprise 17 percent of high-school-aged youth between the ages of sixteen and twenty-four, Latinos/as in 2004 accounted for 40 percent of all high school dropouts, with foreign-born Latinos/as making up 28 percent of this total.[41] What is more, large numbers of our youth are not passing the achievement tests recently instituted as prerequisites to graduation.[42]

Because high school and postsecondary education are strong determinants for socioeconomic class and status, the statistical picture makes for a rather gloomy forecast for most of our youth.[43] Nevertheless, we continue to see more firsts in our ranks. Many of us are the first in our families to graduate from college or receive postsecondary degrees. We, in turn, will expect the same from our children, who will eventually come to see postsecondary education as achievable and part of the normal expectations for their lives. The trend will be slow in changing, however, if we do not mobilize at the micro and macro levels to make a difference.[44]

In short, statistics reveal that we face a battle that is *cuesta arriba* (uphill). Nevertheless, from one border to another Latinos/as and our non-Latino/a sisters and brothers are coming together through ministerial associations, political and labor organizations, and the arts and faith community bases, and they are making a difference.[45]

We should fear not acting prophetically in the world (Matt. 25:31–46). And we must understand that acting on behalf of the least among us today and in the future means access to good housing, good-paying jobs, health care, and education. Who said that Matthew 25 does not necessarily involve us in the world of politics? God's people, especially those who are marginalized, do not have the luxury of not getting involved in politics. To be holy and clean before God is to get our hands and feet in the muck where God is already present. Latinos/as believe that *la regla empieza por la casa*—that is, that as a household, a people, we must model the prophetic ministry of Jesus to address our living conditions.

I end this section of my reflection with the example of a man whose love for God and the congregation left to his care compelled him, many years ago, to begin to explore what it meant to follow the *Jesucristo profeta*. Because of this, the bold red letters he had had painted on the altar wall of the storefront church that read "Santidad a Jehová" (Holiness unto God) took on new meaning for this pastor and his congregation. In the 1970s, this Latino pastor, with his *Taíno* colored skin and his *inglés matao* (broken English), stood up in the middle of a meeting of the city council. Having interrupted the passionate and eloquent speaker, he turned to the group of parishioners who had come with him and had filled up the back seats of the hall. "¿Entienden lo que este hombre dice?" (Do you understand what this man is saying?), he asked the people out loud. Those who came with him yelled, "Noooo!" Surprised and bothered by the audacity of this apparently uncultured and uncouth man, the members of the council and the Anglo audience turned to look at the strangers who had invaded their prestigious meeting. Despite all the years of living in the same city, this would be the first time that many would look at the eyes of those whom they never saw because they were relegated to the other side of town—that section reserved for the new immigrants—the Hispanics, the undesirables. But, in that moment of encounter between two worlds divided by language and by a fecund fear of the stranger, both groups would experience a rebirth. "Did chu underestand guat I just sed?" the pastor asked the mostly Anglo audience present. "Not a word," they responded, rather annoyingly. He then asked them, "Hau can it be dat chu bring soch an important person to speak to the community gwiel chu ignorr a great part of da community dat also peis taxes and contributes to da welferr of its citizens?" he continued, as his accent seemed to flicker off bits of the frustration and weariness he felt over the mistreatment of those God had called to love and serve. The Anglo community heard this man and responded to his and the other half of the community's request for dignity.

That night, both groups left understanding and feeling something new, and this prophetic servant and the members of his church left with their heads held high. From then on, the politicians of that city did not ignore the other half of town. And I, the daughter of this servant of God, have never forgotten the day I learned what it means to serve. I have also not forgotten what I began to learn there—that is, that there is an intrinsic relationship between holiness and prophetic service, also called "social holiness." Those who love God with all their hearts, minds, and strength are known by the way they live that out among the least of these. Needless to say, I continue to be very much convicted by such witness. Hence, I can say with conviction that we dishonor God and the Son who put on humanity and graced the earth by not tending to all the facets of daily living (and God's creation!).

CONCLUSION

I have written some general existential musings concerning the person and work of Christ from a U.S. evangelical (and pentecostal) Latino/a perspective. Although I wanted to provide some insight into the Latino/a experience and understanding of Jesus, I did not seek to represent all Latinos/as in the United States. I focused on certain labels attached to Jesus that come from Scripture or that are important to Latino/a culture. For evangelical Latinos/as, *Jesucristo* is truly the Son of God, the subject and author of our faith. Though one with God in glory, he chose to live among us as a Jew, a member of a humiliated people, conquered and landless. Further, he came as a native of that marginal, insignificant, nowhere place called Nazareth. The divine became incarnate, insignificant, *mestizo, mulato,* crucified, the target of hate and injustice. Through his death and resurrection, we know God's love, grace, community, and new life.

I discussed that in Jesus *el Cristo roto,* in Jesus the fork-Christ, Jesus the prophet, Jesus the *mulato,* Jesus the *mestizo,* God enters history. I indicated that through the continuation of the prophetic witness of Jesus, we learn that prophetic living is inexorably connected to what it means to be "holy" or "sanctified"; indeed, "there is no holiness that is not social."[46] For this reason, he is the one who calls those who love him, and express it through love of neighbor, to inherit God's reign. This *Jesucristo profeta* "examines with justice" and, with God through the Holy Spirit, invites the poor to sing because the Lord "has delivered the life of the needy from the hand of evildoers." (Jer. 20:13). I emphasized *el Jesucristo mulato,* who sees the scandal of difference as divinely ordained. I talked of the mystery of the incarnation in Christ in light of the notion of the body of Christ as a wonderful mixture of race/ethnicities. In this sense, God's people are a *familia* of colors, experiences, potentials, and gifts that are all needed to build up the one body of Christ.

EPILOGUE: AN ALTAR CALL

God has gifted those who struggle with a legacy of power. The story of our communities is one of resilience, fortitude, and the determinate *sí se puede* and *pa'-tras-ni-pa'-cojer-impulso*-attitude and *coraje.* From the Taínos, the Mayas, the Incas, Aztecas, and many others, I have learned that we are not only a people with a history of survival; we are a people with a powerful and inspiring legacy of being builders of nations, innovators, and inventors. Our ancestors were and are scientists, poets, philosophers, mathematicians, historians, theologians, inventors, lovers of life, and world creators. They were warriors![47] And the hope that is Emmanuel, God with us, calls us to build on this dynamic-hope-building fount and warrior legacy so that we can continue to be, not *just* warriors, but warriors on God's mission of establishing a just, peace-full, and compassionate reign. We must be a special kind of warrior—one that our *madres, abuelitas, tías,* and *hermanas* have especially modeled for us. We must be *nursing warriors,* I like to call them; women and men capable of being strong yet sensitive—G.I. moms, grandmas, aunts, sons, fathers, and daughters. You don't need mammary glands to do the kind of nursing to which God calls us. But you do need the kind of womb-love *que te encrespa los cabellos de divino celo, compasión y radicalidad cuando ves que están maltratando, agrediendo, ofendiendo, menospreciando, o ultrajando al hijo o hija que salió de tus entrañas!* You see, nursing warriors get wounded here and there, but we know how to mend our wounds and, in the name of the *roto* but risen *Jesucristo,* get up, and work, and nurse, and care some more. Why? Because we *have to,* because *we must,* because *we can*—¡en el nombre de Jesús! We can do this with the help of the Holy Spirit. She too is a nursing warrior![48] . . . *¡¿Cuántos/as dicen "amen"?*

NOTES

1. "I am Boricua (Puerto Rican). Just so you know!" The expression "Soy boricua pa' que tu lo sepas" was made popular by the 2006 documentary movie by the same title, directed by Rosie Pérez and Liz Garbus.
2. Note that I am not endeavoring to present an empirically based study of the titles used by U.S. Latina/o evangelicals to refer to Jesus—important or useful as this may be. Instead I am writing from my experience as an *evangélica* and the overall language of faith. By "evangelical" I am referring to the historical designation as people who affirm the gospel and its proclamation of the atoning death and resurrection of Christ that is appropriated by faith and lived out in every aspect of our personal, social, political, and economic lives as a witness to and testimony of God's infinite grace, justice, and mercy through the power of the Holy Spirit. Thus, evangelicals affirm Scripture as our "norming norm" and the importance of the preached—and lived—word. By "evangelical," I also want to affirm our connection to the church's tradition. For instance, the Synodical Letter sent to Rome in 382 by the Eastern church uses the term "evangelical faith" to refer to that which the ecumenical church, through the Nicene Council (325), ratified. The letter provides a summary of this early evangelical faith as it pertains to the doctrine of the Trinity and the person of Christ. See *Nicene and Post-Nicene Fathers*, Second Series, Vol. 14, ed. Philip Schaff (Buffalo, NY: Christian Literature Publishing Co., 1900).
3. My experience also includes PhD studies at a Jesuit university (University of St. Louis). I am a member of the United Church of Christ with a Wesleyan-Armenian penchant/foundation.
4. I place "U.S." and "Latino/a" before "evangelical" only to stress the perspective that is being highlighted in the book and which also colors my understanding and experience as an *evangélica*.
5. I assume a Niceno-Constantinopolitan understanding of Jesus as the Son of God, fully human, fully divine, of one substance (*homoousios*) with the Father (Parent).
6. See especially Justo L. González, *Mañana: Christian Theology from a Hispanic Perspective* (Nashville: Abingdon, 1990), 75, and his *Santa Biblia: The Bible through Hispanic Eyes* (Nashville: Abingdon, 1996). See also Luis R. Rivera-Rodriguez, "Reading in Spanish from the Diaspora through Hispanic Eyes," *Theology Today* 54, no. 4 (January 1998): 480–90.
7. E.g., "Chuito" is a nickname for Jesus that I have also heard used by some to express special affection.
8. Unless otherwise referring to one of the titles for the incarnate God, I use the title "Son of God," not only as a statement of faith, but as a way of lifting up our ties to the wider *familia,* past and present, whose witness and confession evangelical Latinos/as affirm. In a very real and critical sense, we, too, are their theological progeny.
9. Growing up pentecostal the idea of having a number of crosses, especially those with a Christ still hanging on it, would have been something very foreign to me. Many Pentecostals see these crucifixes as a form of idolatry. Even now, I collect them more as communal representations of God's self-giving love than as mementos of ongoing suffering.
10. Unfortunately, this also fosters a gender difference that allows our boys to see themselves as "Jesuses" but girls only as "Marias." It would help to make the

connection from *María* to Miriam, the Hebrew form of the name, who was called by God to be leader of God's people with Moses and Aaron (Mic. 6:4).

11. This emphasis is reminiscent of the Antiochene (emphasis on the humanity of Christ over his divinity) vs. Alexandrian (emphasis on the divinity of Christ over his full humanity) christological emphases. For us, Jesus is *Jesucristo,* the incarnate God.

12. Sixto García points especially to the passion plays in which God's suffering and death reveal not only the presence of God in Christ in "sacred time" and "sacred space" but the very basis for a community's ability to relate to God. See "United States Hispanic and Mainstream Trinitarian Theologies," in *Frontiers of Hispanic Theologies in the United States,* ed. Allan Figueroa Deck (Maryknoll, NY: Orbis Books, 1992), 94.

13. "Because of / Through your precious blood, mercy, Lord, mercy. Though my sins [note: *culpa* also implies guilt] be great, greater still is your kindness" (translation mine). I recently found the words of a litany that has the words I remember so well. The images of the suffering of Christ are made vivid through it: "Por tus profundas llagas tan crueles, por tus salivas y por tus hieles perdónale Señor. Por las heridas de pies y manos, por los azotes tan inhumanos perdónale Señor. Por los tres clavos que te clavaron y las espinas que te punzaron perdónale Señor. Por las tres horas de tu agonía en que por madre diste a María, perdónale Señor. Por la abertura de tu costado no estés eternamente enojado perdónale Señor." See www.opcolombia.org/cantoral/5.doc (accessed December 28, 2008).

14. García, in *Frontiers,* 94. Note, although I believe the word "sacrament" is appropriate for its depth and powerful imagery, it is not one that some Latino/a Pentecostals may be comfortable using. The language of "sacrament" is not one that has been fully explored. The term "sacrament" is normally used to refer to the two sacraments of baptism and Communion.

15. See Karl Barth, *Epistle to the Romans,* trans. E. C. Hoskyns (New York: Oxford University Press, 1968), 329, 330.

16. By "white" I am not referring necessarily to skin color. I am following the common use of the term to refer to Caucasians. Rightly or wrongly, the term "white" is used to denote those who have European roots and whose skin color is light. Although my skin color is "white," for instance, I am not "white" in this sense.

17. I developed the notion of the body of Christ as *mulato* for a workshop I titled *Truth Be Told: The Body of Christ Is Mulatto* for Asbury Theological Seminary's Ministry Conference 2004. The early church felt compelled to use philosophical terms familiar to them to explain the mystery of the human and divine in Christ. I am also using terms familiar to our culture, not only to understand the divine and human in Christ, but also to help us understand the wider implications of our connection to each other in the one body.

18. Like its English counterpart "mongrel," *sato* is usually used derogatorily to refer to something that is impure, inferior, dubious, not genuine. See Loida Martell-Otero's article "Of Satos and Saints: Salvation from the Periphery," *Perpectivas: Hispanic Theological Initiative Occasional Papers* 4 (Summer 2001): 7–38.

19. If by *mulato* we do not intend to confound or to separate the divine and human natures in Christ, and if we can affirm that the nature of the incarnation is indeed mystery, then *mulato* becomes a plausible title with which many Latinos/as can resonate.

20. In his book *The Galilean Journey* (Maryknoll, NY: Orbis Books, 1983), Virgilio Elizondo builds on the perception of Jesus (and the Galilean Jews) as

mestizo by virtue of his Galilean birthplace. From this, he develops several principles that speak to the Mexican American experience of marginalization. One of these is the "Galilean principle," that is, "what human beings reject, God chooses as his very own." This *mestizo* Christology provides the springboard for my own understanding of the *mulato* Christ. I go on to build the notion of *mulatez* on the very mystery of the incarnation—that the divine and the human are inextricably entwined in Christ—as constitutive of *Jesucristo* as *mulato*. For a good summary of Elizondo's work, see Eduardo C. Fernández, *La Cocecha: Harvesting Contemporary United States Hispanic Theology (1972–1998)* (Collegeville, MN: Liturgical Press, 2000).

21. I came upon Pedraja's work after I had already developed the section on the *mulato* Christ and a *mulato* "body of Christ" for this chapter. Pedraja explores the idea of a *mestizo-mulato* Christ from various perspectives and is worth reading. See his chapter "Jesucristo" in *Teología: An Introduction to Hispanic Theology* (Nashville: Abingdon Press, 2003), 127–44.

22. Augustine refers to the Holy Spirit as that which bonds the Father to the Son. See his *De Trinitatae.*

23. For a Latino/a understanding of the Trinity, see my chapter "The Trinity," in *Handbook of Latino/a Theologies,* ed. Miguel De La Torre and Edwin Aponte (Atlanta: Chalice Press, 2006).

24. This act of partaking is otherwise known as sanctification. In the New Testament, this sanctification goes hand in hand with the justification of the believer. All those justified by faith in Christ are also sanctified by his Holy Spirit. By the work of divine grace nurtured through our relationship with the Holy One, believers, no matter who they are, live and experience a "condition" or "state" of holiness. It is this same condition of holiness, for instance, that permits Paul to address believers as "saints" (see 1 Cor. 1:1–2; 6:11; Rom. 1:17; 3:21–26; 6:7; Acts 20:32; 26:18).

25. If it is true that we are "holy" in Christ, it is also true that God calls us to "holiness" (1 Pet. 1:15–16ff.). Old Testament: In the book of Leviticus, God tells the Israelite community to "Be holy, for I the LORD your God am holy" (19:2; 11:45; see also Exod. 15:11; 1 Sam. 6:20; Ps. 99:9; Isa. 6, et al.). New Testament: Stressing the divine union between the Father and the Son that would be incarnate in Christ Jesus, the Holy Spirit announces that "the child to be born will be holy; he will be called Son of God" (Luke 1:35). Mary is right to exclaim, "Holy is his name" (Luke 1:49). And so, it is in that triune and Holy God that Paul admonishes us to perfect our holiness out of reverence for God (2 Cor. 7:1c). "Separation" by itself, then, does not sanctify. The condition of "sanctified" or "holiness" stems from our relationship to the God who is holy. The place on which Moses stood was holy because God was in that place. The Holy City and the Holy Mountain were "holy" because God dwelt and manifested God's self in them. It is Christ in us that makes us holy even as we are called to be holy. Nothing nor anyone is intrinsically holy. Only the Holy can sanctify and the only Holy One in essence is God (1 Sam. 2:2). So, holiness comes from God and those whom God calls, God also sanctifies. Note: The term "consecration" is often used interchangeably with "sanctification" and adds to it a sense of being "dedicated," "made new," or "made perfect" (2 Chr. 31:6; Exod. 29:33).

26. Bill Moyers, "Moyers Challenges UCC: 'Drive out the money changers,'" *United Church of Christ News* [Speech, June 23, 2007]; http://www.ucc.org/news/significant-speeches/moyers-challenges-ucc-drive.html (accessed June 25, 2007).

27. Ibid.
28. "Don't be surprised if they fight over it, which is exactly what's happening when people look at their wages and then their taxes and end up hating the government and anything it does" (ibid.).
29. Ibid.
30. Ibid.
31. Marcelo M. Suárez-Orozco and Mariela M. Páez, eds., *Latinos: Remaking America* (Berkeley: University of California Press, 2002), 26. Trumpbour and Bernard report that 40 percent of Puerto Ricans living in New York are poor, a rate that "well exceeds the totals for African Americans." They predict, given the deindustrialization of New York, that the "rapidly expanding Dominican community in New York will suffer a fate similar to that of their Puerto Rican predecessors." See John Trumpbour and Elaine Bernard, "Unions and Latinos: Mutual Transformation," in Suárez-Orozco and Páez, 137–38.
    A recent report states that "although Hispanics represented only 18% of all the children in the U.S., they accounted for almost 1/3 (30 percent) of all children living in poverty" (Suzanne Ryan et al., "Hispanic Teen Pregnancies and Birth Rates: Looking Behind the Numbers," *Child Trends Research Brief*, publication #2005–1 [February 2005]: 6; http://www.childtrends.org/Files/HispanicRB.pdf (accessed July 9, 2007).
32. Barack Obama, "A Politics of Conscience," *United Church of Christ News* [Speech, June 23, 2007]; http://www.ucc.org/news/significant-speeches/a-politics-of-conscience.html (accessed June 25, 2007).
33. This definition is adapted from "What Is 'Racialization' and How Does It Relate to Military Advertising," *United for Peace and Justice;* http://www.unitedfor peace.org/article.php?id=3461 (accessed July 1, 2007). See also *Webster's Third New International Dictionary of the English Language,* Unabridged (Springfield, MA: Merriam-Webster's, Inc., 1993), 1870.
34. Suárez-Orozco and Páez, 22.
35. Ibid., 23.
36. The report further states that Hispanic women in state prisons and jails "are incarcerated at almost twice the rate as of white females (117 persons to 63 persons per 100,000 population)." See The Sentencing Project [posted August 2003]; http://www.sentencingproject.org/Admin/Documents/publications/inc_hispanicprisoners.pdf (accessed July 9, 2007).
37. See "Report: U.S. Criminal Justice System Unfair, Unjust to Hispanics," Michigan State University's *Newsroom.msu.edu* [October 14, 2004]; http://news room.msu.edu/site/indexer/2172/content.htm (accessed July 9, 2007).
38. Ibid. The report calls for and provides ideas for a system that will protect public safety without destroying lives and wasting resources.
39. See Suárez-Orozco and Páez, 28.
40. See Richard Fry, "Hispanic Youth Dropping Out of U.S. Schools: Measuring the Challenge" (Pew Hispanic Center, 2003), iii. Note, the "dropout" status refers to youth between the ages of sixteen and twenty-four who have not graduated from high school or completed a general educational development (GED) program. In the year 2000, 21 percent of Hispanics between the ages of sixteen and nineteen did not finish high school. This difference is stark compared to only 8 percent of European Americans who did not complete high school and 12 percent of African Americans.
41. Child Trends DataBank, "Drop Out Rates" [Report]; www.childtrendsdata bank.org/pdf/1_PDF.pdf. According to research conducted by the National Center for Education Statistics in 2001, 43.4 percent of Hispanics, ages sixteen

to twenty-four born outside of the United States were high-school dropouts.
For more information, see National Center for Education Statistics, "Dropout Rates in the United States: 2001" [Report]; http://nces.ed.gov/pubs2005/
dropout2001/sec_3.asp.

42. Suárez-Orozco and Páez state that in 1999 "over one third of all Latino students failed the Massachusetts Comprehensive Assessment System (MCAS),"
28.

43. According to the 2003 Census Bureau, the difference between European Americans with advanced degrees and Latinos/as was $74,122 to $67,679—a difference of about 10 percent less in income. The bachelor's level, however, accounts
for the greatest disparity, with European Americans earning $53,185 or $12,263
(23 percent) more than Hispanics with an average of $40,949 annual income.
Nicole Stoops, "Educational Attainment in the United States: 2003: Population
Characteristics," United States Census Bureau, publication #20–550 [Report,
June 2004]; http://www.census.gov/prod/2004pubs/p20–550.pdf.

44. A copy of the full 2008 lecture I gave at the first FIEL, USA conference is
forthcoming by this organization of the Church of God (Cleveland).

45. For more on what this difference is, see my chapter to be publised by Fiel USA.

46. I am especially reminded of John Wesley and his insistence that there is no
holiness that is not social.

47. "In Latin America, where liberation theology originated, there have always
been movements of liberation since the early days of the Spanish and Portuguese conquest. Amerindians, slaves, and the oppressed in general fought
against the violence of the colonizers, created redoubts of freedom, such as the
quilombos and *reducciones,* led movements of revolt and independence. And
among the colonizers were bishops such as Bartolomé de Las Casas, Antonio Valdivieso, and Toribio de Mogrovejo, and other missionaries and priests
who defended the rights of the colonized peoples and made evangelization a
process that included advancement of their rights"; http://www.landreform
.org/reading0.htm (accessed August 7, 2007). Note also that another of God's
titles is "warrior" (Exod. 15:3; Ps. 24:8).

48. Pentecostal Christology is very much a pneuma-Christology. I include here a
very brief portion of my sermon "Blessed Are the Breasts" (Luke 11:27–28),
in *Those Preaching Women: A Multicultural Collection,* ed. Ella Pearson Mitch-
ell and Valerie Bridgeman Davis (Valley Forge, PA: Judson Press, 2008).

Chapter 9

El Cristo Migrante/
The Migrant Christ

LUIS R. RIVERA

This chapter explores a christological confession that remains mostly implicit in the spirituality and popular religion of Latin American and Latino/a Christians in the United States[1] as well as in the theological reflection of Latino/a pastoral and professional theologians.[2] This segment of the Christian community confesses that Jesus the Christ is a migrant savior for migrants.[3] In light of their faith perspective, they identify Jesus the Christ as a human-divine savior who was a vulnerable migrant, is still present and active in solidarity among migrants and their allies in justice struggles, and is leading a pilgrim church and a world on a journey toward the kin(g)dom of God.[4] Latin Americans and Latino/a Christians believe, proclaim, celebrate, and follow *el Cristo Migrante* (the migrant Christ) in light of their historical experiences of migrations and their struggles for survival and justice as vulnerable and marginalized migrant people and communities in the United States.

The christological intuition I examine here contests and transforms the adverse policies and racist practices that yet influence the lives of Latin American migrants and the established Latino/a communities in the United States. Followers of *el Cristo Migrante* prophetically call U.S. society and churches to adopt a humanitarian perspective, an ethical stance, and a political agenda for

135

the well-being and rights of documented and undocumented migrants and the established multiple generations of Latino/a communities. This christological confession seeks to empower Latin American immigrants and their Latino/a descendants by providing them with spiritual and ethical resources to develop positive religious and political identities and to critically sanction their struggles for social justice. The confession of *el Cristo Migrante* is an ecumenical contribution to the faith and praxis of the church in a world experiencing the benefits and problems of a globalized and conflictive political economy, which generates massive displacements and flows of migrant workers and refugees.

This chapter seeks to explain the confession of *el Cristo Migrante*. First, I discuss how the experience of migration and the struggle for life and justice of vulnerable and marginalized migrants and their allies are the sociological and spiritual contexts from which the confession of *el Cristo Migrante* emerges. Second, I argue that Christians and theologians who reflect on the religious dimension of these experiences articulate in a variety of ways the christological confessions' spiritual, theological, and ethical wisdom. Third, the constructive theological articulation of this confession engages in the dual tasks of "christifying" migrants and "migratizing" Jesus the Christ by developing a Christology in light of God's *oikonomia* of love and hospitality for the world. Finally, this chapter argues that the praxis and discipleship for building *posadas de hospitalidad para la vida con justicia* (households of hospitality for life with justice) grounds and validates the confession of *el Cristo Migrante*.

THE CONTEXT OF THE CONFESSION

The commitment to *el Cristo Migrante* is grounded in the experience, consciousness, and struggles of migrants from Latin America and their descendants. Contemporary Latin Americans and Latino/a people in the United States know what it means to migrate in the American continent by choice or force. Hispanics are descendants of different migratory ancestral groups, such as people from Asia who came to the Americas and gradually evolved into the Indigenous peoples and civilizations in the American continent; Spanish, Portuguese, and other European people who violently conquered indigenous lands and people in the Americas or populated the continent peacefully; African slaves, Asians, and Middle Eastern people who came as indentured or free workers; and modern and contemporary migrations of Latin American workers, entrepreneurs, refugees, and others who for multiple reasons have traveled throughout Latin America and the Spanish Caribbean or mingled with the established Latino/a communities in the States. These ancient and contemporary migrations from many countries and the mixing of these populations constitute the human and cultural stock that explains the cultural, racial, social, religious, and political differences as well as commonalities among Latin Americans and Latinos/as living in the United States.

Since 1965, the number of people from Latin America and their descendants in the United States has grown.[5] Today, Hispanics are the nation's largest community of color, numbering 45.5 million persons (15 percent of the U.S. population). About 64 percent of Hispanics are native born, and 36 percent are counted as foreign born. Persons of Mexican ancestry represent the largest subgroup of Hispanics, or 64 percent of the U.S. Hispanic population; meanwhile, Puerto Ricans make up 9 percent; Cubans represent 3.4 percent; Salvadorans, 3.1 percent; and Dominicans, 2.8 percent of the total U.S. Hispanic population. Many contemporary immigrants are coming from Central and South America, including Brazilians who speak Portuguese, who are now being called "the other Latinos" to distinguish them from the established and more numerous communities of Mexican, Puerto Rican, Cuban, and Central American populations.[6]

By 1960, only 9.4 percent of the total foreign-born population in the United States came from Latin America, yet by 2000 it was 51 percent of that population. Many foreign-born Hispanics have become U.S. citizens through naturalization,[7] and some have dual citizenship. For instance, ten Latin American countries recognize dual citizenship: Brazil, Colombia, Costa Rica, the Dominican Republic, Ecuador, El Salvador, Mexico, Panama, Peru, and Uruguay.[8] In January 2007, approximately 11.7 million of all foreign-born people in the United States were undocumented, and nearly 7 million of them came from Mexico.[9]

U.S. Hispanic communities are integrated by native-born Latinos/as and foreign-born Latin Americans. Forty-eight percent of the Hispanic-origin population lives in California (13.2 million people) and Texas (8.6 million people). Hispanics have spread out significantly beyond the traditional areas of large concentrations in the Southwest and the Northeast. The following states have at least five hundred thousand Hispanic residents, and in most of them Hispanics constitute the largest minority group: Arizona, California, Colorado, Florida, Georgia, Illinois, Massachusetts, Nevada, New Jersey, New Mexico, New York, North Carolina, Pennsylvania, Texas, Virginia and Washington. The projected total population of all Hispanics combined by 2050 is 132.8 million, which will represent about 30 percent of the U.S. population.

The demographic information helps us understand that the experience, memory, and identities of Latin American migrants and their descendants in the States have a long history of connection. The experience of migration is especially important for those groups that have continued to receive new waves of coethnic migrants over the years. The dramatic growth of the Latin American population, especially through births in the United States, counters the generalized view that most Latinos/as are newcomers; in fact, the majority of Latinos/as are born in the United States, or 64 percent of all Latinos/as.

The politics of race and xenophobia assures that all Latinos/as in the States are viewed as foreigners or permanent outsiders. After September 11, 2001, the unfolding national security ideology in the country also resulted in the criminalization of Latino/a migrants, an increased militarization of the U.S./Mexican border, and regular persecutions of undocumented workers in communities across the country.[10] The majority of native-born Latinos/as and Latin American migrants established in communities in the States insist on being recognized for their legitimate contributions to society. They are not reluctant to publicly advocate for the dignity and human rights of both recent Latino/a migrants, their families, and even the native born.

The experience of migration and settlement influences issues of social identity and cultural awareness differently across generations for Latinos/as in the United States. For instance, social identity and political awareness of the immigrant struggle is close to the experience of first-generation Latinos/as and their U.S.-born children who are connected with migrant families, communities, and organizations. Interestingly, for some second-generation Latinos/as, the experience of being discriminated against because of their ethnic identify, social group membership, and political views permits this generation to compare its experience of marginalization to that known by Latinos/as who equate their life in the States with the condition of exile.[11] In other words, the idea of "exile" has appealed even to second-generation Latino/as.

The metaphor of "being a foreigner in their own country" that best describes the condition of exile is associated with a sense of being treated as "different outsiders" by members of the dominant white and black cultures. Latinos/as who use this symbolic language not only give expression to their sense of being culturally different but they use it to strategically claim social space on the margins of black and white society, the others.[12] In conclusion, the real and symbolic experience of migration and the political commitment to defend the human rights, dignity, and life of Latin American migrants and their descendants is the experiential, social, and spiritual terrain from which the confession of *el Cristo Migrante* issues forth.

THE SUBJECTS OF THE CONFESSION

The confession of *el Cristo Migrante* arises from the experience, work, and reflection of three Christian publics. The subjects of this confession are (1) the Latin American migrant people of faith; (2) the Latino/a migrant churches and their associates that welcome, serve, and defend migrants; and (3) Latino/a lay and ordained leaders and theologians and their partners in denominational bodies, community organizations, and the academy.

Many migrants from Central and South America and the Spanish Caribbean are Christians who belong to a wide variety of churches and denominations. The experience of becoming a migrant due to economic, political, or environmental crises is the basic experience assumed in the confession of *el Cristo Migrante*. Migrants pushed for various reasons from their native lands process and interpret their migration experience in light of their religious faith. Religious meaning is attached to the experience of being forced from their homeland or making a voluntary journey and becoming vulnerable and marginalized foreigners in a new country, *El Norte*. Indirect and direct allusions to the confession of *el Cristo Migrante* appear in Latino/a migrants' prayers, conversations, songs, artwork, celebrations, liturgies, and rituals.[13]

Latino/a migrants have the religious conviction that they find, know, and follow Jesus in the midst of their experiences as newcomers engaged in a struggle for social recognition, respect, and justice. The logic of this belief claims something to this effect: Jesus is among us, inspiring and leading us to become and to do that which (a) overcomes the oppression we suffer as migrants, and which secures us a safe and dignified life; (b) meets our fundamental needs; (c) allows us to be a compassionate, just, loving people of faith for the well-being and justice of other migrants and other people; and (d) empowers us to develop relations, systems, and practices that will bring reconciliation and justice among nationals and foreigners, citizens, and documented and undocumented persons.

In the second public, the confession of *el Cristo Migrante* is embodied in the ministry of congregations that welcome and accompany Latin American migrants and their children. These congregations are part of the large network of community organizations and NGOs that provide services and engage in social rights advocacy for migrants. In particular, Latino/a churches are a safe haven where documented and undocumented migrants find spiritual support, friendship, social services, care for their families, social justice advocacy, respect, and recognition for their contributions to national life. These churches constitute a home away from home where familiar language, foods, festivities, traditions, music, and many other cultural expressions that make sense to them are enjoyed. Latino/a churches that are generally constituted by persons from different national groups typically feel less alien to members of a specific Latino/a cultural background than churches with non-Hispanic members. Latino/a churches help migrants with the process of adaptation and acculturation to the host society. *El Cristo Migrante* appears sociologically and spiritually through the deeds, words, and liturgies of Hispanic churches hosting and serving migrant families and communities.[14]

The third public for the confession of *el Cristo Migrante* is the proclamation and teaching developed by lay and ordained leaders of various denominations as well as Latino/a theologians in the academy. The faith of the migrant people and the challenges of ministry among those who serve them have promoted a reflection and teaching that seeks to discern the spiritual, theological, and ethical meanings of the experience of migration, which presages the struggle for dignity, survival, rights, and social justice for migrants and their communities. Some pastoral and theological leaders are first-generation migrants who know firsthand of the journey from a homeland to a host land. Other Latino/a pastoral and theological leaders identify themselves with the sufferings, struggles, quests, aspirations, and claims of migrants. Second- or third-generation Latino/a and other non-Hispanic religious leaders and theologians share the faith and the religious imagery of first-generation migrants and willingly confess and follow *el Cristo Migrante*.[15]

THE SOURCES OF THE CONFESSION

In and through their experience of migration, many Latino/a Christians believe Christ is one of them and is present among them in solidarity and saving grace. They believe that *el Cristo Migrante* knows their suffering, walks with them in their struggle for new life, and hears their prayers for company on the journey. They spiritually intuit the accompaniment of the resurrected Christ in their struggles for survival, their claim for human dignity, their defense of cultural traditions, and their struggles for social justice. This spiritual discernment comes from the Spirit of Christ in the midst of *la lucha por la vida y la justicia en lo cotidiano* (the struggle for life and justice in daily life). I would say Latino/a migrants sense Christ in (a) the will to survive and resist, (b) the conviction that they are God's children created in God's image, (c) the blessing to find a job to support their families here and abroad, (d) the welcoming and help of family and strangers, (e) the sense that their plight for life and justice is taken up by God, (f) the political advocacy of immigrants rights' organizations, and (g) the faith and hope that a new *mañana* (tomorrow) is God's promise for their lives.[16]

In my view, faith in *el Cristo Migrante* can be found in at least four major sources for Latino/a theological reflection: popular religion, the witness of Scriptures, the militant religious discourse of pro-immigrant churches and grassroots groups, and Latino/a academic theology.[17] Each of these sources provide stories, narratives, testimonies, images, metaphors, concepts, visions, values, propositions, and exhortations that help Latino/a migrant Christians and their allies to articulate and elaborate the theological and ethical vision that encourages persons to embody the life-giving practices of *el Cristo Migrante*.[18]

CRITERIA FOR THE CONFESSION

Latino/a Christologies do not begin with the theoretical and doctrinal debates entertained in the church and academy; instead, they begin with the concrete challenges that living in broken society and in conditions of permanent crisis pose for Christian living. Hence, the confession of *el Cristo Migrante* raises these kinds of questions: How can we be followers of Jesus Christ in an unjust world where the lives of marginalized people and the planet are constantly at risk due to the practices, systems, and ideologies that powerful groups develop throughout the world? How are we going to proclaim, live, and practice the gospel of Jesus Christ in a country where a great majority of Latino/a people and communities are poor, economically exploited, political marginalized, racially excluded, culturally dominated, and victimized by many forms of violence?[19] How can we realize the vocation to be transformed into the image of Christ in a society where the lives of documented and undocumented migrants are under siege due to the criminalization of migrants, the militarization of the border, and raids on homes and workplaces? How can we have table communion with the Christ who is present among strangers in a society that makes migrant newcomers invisible or treats them as criminals and enemies?

Latino/a Christologies interpretively confessing *el Cristo Migrante* are reflective works that render explicit two interrelated themes. First, they clarify in religious terms the liberating or redemptive character of the political praxis of marginalized and poor migrants who along with allied groups find multiple ways to resist oppression, social injustice, and the denial of their human rights. The struggle for a dignified and just life here is nothing less than a sign for the God who is present redeeming the world. Second, these Christologies clarify the connection of faith to the liberative life, message, and actions of the resurrected Christ. These Christologies that promote the following of *el Cristo Migrante* motivate a concern for bringing about just living conditions for Latin American migrants and Latino/a communities. Thus, the Christian commitment to join migrants in their existential struggle for a new life through ministries of service and advocacy become faithful responses to Jesus the Christ in a world in need of humanizing renewal.

In other words, Jesus the Christ is present and active among poor, marginalized, and vulnerable Latino/a migrants, empowering them to secure (a) the survival of their families, (b) the recognition of their human dignity and human rights, and (c) respect for their right to belong in national society and be protected by the States where their labor brings societal benefits. *El Cristo Migrante* is redeeming migrants and the larger society through the redemptive struggles of unwanted strangers who seek justice and life. One could say to the wider church that *el Cristo Migrante* calls the church and society now to practice hospitality by building households that sustain the dignity, serve the needs, and defend the just causes of documented and undocumented migrants.

To explore more deeply, there are five key criteria for doing Christology present in the work of Latino/a theologians that frame their interpretive scheme in light of *el Cristo Migrante*. A first criterion for our Christology is a *commitment to liberating praxis*. For Latino/a theologians, liberating praxis refers to collective and reflective human/divine actions that seek to transform relations, practices, ideologies, and institutions that generate all sorts of human inequalities, divisions, and injustices. This transformative Christology of political action seeks the goal of economic, political, cultural, racial/ethnic, gender, and ecological justice, which is interpreted as one of the main goals of God's creative and redemptive activity—a God who redeems by taking a preferential option for the poor as shown in the experience of Israel and of Jesus the Christ.[20] The resurrected Christ and the abiding Spirit are still animating and sustaining the redemptive and liberating praxis that takes place in the world and the church.

The second Latino/a Christology criterion is the centrality of *liberating discipleship*. What we have here is an emphasis on living out the Christian life and witness for the purposes of reconciliation in all fundamental relations (right relations with God, others, nature) and for comprehensive justice.[21] A third criterion in Latino/a Christology is the interdependence of Christology and soteriology, which are centered in the hope and praxis for the kin(g)dom of God. Along with other liberationist theologians, Latino/a theologians are committed to highlight the hope for God's kingdom and the centrality of the political and historical dimension of salvation, including God's preferential option for the poor.

A fourth criterion present in the christological reflection of many Latino/a theologians is a commitment to work *critically* within the boundaries of a Nicean-Chalcedonian Christology and a Trinitarian understanding of God with a methodological emphasis on the "economic Trinity."[22] It is through the liberating presence and ministry of the Son and the Spirit in the poor and faithful Jesus, who lived and died for the sake of God's kingdom for the poor and salvation for all people, that we come to know the liberating work and identity of the Triune God. The God who continuously makes a preferential option for the poor and seeks to liberate creation from all oppressions and injustices is the Trinitarian God who through the Son in the power of the Spirit became incarnate in *el Cristo Migrante*.

Finally, christological discernment and doctrinal construction among Latino/a theologians is informed by the following set of theopolitical commitments: (1) the emergence of a just and participatory, ecologically responsible, and multicultural society as a historical and limited expression of the presence of the kin(g)dom of God; (2) the affirmation and advocacy of human dignity, human rights, and the moral and political agency of the poor, marginalized, and oppressed people as creatures of God created in God's image; (3) the economic, political, social, and cultural survival and development of Latino/a communities as part of the multicultural humanity God intends; (4) the recognition, celebration, and development of those liberating expressions in Latino/a Christian popular religion that are faithful and living manifestations of the Christian faith; and (5) the development of Latino/a churches and discipleship oriented to a praxis of compassion, justice, solidarity, service, and community building in the following of Jesus Christ.

ELABORATING THE CONFESSION

The confession of *el Cristo Migrante* makes two interdependent claims: (1) the "christiphication" of migrants and (2) the "migratization" of Jesus Christ. The first claim attempts to clarify the Christic or sacramental role of migrants. The second claim seeks to discern the centrality of migration to the identity, praxis, and saving role of Christ.

The "Christiphication" of Migrants

Latino/a theologians proclaim and defend the dignity, gifts, and aspirations of documented and undocumented migrants in the sight of God. Their dignity and rights are based on the belief that they are God's subjects empowered by the Spirit, loved by God, created in God's image, and called to be responsible members of God's creation. According to the Deuteronomist and prophetic traditions, the God of compassion and mercy defends the cause of justice for poor and oppressed people, including migrants. Another way of making this emphasis is by advancing the christological argument that Christ is graciously present among and for migrants. The solidarity of the resurrected Christ who accompanies migrants in their struggle for life assures that migrants become visible and others in the Christian community. In other words, the church should be mindful of migrants, for they reveal the Christ who calls us to serve him by loving the stranger.

Migrants are more than objects of Christian compassion, love, and service, however. They are subjects and agents in the company of Christ. In the Latino/a theological imagery, Jesus Christ's presence among and for migrants turns them into *alter Christi*. In this regard, the christiphication of the migrants by Christ's presence suggests several ways to interpret the theological importance of migrants. In light of Christ alive among them, migrants perform a revelatory, liberating, and sacramental function that benefits the Christian community.

First, vulnerable and marginal migrants reveal Christ's presence, judgment, and love. Christ's love encompasses the vulnerable, needy, marginalized, and oppressed people in the world. *El Cristo Migrante* not only opts for migrants, but stands with those who minister to them. Christ is the inviting savior for both migrants and hosts. Christ seeks to be present with and for a community of hospitality where migrants and hosts engage in relationships that promote values and practices of solidarity, care, justice, and inclusion. The opportunities to relate and behave in such ways become the occasion for either divine judgment or divine communion. The denial of hospitality, care, and justice separate us from Christ. The practice of love and service for the migrant allows the Christian community to serve and be in communion with Christ.

Second, the multiple needs of migrants provide the occasions for Christians to respond and engage in practices of hospitality and justice that make present the kin(g)dom. In these caring actions, God's kin(g)dom is embodied "on earth as it is in heaven." Christians and societies that serve migrants experience collective and personal liberations from structures and dynamics of indifference, exploitation, oppression, marginalization, violence, racism, ethnocentrism, cultural imperialism, and other forms of violence. In other words, migrants and those engaged in relationships of hospitality are agents of God's alternative order for the mending of the world.

Finally, the relationship between migrants *en la lucha* (in the struggle) and persons in solidarity with them makes possible the partial but real formation of new communities and new people. The praxis for hospitality and justice becomes a discipline for the spiritual, ethical, and communal formation of a renewed church working for an alternative human society. Character and community formation go hand in hand and take a particular direction in the presence of migrants. *El Cristo Migrante* reveals and works through *los migrantes,* making them sacraments for the kin(g)dom.

In summary, the confession of the presence of el *Cristo Migrante* with migrants is a way to make the Christian community accountable and active in Christ's presence and mission to one segment of vulnerable and marginalized people and in the transformation of the world. The Christian duty to practice hospitality and justice with migrants is a response to the living Christ who calls, judges, and transforms the world by the ways followers respond to the divine-human dignity of migrants (documented or undocumented), their human rights as persons and workers, and their rightful expectation for justice from society and governments.

The "Migratization" of Jesus Christ

Latino/a Christians and theologians can confess that Jesus Christ is a migrant in two ways. As we have seen before, the resurrected Christ can be called *migrante* because of his presence and solidarity (association and identification) with migrants who pray and search for hospitality and justice. The other way is to speculate on the importance of a "migratory and hospitality paradigm" as key to understanding Jesus' identity and work as the Christ. Can the symbols of migration and hospitality help Christians understand who Jesus Christ is for us in the context of international migrations in a globalized world? What are the implications for Christology if we confess that the resurrected Jesus was and is a "migrant for migrants" in his work and identity as Christ? The rest of this chapter explores and illustrates this second strategy of doing Christology, focusing on human/divine migratory dynamics in Jesus' life and ministry.

El Cristo Migrante in Light of God's *Oikonomia* of Love and Hospitality

Latino/a theologians work with at least three fundamental affirmations about the God revealed in Israel and through Jesus Christ and the Spirit. First, God created and is leading and transforming a dynamic creation into God's commonwealth, temple, and household. In God's kin(g)dom or household, Israel is invited to live by loving God and others in communities of right relations. In God's household, justice and care prevail, and a livelihood is provided to all, especially the vulnerable and destitute group. God's household is a community of life against death and freedom against slavery. In other words, God is active in the universe and history, promoting the cause of liberation for creation and human beings and creating a new household (heaven and earth) defined by love, justice, peace, and freedom in all fundamental relationships (God, others, nature). In God's household, social systems and relational dynamics support and defend the promise of abundant life in shared creation. In God's household, life, mercy, and justice are the causes taken up by the church in defense of the vulnerable, destitute, oppressed, and marginalized people in the world, including Hispanics in the United States. In summary, the God of life who creates, liberates, and redeems creation in and through love is empowering and leading it to become God's household of life with justice. The mission of the Son and the Spirit among the wretched of the earth, which constitutes the theological framework for the confession of *el Cristo Migrante,* then reflects God's *oikonomia.*

Second, the God of love and the love of God are core beliefs in the faith and message of Latino/a theologies. The living and liberating God who created the world and is redemptively active in history is the God who fashioned, inhabits, leads, and redeems creation with love. God's life, liberating power, and redemptive mission to mend and transform creation must be conceived and responded to in light of the gracious and beneficial sharing and praxis of divine love (*agape*). Divine love was revealed to the world in God's liberation of the Hebrews from slavery and covenantal formation of a new nation. Those set free were called to love God and others by creating a community for life and justice with a special concern for the poor, the widow, the orphan, and the stranger. Divine love was radically revealed in the life, ministry, death, and resurrection of Jesus the Christ and by way of the sending and ministry of the Spirit. The God of love and compassion seeks to restore and build a community of loving relationships with God, others, and the world where life, justice, well-being, peace, solidarity, and freedom are shared and prevail for all, especially for the poor, marginalized, and oppressed. By way of compassionate love, God is revealed as a God-for-others, or Divine love is "God's being-for others."[23]

Finally, the God of love and justice is a hospitable God who is concerned with creating and sustaining communities that welcome others and nurture relationships and systems that secure and promote life, especially for the poor of the earth. The God of Israel and Jesus Christ is a God who practices a compassionate and just hospitality of life. The migrant and hospitable God is disclosed in acts of creation (first and continuous), liberation (the exodus; life-cross-resurrection-exaltation of Jesus), and redemption (realization of God's kin[g]-dom in a new heaven and earth). In all of God's *oikonomia,* God is seeking to be host and guest of a renewed human community that is empowered by Divine love to promote and sustain practices that create fullness of life and hospitality toward one another.[24] God is seeking to bless creation and all people by turning them into the hospitable household of God defined by God's righteousness and compassion that rules people's hearts and guides the actions of nations. God's love is the heart of God's hospitality, and God's hospitality for a household of life with justice is the praxis of God's love.[25] For many Latino/a believers and theologians, *el Cristo Migrante* is a radical revelation in human flesh of God's liberating love and hospitality.

El Cristo Migrante: Prophet and Agent of God's Hospitable Household of Life with Justice

According to the scriptural narrative, Jesus' life and ministry were shaped by different experiences of migration. The Gospel of Matthew represents the family of Jesus and the child Jesus as political refugees in Egypt and as internally displaced people in Nazareth. Furthermore, the Gospels present Jesus as an itinerant prophet and preacher, moving across regions, cities, and villages in Palestine. Throughout his journeys and ministry, he encountered and preached preferentially the kingdom to poor and marginalized people, including internal and external migrants or foreigners with migrant backgrounds. His adoption of a migratory lifestyle made him experience similar negative consequences that vulnerable and unwanted internal or external migrants experience today. In the narrative, Jesus becomes the object of prejudice, rejection, threats, and violence, as many migrants do.

In all his human and divine wanderings, the migrant Jesus became host and guest of human and divine hospitality. In his preaching and teaching, forgiveness of sin, healing, meals, and sharing, Jesus extended God's compassion and hospitality to destitute, marginal, and despised populations: poor, sinners, the sick and crippled, tax collectors, women, children, prostitutes, gentiles, and persons considered unclean. He also became guest and host in houses and at tables of friends, powerful people, strangers, and sinners. Jesus proclaimed, enacted, and invited people to engage in the hospitality of God's kingdom by welcoming vulnerable and destitute people, and he promised to be present as guest and host in the acts of hospitality performed by Christian communities.[26]

The hospitality that Jesus practiced and invited others to offer was a call to accept and promote God's gracious hospitality to all, especially to the last, the least, and the lost. Jesus advanced in his ministry an alternative household of God which was characterized by the welcoming of the destitute, the provision of livelihood to the poor, and equality in the community of followers. This hospitality was an affront and an alternative logic to the systems of economic, political, and religious oppression that typified the Roman colonial agrarian society of Jesus' day, which was partly defined in Palestine by an aristocratic patronage system.[27]

In the most profound sense, the hospitality that Jesus embodied and practiced was the manifestation of God's love, mercy, and justice taught by the Torah and the prophets. *El Cristo Migrante* of Hispanic faith and theology was and is a migrant prophet who embodies the hospitality of love and justice in God's household. In and through this hospitality of service (*diakonia*) and communion (*koinonia*), he lives, reveals, and exercises God's love and justice, that is, the God-for-otherness. In making this confession, Hispanic Christians trust that they live and struggle in the company (presence, blessing, solidarity) of this human and divine savior who is still with us through the hospitality of many and at the table where he presides as resurrected host and guest, extending hospitality to disciples, sinners, the poor, and all who care to share.[28]

El Cristo Migrante: Mediator of God's Love and Hospitality for a Kin(g)dom of Life with Justice

The Latino/a understanding of the salvific identity of Jesus seeks to clarify the faith conviction that the resurrected One identifies with and accompanies

Latino/a migrants and their communities in the sufferings and struggles for life with justice. These Christians believe that the aspiration for households of life with justice at home and their new context is part of God's salvation for creation and humanity and, as such, a human vocation and part of the church's mission. God's salvation has to do with the establishment of a new life-giving household that dispenses justice and equality. In this new community, God and the neighbor are loved and the excluded and harmed by all systems of injustice are welcomed, healed, and released from their sufferings and burdens. This is the hope for which Jesus lived, ministered, died, and was resurrected; moreover, this hope is a nonnegotiable component in Latino/a Christology.

In his proclamation and enactment of God's kin(g)dom, Jesus saved people through his acts of forgiveness, teaching, healing, and table fellowship. In these acts, he manifested and mediated God's hospitality, that is, God's concern for life and faithfulness to the covenant. Jesus issued a prophetic call for the reordering of life in Israel to conform to the Torah's call to love God and neighbor and to care for the destitute and vulnerable. He opposed the economic, political, and religious systems that brought destitution and death to the excluded and poor masses, especially by way of an onerous taxation system. These systems condemned the poor and marginal populations with the sense of not belonging to the people of God because of their impurity due to their inability to make payments of religious tithes and taxes; however, Jesus brought the excluded a sense of blessing, belonging, and honorable status by teaching about and practicing God's compassion, forgiveness, care, and justice. The masses experienced salvation from material exclusion in the meals he hosted; reconciliation from religious rejection in his words of forgiveness and acts of healing; and liberation from spiritual, patronage, and imperial subjugations through his exorcisms. Jesus was perceived as the prophet and broker of God's salvation and hospitality that cancels debts, forgives sins, and makes people clean, whole, and free.

Latino/a theologians confess *el Cristo Migrante* as a savior who in his past and present ministry makes available God's justice and liberation. This savior empowers migrants, churches, and other people with the Spirit in order for them to practice God's love and hospitality, which contributes to the construction and reformation of households for life with justice, freedom, equality, and peace. Jesus saves us from the powers of sin, death, idolatry, and injustice that make us hostile and inhospitable to others and impede us to fulfill our vocation of loving God and others. Jesus saves us to benefit and share God's gracious and saving hospitality by empowering us with the Spirit to be faithful disciples of a Messiah who has come to be a steward and mentor of life with justice in the household of God.

El Cristo Migrante: Embodiment of the Love and Hospitality of the Triune God

One of the ways Latino/a believers and theologians affirm the dignity and rights of migrants is by making a couple of christological affirmations drawn from the Gospel of Matthew. In that scriptural narrative, Jesus is God's Son who became a migrant and is present in the lives of foreigners and strangers calling people to their service. This divine call to practice hospitality to strangers and migrants is a moral call and mission convocation issued to human and Christian communities alike. The Son of God embodied in the flesh of the migrant Jesus and the migrants of Jesus reveals that rejected others count for God. But what does the divine presence in the migrant and hospitable Jesus and other migrants reveal about God? More specifically, what does the experience of migrations in Jesus' life and his commitment to the poor as well as his resurrected presence among strangers and migrants reveal about God-in-Christ? God's "economic" presence, solidarity, and hospitality in Jesus and other migrants reveals *migratory, hospitable communion and praxis* as qualities of the love and mission of the Triune God.

The Triune God has revealed God's love and justice for the world in creation and redemption.[29] In creation and redemption, God is a hospitable and loving God "making room" and welcoming the world through the shared creative missions of the Spirit and the Son. In continuous creation and the history of salvation, God has become a "pilgrim and guest" God by coming to and inhabiting the world in the shared redemptive missions of the Son and the Spirit who lead creation full of life in the journey toward God's kin(g)dom of freedom and justice. In summary, God relates to and redeems the world in love and justice as a pilgrim and hospitable creator/savior through the loving pilgrimage and hospitality of the Son and the Spirit, who bring God to the world and the world to God in creation and redemption.

The God who in creation and redemption walks with the world (pilgrim God) and comes to the world as host and guest (hospitable God) is a Triune God who lives in an eternal communion of love, God-for-others in the world. The Triune God lives in the unity and communion of love where the divine persons engage in eternal generative loving processions and relations of visiting and welcoming. God's *koinonia* of love constitutes the ecstatic and generative praxis of mutual *perichoresis* (interpenetration which implies pilgrimage and hospitality to one another) that constitutes the communal life and unity of the Triune God. The life of the one God happens eternally in the pilgrimage and hospitality of *agape* in the divine community. This Triune God welcomes and comes to the world in creation and redemption through the "way of the Son of God into the Far Country"[30] and by way of the outpouring of a gathering Spirit.

El Cristo Migrante in the power and company of the Spirit is embodiment and agent of the pilgrim and hospitable Triune God who makes God the host and guest to migrants struggling to build households where life with justice is possible for them. This happens in a world where the majority of people suffer the negative impact of the injustice, inequality, and rejection generated by unjust systems that benefit those in power. Given this grim reality, *el Cristo y el*

Espíritu Migrante create and empower the church to be both a migrant people in solidarity with and a welcoming household for migrants.

THE PRACTICE OF THE CONFESSION AND ITS CHRISTOLOGICAL MEANING

Latino/a theologians subscribe to the principle that discipleship is organically connected to Christology. What is important in the following of Christ is not so much what we say but what we do. The confession of *el Cristo Migrante* becomes a truthful doctrinal or liturgical confession within a practice and lifestyle committed to pursue the values, interests, and goals of the one who from strangers and migrants calls churches to become *posadas hospitalarias para la vida* (hospitable inns for life).

El Cristo Migrante calls the community of disciples to become hospitable households for migrants who aspire and struggle for life with justice. Hospitality involves several practices. Hospitality requires a welcome by accepting those "knocking at the door" or inviting those "on the roads" of our barrios and cities. In the welcoming of strangers and migrants in need, the church reaffirms its vocation to be a hospitable household of God that offers life. The church becomes a *posada* (hospitable shelter) that provides a safe place where migrant people can find acceptance, protection, help, and care. Hospitality involves the sharing of resources and services to attend to the multiple needs of migrant people and families. This sharing should be done without paternalism and manipulation, and mindful of the human capital (resources, gifts, rights) that migrants have. True hospitality allows for role reversal of hosts and guests in the sharing of the resources, gifts, and blessings that each have and can share with one another. In true hospitality, hosts and guests engage in a mutual passing of peace (*shalom*). Hospitality allows for and culminates in short- or long-term fellowship, that is, face-to-face human relations that recognize the names, dignity, stories, feelings, and aspirations of those who speak. These respectful, kind, and cordial relations create the possibility for bonds of friendship and spiritual kinship that give humane depth to the necessary social acts of service and protection.

Christian hospitality is a practice for life with justice that confronts the powers of death, injustice, and alienation that affect the lives of poor migrants. In the welcoming of sojourners, the church becomes a household for the protection and wellness of life. In the sharing of resources through services (*diakonia*), the church works for wholeness of life, that is, the satisfaction of basic needs that sustains human life with dignity. In the fellowship of friendship (*koinonia*), the church creates the opportunity for fullness of life in love that empowers people to reaffirm and claim their dignity and honor as human beings and as children of God. *El Cristo Migrante* promises surprising things to nations and churches that become *posadas* (households of hospitality) in the process of welcoming and serving strangers and migrants: "as you did to one of the least of these who are members of my family, you did it to me" (Matt. 25:40).

In the service to *los migrantes de Cristo y al Cristo Migrante* (the migrants of Christ and the migrant Christ), the church joins Christ in three ways: sharing the mission, becoming disciples, and growing in the union and image of *el Cristo Migrante*. First, churches that engage in ministries of care and advocacy with migrant populations participate in the mission of *el Cristo Migrante,* who is present among migrants advocating and caring for them. Second, through engagement in this mission of hospitality, Christians become true and truthful disciples. Paraphrasing the Gospel of Matthew (7:21): "Not everyone who says to me, '*Cristo Migrante, Cristo Migrante,*' belongs to the hospitable house of God, but only the one who does according to the hospitality of *el Cristo Migrante.*" Finally, in the praxis of becoming *posadas,* churches and Christians experience a deeper communion and identification with Christ. In other words, in the collaboration with the mission of *el Cristo Migrante,* the community of disciples is empowered by the Spirit to imitate Christ (*imitatio Christi*), which leads to their transformation into Christ's image (*imago Christi*)[31] in order to be "sacraments" of Christ's presence (*alter Christi*) for migrants.

There is a deep spiritual transfiguration that takes place in practicing hospitality with migrants. Through a veiled and shared presence in hosts and guests, *el Cristo Migrante* makes possible a mutual redemptive communion and community of hospitality. The migrants become the "guest Christ" who asks the church for hospitality, and the church in hospitality becomes the "host Christ" to migrants; they find and bring Christ to one another. In the needed, challenging, and at times messy ministries of hospitality to migrants, the world and the church are "christified" because Christ remains incarnate in households and practices of hospitality.

CONCLUSION

This chapter argued and explained that the title and confession of *el Cristo Migrante* is part of the faith experience and theological and ethical discernment of Latino/a Christians and theologians. The reality of Latin American migrants and their children in the United States challenges Christians to develop ministries of Christic hospitality and to turn churches into a hospitable household of life with justice. Christians and churches discern and confess *el Cristo Migrante* by experiencing the life of migrants and by participating in their struggles for a more just life. From the experiences and praxis of these publics, this christological confession makes sense and is valid for Latino/a believers, theologians, and the wider Christian community. *El Cristo Migrante* is one among many titles that are needed to express the life-giving faith and discipleship of Latino/a Christians and churches that discern and respond to the liberating presence and ministry of the resurrected Christ in the faces, aspirations, and struggles of Latin Americans in the United States and around the world.

NOTES

1. In this chapter we make the distinction between Latin Americans living in the United States and Latinos/as in the United States. The first group is composed of citizens from Latin American countries who are recent migrants or settled residents (authorized or not) living and working in the United States. Latinos/as is an inclusive noun that substitutes the former "latino/a" and refers to two main groups: U.S. naturalized citizens from Latin America and the children of all Latin American migrants who are U.S. citizens by birth or naturalization. Latino communities in the United States are integrated by all these people, and we need to admit that these distinctions are not of much importance to many of them.

2. The importance of this christological motif or title is not recognized by Michelle A. Gonzalez in her brief but important typology developed in her article on Jesus in *Handbook of Latino/a Theologies,* ed. Edwin D. Aponte and Miguel De La Torre (St. Louis: Chalice Press, 2006),17–24.

3. Lutheran theologian José David Rodríguez speaks about "confessing the faith in Spanish, that is, confessing the faith in a way that brings our Hispanic history and perspective to bear on our interpretation of the gospel." See "Confessing the Faith from a Hispanic Perspective," in *Protestantes/Protestants: Hispanic Christianity within Mainline Traditions,* ed. David Maldonado Jr. (Nashville: Abingdon Press, 1999), 112–13.

4. We use the awkward expression kin(g)dom of God to do two things. One is to recognize the anti-imperial discourse in the Gospels by using the image of God's kingdom or reign in the context of the Roman Empire. The other is to recognize the critique of the imperialistic, hierarchical, and patriarchal dimensions of the kingdom language as stated by Ada María Isasi-Díaz and her alternative expression of kin-dom, that is, a household of kinship and solidarity or God's family. For an extended commentary on "kin-dom," see *La Lucha Continues: Mujerista Theology* (Maryknoll, NY: Orbis Books, 2004), 243–51; also her brief comments in *En la Lucha, In the Struggle: Elaborating a Mujerista Theology* (Minneapolis: Fortress Press, 2004), 213 n. 1; also *Mujerista Theology: A Theology for the Twenty-First Century* (Maryknoll, NY: Orbis Books, 1996), 89, 103 n. 8.

5. The source of information for this and following paragraphs is http://www .census.gov/Press-Release/www/releases/archives/facts_for_features_special_ editions/012245.html.

6. Jose Luis Falconi and Jose Antonio Mazzotti, eds., *The Other Latinos: Central and South Americans in the United States* (Cambridge, MA: Harvard University Press, 2007); Manuel A. Vásquez, "Central and South Americans, and 'Other Latinos/as,'" in *Handbook of Latino/a Theologies,* ed. Edwin David Aponte and Miguel A. De La Torre (St. Louis: Chalice Press, 2006), 160–68.

7. http://www.dhs.gov/xlibrary/assets/statistics/publications/natz_fr_07.pdf.

8. Reed Ueda, "Immigration in Global Historical Perspective," in *The New Americans: A Guide to Immigration since 1965,* ed. Mary C. Waters and Reed Ueda (Cambridge, MA: Harvard University Press, 2007), 22.

9. http://www.dhs.gov/xlibrary/assets/statistics/publications/ois_ill_pe_2007.pdf.

10. http://www.migrationinformation.org/charts/spot-mar07-fig1.cfm; http:// www.ice.gov/doclib/pi/news/ factsheets/fy07accmplshmntsweb.pdf.

11. See the discussion of the "exilic paradigm" in Justo L. González, *Santa Biblia: The Bible through Hispanic Eyes* (Nashville: Abingdon Press, 1996), 91–102; also Fernando F. Segovia, "In the World but Not of It: Exile as Locus for a

Theology of the Diaspora," in *Hispanic/Latino Theology: Challenge and Promise,* ed. Ada María Isasi-Díaz and Fernando F. Segovia (Minneapolis: Fortress Press, 1996), 195–217.

12. See the discussion on otherness in Fernando F. Segovia, "Two Places and No Place on Which to Stand: Mixture and Otherness in Hispanic American Theology," in *Hispanic Americans in Theology and the Church,* ed. F. F. Segovia, special issue of *Listening; Journal of Religion and Culture* 27, no. 1 (Winter 1992): 26–40; also, Fernando F. Segovia, "Toward a Hermeneutics of the Diaspora: A Hermeneutics of Otherness and Engagement," in *Reading from this Place,* vol. 1, ed. Fernando F. Segovia and Mary Ann Tolbert (Minneapolis: Fortress Press, 1995), 57–73.

13. For an empirical and sociological study of the role of faith and religious interpretation among undocumented migrants, see Jacqueline Maria Hagan, *Migration Miracle: Faith, Hope and Meaning on the Undocumented Journey* (Cambridge, MA: Harvard University Press, 2008).

14. Ibid., 82–132. For the public ministries and politics of Latino/a churches, see Gastón Espinosa, Virgilio Elizondo, and Jesse Miranda, eds., *Latino Religions and Civic Activism in the United States* (New York: Oxford University Press, 2005). For an account of the impact of the Christian practices of Central American Christians on Latino/a churches in the United States, see Harold J. Recinos, "The Barrio as the Locus of a New Church," in *Hispanic/Latino Theology: Challenge and Promise,* ed. Ada María Isasi-Díaz and Fernando F. Segovia (Minneapolis: Fortress Press, 1996), 183–94. For the praxis of social justice among religious groups working with immigrants in the United States, see *Religion and Social Justice for Immigrants,* ed. Pierrette Hondagneu-Sotelo (New Brunswick, NJ: Rutgers University Press, 2007).

15. See the collection of brief essays on immigration in Hispanic Theological Initiative, *Perspectivas: Occasional Papers* (Fall 2006); M. Daniel Carroll R., *Christian at the Border: Immigration, the Church, and the Bible* (Grand Rapids: Baker Academic, 2008); *A Promised Land, A Perilous Journey: Theological Perspectives on Migration,* ed. Daniel G. Groody and Gioacchino Campese (Notre Dame, IN: University of Notre Dame Press, 2008); and *Migration, Religious Experience, and Globalization,* ed. Gioacchino Campese, C.S., and Pietro Ciallella, C.S. (New York: Center for Migration Studies, 2003). It is important to consult the pastoral letters, church statements or declarations, press releases, and educational materials developed by different Christian denominations to support the work and ministries with migrant people.

16. For a theological reflection on the Spanish word *mañana,* see Justo L. González, *Mañana: Christian Theology from a Hispanic Perspective* (Nashville: Abingdon Press, 1990), 157–67.

17. The original version of this chapter had a discussion of the popular religious ritual of Las Posadas that had to be omitted because of space limitation. Las Posadas (the inns, lodgings, or shelters) is a religious ritual and festivity of Mexican Catholic origins that commemorates the journey and hardships of Joseph and Mary from Nazareth to Bethlehem in search of an inn where Mary could give birth to Jesus. When they were unable to find lodging in Bethlehem, they were forced to seek shelter in a stable, where Jesus was born. From December 16 to December 24, many Latino/a families in communities and churches engage in a reenactment of this story. They dramatize both the experience of displacement of the Holy Family and their own experience of migration and the search for a safe place for their families. See the brief theological reflections on Las Posadas by two Latino/a Catholic theologians: Ana Maria Pineda,

"Hospitality," in *Practicing Our Faith: A Way of Life for a Searching People,* ed. Dorothy C. Bass (San Francisco: Jossey-Bass Publishers, 1997), 29–42; and Virgilio P. Elizondo, "Living Faith: Resistance and Survival," in Virgilio P. Elizondo and Timothy M. Matovina, *Mestizo Worship: A Pastoral Approach to Liturgical Ministry* (Collegeville, MN: Liturgical Press, 1998), 7–12. On the religious practices of Mexican popular Catholicism, see *Horizons of the Sacred: Mexican Traditions in U.S. Catholicism,* ed. Timothy Matovina and Gary Riebe-Estrella (Ithaca, NY: Cornell University Press, 2002).

18. The original version of this paper had a section discussing material in the Gospel of Matthew that represents Jesus as a refugee in Egypt and a displaced person in Nazareth (Matt. 2), in his encounters with migrants (Matt. 8:5–13), and as the Son of Man present among strangers (Matt. 25:1–46). Due to space limitation this material was omitted. See the hermeneutical contribution of David Cortés-Fuentes in his brief commentary to this Gospel in *Mateo* (Minneapolis: Augsburg Fortress, 2006).

19. Ismael García, *Dignidad: Ethics through Hispanic Eyes* (Nashville: Abingdon Press, 1997), 21–28.

20. "Rather than asking what Jesus would do, we might be better served in asking what Jesus is doing and where. When we consider that God's work continues today through us and through the work of the Holy Spirit in our lives, in the church, and in the world, we are called to the recognition that Jesus' work does indeed continue today. If we look closely at the stories of the New Testament we can gain a deeper insight into where Jesus is today and what Jesus is doing in the world. In the New Testament accounts, Jesus dwelt among the poor, among those living in the margins of society. . . . Today, it is in those very same places that we must look to see Jesus. We must look to the poor and to those living in the margins of society. That is where the Holy Spirit is at work today. It is there that we find Jesus actively present today" (Luis G. Pedraja, *Teología: An Introduction to Hispanic Theology* [Nashville: Abingdon Press, 2003], 162). On the preferential option for the poor, see Roberto S. Goizueta, *Caminemos con Jesús: Toward a Hispanic/Latino Theology of Accompaniment* (Maryknoll, NY: Orbis Books, 1995), 173–211; Carmen Marie Nanko, "Justice Crosses the Border: The Preferential Option for the Poor in the United States," in *A Reader in Latina Feminist Theology: Religion and Justice,* ed. María Pilar Aquino, Daisy L. Machado, and Jeanette Rodríguez (Austin: University of Texas Press, 2002), 177–203.

21. For Latino/a theologians on justice, see García, *Dignidad,* 77–116; Isasi-Díaz, *Mujerista Theology,* 29–34, 105–27; Isasi-Díaz, *La Lucha Continues,* 186–218, 219–39; María Pilar Aquino, "Feminist Intercultural Theology: Toward a Shared Future of Justice," in *Feminist Intercultural Theology: Latina Explorations for a Just World,* ed. María Pilar Aquino and María José Rosado-Nunez (Maryknoll, NY: Orbis Books, 2007), 9–28.

22. For Latino/a theologians on the Trinity, see González, *Mañana,* 101–15; Justo L. González, *A Concise History of Christian Doctrine* (Nashville: Abingdon Press, 2005), 71–90; Pedraja, *Teología,* 117–20; Luis G. Pedraja, "Trinity," in *Handbook of U.S. Theologies of Liberation,* ed. Miguel A. De La Torre (St. Louis: Chalice Press, 2004), 46–58; Zaida Maldonado Pérez, "The Trinity," in *Handbook of Latino/a Theologies,* ed. Edwin David Aponte and Miguel A. De La Torre (St. Louis: Chalice Press, 2006), 32–39; Teresa Chavez Sauceda, "Love in the Crossroads: Stepping-Stones to a Doctrine of God in Hispanic/Latino Theology," in *Teología en Conjunto: A Collaborative Hispanic Protestant Theology,* ed. José David Rodríguez and Loida I. Martell-Otero

(Louisville, KY: Westminster John Knox Press, 1997), 22–32; Sixto J. García, "U.S. Hispanic and Mainstream Trinitarian Theologies," in *Frontiers of Hispanic Theology in the United States,* ed. Allan Figueroa Deck, S.J. (Maryknoll, NY: Orbis Books, 1992), 88–103; Sixto J. García, "A Hispanic Approach to Trinitarian Theology: The Dynamics of Celebration, Reflection, and Praxis," in *WE ARE A PEOPLE! Initiatives in Hispanic American Theology,* ed. Roberto S. Goizueta (Minneapolis: Fortress Press, 1992), 107–32; Miguel H. Díaz, "A Trinitarian Approach to the Community-Building Process of Tradition," in *Futuring Our Past: Explorations in the Theology of Tradition,* ed. Orlando O. Espín and Gary Macy (Maryknoll, NY: Orbis Books, 2006), 157–79.

23. González, *Mañana,* 131–32,152–54.

24. John Koening, *New Testament Hospitality: Partnership with Strangers as Promise and Mission* (Philadelphia: Fortress Press, 1985); Elizabeth Newman, *Untamed Hospitality: Welcoming God and Other Strangers* (Grand Rapids: Brazos Press, 2007); *You Welcomed Me: A Sourcebook on Hospitality in Early Christianity,* ed. Amy Oden (Nashville: Abingdon Press, 2001); Thomas Ogletree, *Hospitality to the Stranger: Dimensions of Moral Understanding* (Philadelphia: Fortress, 1985); Christine Pohl, *Making Room: Recovering Hospitality as a Christian Tradition* (Grand Rapids: Eerdmans, 1999); Arthur Sutherland, *I Was a Stranger: A Christian Theology of Hospitality* (Nashville: Abingdon, 2006); Amos Yong, *Hospitality and the Other: Pentecost, Christian Practices, and the Neighbor* (Maryknoll, NY: Orbis Books, 2008).

25. For the theological importance of the image of the household of God and the economy, see M. Douglas Meeks, *God the Economist: The Doctrine of God and Political Economy* (Minneapolis: Fortress Press, 1989).

26. Matthew 25:1–46.

27. William R. Herzog II, *Jesus, Justice, and the Reign of God: A Ministry of Liberation* (Louisville, KY: Westminster John Knox Press, 2000); Bruce J. Malina, *The Social Gospel of Jesus: The Kingdom of God in Mediterranean Perspective* (Minneapolis: Fortress Press, 2001).

28. Eliseo Pérez Alvarez, "In Memory of Me: Hispanic/Latino Christology beyond Borders," in *Teología en Conjunto: A Collaborative Hispanic Protestant Theology,* ed. José David Rodríguez and Loida I. Martell-Otero (Louisville, KY: Westminster John Knox Press, 1997), 32–49.

29. David S. Cunningham, *These Three Are One: The Practice of Trinitarian Theology* (Oxford: Blackwell Publishers, 1998); Veli-Matti Kaerddaeinen, *The Trinity: Global Perspectives* (Louisville, KY: Westminster John Knox Press, 2007).

30. Karl Barth, *Church Dogmatics,* IV/I, ed. G. W. Bromiley and T. F. Torrance (New York: Charles Scribner's Sons, 1956), 157–10.

31. On the image of Christ and Christ as God's image, see Rom. 8:29; 2 Cor. 3:18; 4:4; Col. 1:15; 3:9–11.

PART 2
POPULAR RELIGION

Speak
Harold J. Recinos

I sit and hear
about the man
from Guatemala

shot last week
by cops who never
sob about wrong

doing. I see
bony children in
unlit apartments

neglected, abused,
desperately crying
in beaten mothers'

arms. I hear people
talk about martyrs, agony
without end, the death

of the world, the vain
cries everywhere, the
churches unable to see

and hear beyond their
sullen Sabbath. I
dwell on the silence

of God.

Chapter 10

Qué Lindo Es Mi Cristo

The Erotic Jesus/Christ in the Caribbean, Latin American, and Latino/a Protestant Christian Music

CARLOS F. CARDOZA-ORLANDI

In a wonderful essay on spirituality and sexuality,[1] Lee Butler paints a picture that I think beautifully captures the grassroots Protestant Caribbean and Latino/a rhetoric of sexuality and spirituality:

> When most Christians are asked to think about body issues, notions of purity are frequently central to those considerations. The ideology that resounds throughout the Christian community is that the body is a temple, and we must always put forth great effort to keep the temple pure. These ideas are quite pervasive because of a deep sense that the body and bodily activities are sinful, corrupted, and impure. This understanding has often resulted in an attempt to be disembodied. Having the feeling that the impure activities of the body are unavoidable, Christians have attempted to minimize or escape the body in the name of sanctification.[2]

Butler recognizes, however, that African—and I add Caribbean, Latin American, and Latino/a—spirituality "is the active integration of our humanity resulting in a singularly directed effort to be in communion with God and others. It is the human spirit moving and being drawn toward God's Spirit."[3] Through this integration, a contested human response to the division between body and spirit, we discover unexpected expressions that implicitly challenge the rhetoric which splits the body and spirit in many Caribbean, Latin American, and Latino/a Protestant communities.

In this essay I examine grassroots Caribbean, Latin American, and Latino/a Protestant hymnody and *coritos*,[4] which express a unique relationship between spirituality and the erotic. The dominant theological discourse in our communities has for too long denied an explicit erotic language of spirituality while, on the other hand, our music, lyrics, and celebratory worship invite the body to become intertwined with the seductive power of the Holy Spirit. Therefore, I want to do three things in this essay: (1) identify the explicit erotic language in some of our grassroots musical production; (2) identify this erotic language in the ways Latino/a communities name and relate to Jesus Christ—the erotic Jesus; and (3) suggest that when our communities rediscover this erotic Jesus with whom we relate, we, as a Christian community, are able to engage in spiritual formation activities that begin to challenge the body-spirit divide, and seek an intentional integration of our spirit and body.

SOME THEOLOGICAL
AND HISTORICAL CONSIDERATIONS

There is an important similarity between African Christianity and Caribbean, Latin American, and Latino/a Protestant Christianity. Both of these Christian expressions seek "a 'communicative' discipline, in which the overriding question" is "How can we best do our theology so that the Gospel will touch Africans [and Caribbeans, Latin Americans, and Latinos/as] most deeply?"[5] While the focus in many Western Christian circles is to articulate a denominational or confessional theology,[6] setting boundaries, and reclaiming a particular and frequently rigid identity, many African, Asian, Caribbean, Latin American, and Latino/a Christian communities articulate the gospel experience in terms of communicative action. The focus of our theology and practices of ministry is on a risky transmission of the gospel experience: deeply biographical, contextual, filled with daily life language, and proposing an alternative religious grounding and identity, which creates a healthy and integrated human being. While many Western Christians focus on making what we have better, African, Asian, Caribbean, Latin American, and Latino/a Christians focus on offering what we have so that we can all seek to be better.

This communicative action is embodied testimony.[7] The grassroots musical production and use of local hymns and *coritos* is a testament to the people's experience with the gospel of Jesus Christ and their agency in communicating the gospel to their broader community. Hence, this is theology deeply grounded in communal mission practice. While many Caribbean, Latin American, and Latino/a Protestant theologians find a split of the body and spirit in classical theological formulations and propose formal theological correctives and guide-lines for healing that split,[8] we frequently dismiss how our Protestant authors and artists address and attempt to correct, in their musical creativity, the dam-aging split. Their theological insight usually proves to have immediate access through the communicative action of a transformative gospel experienced in community. It has a much more permeable and integrative presence because it is a communicative and community activity.

In describing this same situation in the African context—related to the world of spirits and exorcisms—anthropologist Todd M. Vanden Berg gives us a clari-fying statement of the limits and ideological risks of the professional theologian and the potential theological wealth at the grass roots:

> At the ground level the spirit moves in mysterious ways—apparently too mysterious for some theologians. Not only [does] theologians' discomfort reflect the unusual nature and character of the specific areas of integration that occur at a grass-roots level but also it may reflect the challenge they may feel on issues of identity, power and authority.[9]

In my view, the hymns and *coritos* discussed here are an integration of the spirit with the body, an erotic expression of a relationship with God. They are a grass-roots theological proposal that challenges the classical and popular Protestant rhetoric of the spirit-body divide in many of our Caribbean, Latin American, and Latino/a Protestant communities.[10]

Although I am not following a strict chronological order, the hymns and *coritos* represent three different historical stages in Caribbean, Latin American, and Latino/a Protestant Christianity.[11] I focus on the explicit erotic representa-tion of Jesus Christ and his relationship with believers and nonbelievers, and not the historical development of grassroots Protestant thought and worship practices.[12] The first historical stage, represented by Rafael and Luz Ester Rios de Cuna, Puerto Ricans, dates to the 1940s, and represents the first musical production by the first generation of Puerto Rican Protestants. The second his-torical stage, represented by Mexican and Mexican American Antonio Rivera and Freddie Duran, is approximately dated between the mid-1960s and the mid-1970s. Rivera and Duran represent the latter part of the second generation of grassroots Mexican and Mexican American Protestants. The third histori-cal stage, represented by Abigail Ortega, is the contemporary Latina-Hispanic youth expression that I place in the late 1990s and 2000s. Contemporary Latino/a-Hispanic Protestant artists who represent what I call "transitional embodiments." Their musical style is different from that of the previous gen-erations. Cuna's work, for instance, has a musical structure distinct from the traditional translated-to-Spanish hymns typically found in the *Himnos de la Vida Cristiana* hymnal. Rivera and Duran employ the bolero as their musical medium for their hymns. Meanwhile, Ortega uses reggaeton and hip-hop to communicate her Christian experience.

DEFINING THE EROTIC

Karen Baker-Fletcher reminds us that the Greeks "understood *eros* as a unifying force."[13] She writes, "Black women . . . are often suspicious of *eros* associating popular understandings of the *'erotic'* in pornography or with 'doing the nasty.' . . . But this is a false understanding of *eros* and the *erotic* learned from patriarchal structures that denigrate women's power *[and men's psyche]* to love in a way that unites body and spirit."[14] Baker-Fletcher defines *eros* as "the desire for union with the sacred," and "the desire for union with the other . . . The *erotic* satisfies more than physical hunger and tastes. The power of it heals the souls and the bones."[15]

As we seek to discover the erotic in Latino/a hymns and *coritos,* I build upon Baker-Fletcher's definition of *eros* and the erotic, and suggest the following additional criteria. First, the erotic seeks intimacy with the body. The expressions of love and care are bodily related; the relationship is one of body to body. Second, the erotic points to an experience with the beautiful. Third, the erotic uses body language to point to a spiritual condition, whether one that needs or describes redemption and liberation. The relationship in language between body and spirit is in itself a way of challenging the body-spirit divide. Fourth, the erotic language refers to the relationship of the believer or nonbeliever with the divine—in our case, Latino/a communities with Jesus Christ—and yet the language is interchangeable to refer to the relationship between love partners. For instance, if I change the term "God" or "Jesus Christ" in these hymns and *coritos* for the name of my wife—Lizzie—it partially describes the nature of our love relationship. Finally, the erotic power of the language of these hymns and *coritos* is multiplied by the musical genre used by these grassroots Protestant artists. Jesus as a divine companion imagined in the music of a bolero creates a different aura of relationship, where expectation, pleasure, satisfaction, and faithfulness are embodied.[16]

THE HYMNS AND *CORITOS*:
REDISCOVERING THE EROTIC JESUS CHRIST

As a reminder, the objectives of this essay are to identify the explicit erotic language in some of our grassroots musical production, to identify this erotic language with ways our communities name and relate to Jesus Christ—the erotic Jesus—and to suggest that when our communities rediscover this erotic Jesus with whom we relate, we, as a Christian community, are able to engage in spiritual formation activities that begin to challenge the body-spirit divide, and which seek an intentional integration of spirit and body. I address the first two objectives in this section.

Four of the seven hymns discussed in this essay are provided at the end of the essay. For the other three hymns, the reader is encouraged to find the lyrics in the Internet. Web addresses are provided in the endnotes for each of these three hymns. Moreover, I strongly recommend the reader to search the Internet for performances of all of these hymns. The fact that these hymns are found all over the Internet—lyrics and performances by different artists, from professional Christian singers to amateur videos in local congregations—points to their popular character in Protestant, pentecostal, and charismatic circles in Latin America, the Caribbean, the United States, and Canada.[17] I quote some sections of the hymns and *coritos* where I believe that the explicit erotic language is fully expressed in relationship to Jesus Christ. The reader should remember that these hymns and *coritos* are congregational songs. They are sung as specials in worship services, sung by the whole congregation, and celebrated as spiritual and praise gifts from the community to Jesus Christ.

Rafael Cuna is a child of the *Avivamiento del 33* (Protestant charismatic renewal of 1933) in Puerto Rico.[18] He was a member of a Disciples church in Corozal, Puerto Rico, but was later ordained by one of the pentecostal traditions in the United States. Cuna published *Cuna de Flores* in 1948, a collection of hymns and *coritos* he wrote during the 1940s. Regarding this personal publication, he writes in the introduction,

> La inspiración de algunos de estos himnos fue cosa dramática, pues ciertas veces yendo de camino tuve que detener el vehículo a la orilla de la carretera para escribir la melodía; otras veces levantarme de noche a hacer lo mismo; así en distintos lugares, cuando menos lo esperaba aparecía la melodía.[19]

Cuna states the purpose of this hymnal, saying,

> Las angustias y sinsabores que vencí, me hacen acreedor de un contentamiento espiritual bello, y más bello aún si supiera que éstos himnos fuesen un aliciente benéfico y positivo en la salvación de algún alma.[20]

In the introduction to *Cuna de Flores,* Cuna sets the tone of the hymns and *coritos.* They are the result of a deep and beautiful spiritual joy for conquering difficult situations. They are testimonies of Jesus' intervention in his life, and their inspiration comes not only from daily life, but during daily life tasks.

In his hymn *El Amor de Dios,*[21] Cuna names the love of God in Jesus as a powerful force that penetrates and inspires his life. This powerful love eliminates rebellion and comforts, protects, redeems, and sustains the believer's faith. Such a powerful love only comes from the Lord! Yet the chorus changes the tone of the power of love from one that transforms to one that renews, is sweet, tender, and pure. The juxtaposition of a powerful, transforming love with a sweet, tender love seems to be a play between an omnipotent God and a more intimate, beautiful, caring Jesus. Jesus is love, and as love Jesus comes close, Jesus is intimate, Jesus brings peace, Jesus is comfort, Jesus is tender, and Jesus is sweet. In other words, Cuna's *El Amor de Dios* is a testimony to Jesus' love. The hymn focuses exclusively on Jesus' loving character and the believers' (and nonbelievers') passive role in experiencing this love. All intimate initiative is in Jesus, and the believer experiences the penetration and inspiration of the Lord's love in both tender and redeeming ways.

Cuna's hymn *Al Abrigo del Altísimo* based on Psalm 91 takes a different direction. The strophes give witness to God's protective character. God will protect the believer from darkness, from the temptor's arms, from stumbling and falling, and from death. However, in the hymn Cuna emphasizes the action of dwelling in God. The believer knows God's protective and caring character; hence, the believer needs to want to dwell in God's peaceful and loving being. Dwelling in God not only results in protection but is also an experience of pleasure. Dwelling in God is a delight, and the believer enjoys and praises forever.

Antonio Rivera's *Divino Compañero*[22] is a tender account of the Emmaus story in the Gospel of Luke. In a bolero style, Rivera describes the overwhelming presence of Jesus, which dissipates shadows and brings the light of love. For Rivera, light is not about seeing, but rather about warmth and love. Jesus' presence in the journey is comforting and protective. The chorus is a beautiful invitation for Jesus to stay, for Jesus to dwell in the believer's being. Rivero invites the Lord to make the believer a permanent resting place, and he pleads to Jesus to accept this new resting place. The hymn concludes with another plea: Don't leave me alone in the journey; help me until the end.

In Rivera's hymn, the believer takes initiative in seeking the love and companionship of Jesus. The believer invites intimacy and a permanent relationship of accompaniment. Recognizing Jesus as a divine and protective presence results in a passionate invitation from the believer for a permanent companionship in the faith journey.

Freddie Duran's *Qué Lindo Es Mi Cristo*[23] reveals a very intimate relationship between the believer and Jesus Christ. Perhaps one of the most surprising references to Christ is that he is *lindo*—beautiful. This image of a beautiful Christ is enriched by the fact that this hymn is a bolero, a musical beat that invites intimacy and desire. In the strophes, Duran relates Christ's beauty with tender hands that caress and cradle the believer. Tender touch and beauty are Christ's gift to the believer and the sinner. But Christ is beautiful because he is tender and loving; he caresses his followers. Moreover, Christ's *kenosis,* God's emptying of Godself in Jesus Christ, is Christ's beauty and intimate love. *La entrega total de Cristo* (Christ totally giving himself) can only be embodied in the sweet and tender caresses of Christ to the believer and the sinner.

Duran uses erotic language to refer to the passion and relationship that Christ has with the believers—and what Christ offers to the nonbeliever. Duran does take the image of Christ to a new level. Christ's hands are tender, and Christ's tender hands caress the believer. Additionally, for Duran, Christ's tender hands caress and fill the believers' soul with love. After this tender touch of Christ, the believer finds in Christ's voice the assurance of love.

Vivir Prendado[24] is an anonymous hymn that follows the same erotic pattern of Duran's *Qué Lindo Es Mi Cristo.* The strophes immediately show the need of the believer to be close to Christ. The imagery of closeness, based on the Gospel of John and the traditional assumption that John is the Beloved Disciple, is tender and mystical. The hymn writer desires to lie on Jesus' chest, to feel Jesus' heartbeat, to listen closely to Christ's holy secrets. With a *paso-doble* rhythm, the hymn infuses the urgency of this intimate encounter—an encounter of fire and intoxicating perfume, an encounter that engenders courage. Interestingly, the phrase *vivir prendado* is commonly used to refer to a deep attachment to someone. When I shared with a colleague the lyrics of this hymn, he immediately asked whether this was a poem by San Juan de la Cruz, the Spanish mystic. In *Vivir Prendado* the erotic agency falls on the believer. The believer wants this close encounter of the body with the body of Jesus.

Perhaps the most striking rhythm and lyrics come from Abigail Ortega, a young Latina from Georgia. Playing the basic rhythm of reggaeton and hip-hop, *Acaríciame*[25] names what Ortega needs from her Lord: *una caricia*—a caress. In her first hymn her desire for Christ's caress is reflective of her needs—she is alone, she is overwhelmed, she needs help. She needs Christ's caress because she experiences abandonment, uncertainty, and exhaustion. The desire for care is radically expressed in a seductive rhythm and with the typical repetition inducing a demand: *acaríciame, acaríciame, acaríciame.* In the second strophe she is hurting and wants to laugh; she wants the end of her suffering. She wants her life to be joyful, and this only happens when she is close to Christ.

Ortega's second hymn, *Mi Testimonio,* narrates her family context and life. The ways in which she names the suffering, the turmoil in family relationships, and her own devastated self is totally dependent on body imagery and relationships. Perhaps the English translation does not capture how strong the body language is in Spanish, especially when she says, *con un padre no de sangre, por qué siento dolor, por qué mi vida no tiene calor, mi corazón se está muriendo por falta de amor* (with a father not of flesh, why do I feel pain, because my life is empty, my heart is dying for lack of love). All of these phrases locate Ortega's suffering in the body-spirit intersection.

Ortega's narrative of redemption is brief, but to the point. She returns, perhaps, to a common theme: *alguien me abrazó, alguien me acarició, me dijo ¡yo te amo!* (Someone embraced me, someone caressed me, told me, "I love you!"). She also includes in her hymn the term *Mija,* a typical term of endearment and care among Mexicans and Mexican Americans. It is the diminutive, a kind, tender term for *mi hija*—my child. Ortega concludes her testimony with affirmations of Christ's work in her life and the complete assurance that she only trusts in him—and all of these because of a hug, a caress, and the ultimate words of love, "I love you!" from Jesus the Christ.

CONCLUSION

These hymns and *coritos* are an erotic communicative action. Jesus Christ is portrayed as one whose love is embodied in intimacy, closeness, caress, and embrace. The power of Christ against evil is channeled through an imagery of tenderness and intimacy, not conflict and warfare. Jesus Christ's erotic nature conquers fears, dissipates darkness, and restores peace and hope. Jesus Christ's erotic nature reveals a desire from Jesus to be close to the community. Jesus' saving power is translated into a loving and palpitating heart, tender and embracing hands, and seductive, intoxicating aroma. Jesus' erotic nature invites the believer to a deeper intimate relationship and seduces the nonbeliever into a tender encounter. In other words, Jesus' erotic nature creates discipleship and evangelizes the world.

These hymns and *coritos* reveal the erotic nature of the Christian community. These grassroots Christian artists desire, want, and long for intimacy with Christ. The response of our Caribbean, Latin American, and Latino/a Protestant communities is a charismatic eroticism that seeks intimacy with Jesus. In this desire for intimacy, expressed in bodily functions, strong feelings, and with biblical connections, the community discovers the embodied intensity of Christ's love.

Notice how these hymns and *coritos* question rigid gender-based relationships with Jesus Christ. *Qué Lindo Es Mi Cristo* and *Vivir Prendado* are two unique examples of male Protestant artists relating to Jesus Christ with typical serenade music and imagery. While it is very typical for Roman Catholic Mexicans and Mexican Americans to serenade *La Morenita*—the Virgin of Guadalupe, Mexicans and Mexican American Protestants serenade Jesus Christ, naming their relationship with Jesus Christ as one of yearning for the beauty and love of Jesus' caress.

Finally, these hymns and *coritos* remind us of the wisdom and creativity found in the grassroots experience of Jesus Christ. These musical resources are worship and educational opportunities to address questions and concerns in our community about sex, relationships, and the need for a faith that integrates our daily life experience. These resources become an invitation to remind our communities that all is sacred.

TRANSLATION OF HYMNS

El amor de Dios/The Love of God[26]
RAFAEL CUNA[27]

(1) No hay amor como el de Dios;/There is no love like God's;
Que me llena el corazón;/It overwhelms my heart;
Que penetra en mi, que me inspira más;/It penetrates me, it inspires me on;
El amor de mi Señor./My Lord's love.
(*Chorus*) El amor de mi Señor,/My Lord's love
Me renueva el corazón;/Renews my heart;
Dulce amor de Dios;/Sweet love of God;
Tierno y puro es;/Tender and pure it is;
El amor de mi Señor./My Lord's love.
(2) Borrará mi rebelión;/It will eliminate my rebellion;
El amor de mi Señor;/My Lord's love;

La bondad de él;/God's kindness;
Es consuleo en mi;/Comforts me;
Pone paz en mi aflicción./Brings me peace in my sorrow.
(3) No hay amor como el de Dios;/There is no love like God's;
Que me imparte protección;/It grants me protection;
Me redimirá y me sostendrá;/It will redeem and sustain me;
El amor de mi Señor./My Lord's love.

Al Abrigo del Altísimo/Under the Care of the Most High
Based on Psalm 91
RAFAEL CUNA

(1) El que habita al abrigo de Dios;/One who dwells under God's care;
Morará de su sombra al calor;/Will move from one's own darkness to warmth;
Confiado y seguro estará;/One will trust and be safe
De los brazos del vil tentador./From the vile temptor's arms.
(**Chorus**) Oh yo quiero habitar al abrigo de Dios;/Oh I want to dwell in
    God's care;
Sólo allí encuentro paz y profundo amor;/Only there do I find peace and
    deep love;
Mi delicia es con él;/My pleasure is with Him;
Comunión disfrutar y por siempre;/Delightful communion with God
    and forever;
Su nombre alabar./Praise God's name.
(2) El que habita al abrigo de Dios;/One who dwells under God's care;
En sus alas seguro estará;/Under God's wings will be safe;
Caerán mil y diez mil por doquier;/Thousands may fall on your sides;
Más a él no vendrá mortandad./But death will never reach.
(3) El que habita al abrigo de Dios;/ One who dwells under God's care;
Ciertamente será muy feliz;/Will certainly be joyful;
Angeles guardarán su salud;/Angels will protect one's health
Y su pié nunca resbalará./And one's feet will never stumble and fall.

Acaríciame/Caress Me
ABIGAIL ORTEGA[28]

Acaríciame, porque a veces/Caress me because sometimes
Me siento que ando sola./I feel I'm walking alone.
Acaríciame, porque siento/Caress me because I feel like
Que me ahogan las olas./The waves are smothering me.
Acaríciame, cuando veas/Caress me when you see
Que ya no puedo más,/that I cannot go on,
Y dime que Tu me ayudarás/And tell me that you'll help me
Y me amas. . . ./And love me. . . .
Yo no sé qué me pasa, Señor/I don't know what is going on, Lord
Yo me siento con mucho dolor,/I feel a lot of pain,
Me ha llegado una situación,/Something has come over me,
Que me da mucha desilusión./That leaves me empty.
Yo quisiera dejar de sufrir;/I want to stop suffering;
Yo quisiera reir y reir,/I want to laugh and laugh,

Que mi vida fuera muy feliz,/That my life could be joyful,
Yo quiero estar junto a Ti./I want to be close to you.[29]

Mi Testimonio/My Testimony
ABIGAIL ORTEGA

Desde niña yo he llorado,/Ever since I was a girl I cried,
Desde chica yo había sufrido,/Since I was a little one I'd suffered,
Y yo no entendía porqué,/And I didn't understand why,
Era así mi vida./My life was just that way.
Tan pequeña y yo sin padre,/So small and without a father,
Y con una joven madre,/And with a young mother,
Era un mundo diferente,/It was a different world,
Con un padre no de sangre./With a father who was not my father.
Muchas cosas malas pasaron;/Many bad things happened,
Cosas malas que me hicieron,/They did bad things to me;
Yo era inocente y con una sana mente;/I was innocent and had no malice;
Destruyeron mi confianza, mi niñez/They destroy my trust, my childhood
Y mi esperanza,/And my hope,
Yo no encontraba salida,/I didn't know where to go,
Muchos pleitos y amenazas./So many fights and threats.
Todo mi mundo no tenía color/My world was colorless
No sentía el frío tampoco el calor,/I felt neither cold or heat,
Sentía miedo también depresión,/I was afraid and depressed,
A Dios gritaba en mi oración,/I screamed out to God in my prayers,
Que me sacara de este infierno./Take me out of this hell.
(Chorus) Dime por qué, por qué siento mucho dolor,/Tell me why, why I feel so
    much pain,
Dime por qué, por qué mi vida no tiene color;/Tell me why, why there is no
    color in my life;
Dime por qué, por qué no siento Tu calor;/Tell me why, why I do not feel your
    warmth;
Mi corazón se está muriendo por falta de amor./My heart dies for want of love.
Pasaron años y todo cambió,/The years passed and everything changed,
En vez de bueno se puso peor;/Instead of getting better it just got worse;
Mi hermano el mayor irse de la casa decidió,/My older brother left home,
Porque su corazón no aguanto,/Because his heart could not take more,
Tanta tragedia, tanto dolor,/So much tragedy, so much pain,
La única salida la encontró en la pandillas,/He found in gangs his only hope,
El era mi ejemplo yo también hice lo mismo,/He was my role model so I did
    the same,
Estábamos pérdidos tratando de encontrar amor,/We were lost trying to
    find love,
Haciendo cosas para robar la atención./Doing things to make anybody care.
Pero mi hermano siguió más profundo,/But my brother sank deeper,
El se fue como para otro mundo,/He went to another world,
El ya no era el mismo,/He wasn't the same;
No se parecía mi hermano,/He wasn't the brother I knew,
Ahora me sentía sola,/Now I felt alone,
Sentía que me ahogaban las olas,/Like the waves were going to smother me,
Yo lloraba cada noche,/I cried every night,

Todos los días a cada hora./Every day every hour.
(Chorus)
Mi corazón endureció,/My heart was hardened,
Día a día guardaba rencor,/Day by day I grew more bitter,
Yo ya no podia,/I couldn't anymore,
Hasta quise quitarme la vida,/I even thought of taking my life,
Teniendo tantos problemas,/With so many problems
Y ahora mi hermano encarcelado;/And now my brother in prison,
Y a mi madre suifriendo, llorando y orando./And my mother hurting, crying,
    and praying.
Yo caí, desmayé, yo sufrí y lloré,/I fell, fainted, I suffered and cried,
Pero algo paso, alguien me abrazó,/But something happened, someone
    embraced me,
Alguien me acarició, me dijo ¡yo te amo!/Someone caressed me, told me, I love you!
Deja de llorar, seca tus lágrimas,/Stop crying, dry your tears;
Yo nunca te abandoné,/I never abandoned you,
Ni siquiera te dejé,/Not even took one step away from you,
Mija siempre te cuide, *Mija*/I always cared for you,
Yo siempre te he sido fiel. ¡Levántate!/I always been faithful to you. Rise!
El sanó mi corazón, vida nueva él me dio,/He healed my heart, new life he
    gave me,
El murió por mí en la cruz,/He died for me on the cross;
Por completo se entregó,/Wholly He gave himself;
Pase, pase lo que pase,/No matter what happens
Venga, venga lo que venga,/No matter what may come,
Sólo en Cristo confío,/I trust only Christ,
Y no hay nada que me detenga./And nothing holds me back.

NOTES

1. Lee Butler, "The Spirit Is Willing and the Flesh Is Too: Living Whole and Holy Lives through Integrating Spirituality and Sexuality," in *Loving the Body: Black Religious Studies and the Erotic*, ed. Anthony Pinn and Dwight N. Hopkins (New York: Palgrave Macmillan, 2004), 111–20.
2. Ibid., 111.
3. Ibid., 117.
4. *Coritos* is the term used by Latino/a congregations to refer to Christian songs.
5. Kwame Bediako, "'Whose Religion is Christianity?' Reflections on Opportunities and Challenges in Christian Theological Scholarship: The African Dimension," in *Mission in the Twenty-First Century: Exploring the Five Marks of the Global Mission,* ed. Andrew Walls and Cathy Ross (Maryknoll, NY: Orbis Books, 2008), 110.
6. Ibid.
7. For a further discussion on testimony as a practice of mission, communicative action, and congregational practice, see my essays "Mission at the Borders," in *Teaching Mission in a Global Context,* ed. Patricia Loyde-Siddle and Bonnie Sue Lewis (Louisville, KY: Geneva Press, 2001), 25–39, and "What Makes Preaching 'Missional'?" *Journal for Preachers* 22, no. 4 (Pentecost 1999): 3–9.

8. The contribution of Caribbean, Latin American, and Latina feminist and *mujerista* theologians has been crucial in my own awareness regarding issues of the body. Without this contribution it would have been impossible to look at these hymns and *coritos* with what I call "an erotic eye." My critique is not in relation to the formal theological contributions, but to the false assumption that the grassroots has not addressed the spirit-body divide in our Protestant communities. For some of the most recent Latin American and Latina works addressing some of these issues, see Maria Pilar Aquino and Maria Jose Rosado Nuñez, *Feminist Inter-cultural Theology* (Maryknoll, NY: Orbis Books, 2007), and Marcella Althaus-Reid, *Liberation Theology and Sexuality* (Aldershot, England: Ashgate, 2006).

9. Todd M. Vanden Berg, "Culture, Christianity, and Witchcraft in a West African Context," in *The Changing Face of Christianity,* ed. Lamin Sanneh and Joel Carpenter (New York: Oxford University Press, 2005), 47.

10. Regretfully, many Christian leaders and theologians spiritualize these hymns and *coritos,* domesticating their spirit-body integration. Nevertheless, the resources are available, accessible, and frequently used by the community. As any good and vital symbol, they carry layers of meaning waiting to be uncovered.

11. See pages 164–67 for hymns and *coritos.*

12. One of the challenges of grassroots Caribbean, Latin American, and Protestant music is finding precise historical data. Except for one "official" publication and two interviews, most of the music comes from two sources: church or local publications of hymns and *coritos* with no music—which assumes that people know the music of the hymns and *coritos*—and recent CDs advertised as *Clásicos de Siempre* or *Música del Ayer* with no date of the musical production.

13. Karen Baker-Fletcher, "The Erotic in Contemporary Black Women's Writings," in Pinn and Hopkins, *Loving the Body,* 201.

14. Ibid., 201–2 (italics added).

15. Ibid., 202–3.

16. I am well aware of our Spanish mystical heritage in figures like San Juan de la Cruz and Santa Teresa de Avila. Because of limited space, I decided not to discuss the historical connections between these mystics and our Caribbean, Latin American, and Latino/a Protestant erotic music.

17. See pages 164–67 for hymns and *coritos.*

18. The historical information for Rafael Cuna comes from Rev. Hector J. Gonzalez, ordained minister of *La Iglesia Cristiana (Discípulos de Cristo) en Puerto Rico* (personal and phone interviews with author, January and February 2009).

19. Rafael Cuna, *Cuna de Flores* (Puerto Nuevo, Puerto Rico, 1948), 2. "The inspiration of some of these hymns was a dramatic thing, for certain times as I was traveling I had to stop the vehicle at the side of the road to write the melody; other times I would get up at night to do the same; like so in different places, when I least expected it" (author's translation).

20. Ibid. "The afflictions and bitterness which I conquered make me a recipient of a beautiful spiritual joy, and more beautiful it would be if I knew that these hymns were a beneficial and positive enticement in the salvation of a soul" (author's translation).

21. Cuna's hymns are provided at the end of the essay. Performances of these hymns can be seen in Youtube.com under the title of the hymns and/or using the first sentence of the hymn. The reader can also find the hymns in www

.coroguadalajara.org, www.justsomelyrics.com, www.stevegreenministries.org/ lyrics, and other links. The hymns are also available in the following hymnals: *Caliz de Bendiciones* (St. Louis: Chalice Press, 1996), *Mil Voces para Celebrar* (Nashville: Abingdon Press, 1996), and *El himnario presbiteriano* (Louisville, KY: Geneva Press, 1998). The lyrics of *Al Abigo del Altisimo* are by Luz Ester Rios de Cuna.

22. The following three hymns, *Divino Compañero, Qué Lindos Es Mi Cristo,* and *Vivir Prendado,* are not provided at the end of the essay. The reader is encouraged to find the lyrics and performances on the Internet. For *Divino Compañero* and *Qué Lindos Es Mi Cristo* see www.Youtube.com, with the key words of Marcos Witt and Manuel Bonilla. The reader will also find the hymns performed in local Christian communities. I personally recommend Manuel Bonilla or the local Christian communities' performances. Other Web sites for lyrics are www.allthelyrics.com, www.justsomelyrics.com, and www.Esnips.com, using the key words "Vivir Prendado." Furthermore, these three hymns are available in the iPod store.

Very little information is available about Antonio Rivera and his music. I grew up with these hymns in local Puerto Rican congregations, and these hymns were (and in some circles continue to be) widely known in Latin America, the Caribbean, and many Latino/a congregations. I was able to find these hymns in popular church publications such as *Nuevo Himnario Canticos Especiales* (Las Piedras, Puerto Rico: n.d.), Arroyo Distribution Group, and *Himnos de la Iglesia* (n.p., n.d.). More important, however, is the fact that these hymns, after many years, have been put on the market advertised as *Himnos del Ayer* (Hymns of Yesterday) by Mexican and Mexican American Protestant singers such as Manuel Bonilla and Ricardo Rodriguez.

23. There is little information about Freddie Durán. However, as stated in the previous note, this hymn is part of multiple local congregations' worship services in Latin America, the Caribbean, and many Latino/a congregations, particularly Pentecostal congregations. This hymn was and continues to be marketed and advertised as *Himnos del Ayer* (Hymns of Yesterday) by Mexican and Mexican American singers, and some of the more current Christian singers in the Latino Christian music business.

24. I was unable to find the author of this hymn. The information found was confusing and uncertain, hence I decided to label it as anonymous. However, this hymn is found in the collection of *Clásicos de Siempre II* by Ricardo Rodriguez, a former member of the Mexican American Christian group *Los Latinos.* Once more, it shows how these hymns belong to a previous generation, and yet continue to be used—and marketable—among Latin American, Caribbean, and Latino/a Protestant Christians.

25. Ortega's hymns are provided at the end of the essay and used by permission. Given the recent production of these hymns, they are not in the public domain.

26. All translations by Carlos F. Cardoza-Orlandi. Hymns were translated to English trying to capture the meaning of the Spanish language rather than following any poetic or rhythmic pattern that would allow the hymn to be sung in English with the original beat.

27. Originally published by Rafael Cuna, *Cuna de flores: Himnos y coritos de Rafael Cuna* (Puerto Nuevo, Puerto Rico: 1948), 16. Copy of this hymnal was provided by Rev. Héctor J. González, ordained minister, *Iglesia Cristiana (Discípulos de Cristo) en Puerto Rico*. More recent publications of these hymns are found in *Caliz de Bendiciones* and *Mil Voces para Celebrar*.

28. Abigail Ortega is a member of the *Iglesia Cristiana (Discípulos de Cristo) El Aposento Alto* in Lake City, Georgia. Of Mexican background, Ortega represents Latino/a youth in many local charismatic congregations. She is a community college student discerning her future in ministry. Her reggaeton and hip-hop styles are a clear appropriation of current popular musical styles and the Christianization of these styles in the context of local congregations.

29. This section of this hymn was written by Ortega.

Chapter 11

Three Visual Images of Jesus the Christ from the Latino/a Community

God the Vulnerable; God the Broken; God the Loving

EDUARDO C. FERNÁNDEZ, S.J.

> *The Holy One and those who are made one in him set about changing the world's mind by first seizing the world's imagination through acts of powerlessness. In doing so they tapped into the most awesome source of power there is.*
>
> Aidan Kavanagh, *On Liturgical Theology*[1]

In Michelle González's "Jesus" entry in the *Handbook of Latina/o Theologies,* among the three challenges in the field that she identifies is that of wrestling with the contours of a Latino/a Christology. Summarizing the important contributions of Virgilio Elizondo, Luis Pedraja, Roberto Goizueta, Ada María Isasi-Díaz, Miguel De La Torre, and a few others, she argues for a greater critical development in the area of Latino/a Christology. She writes: "While the centrality of the crucified Christ in the faith and religious practices of Latino/a communities is clear, the centrality of Christology within Latino/a theology is not."[2]

I wish to express my gratitude to Mia Mochizuki, Virgilio Elizondo, Thomas Steele, S. J., and Charlie Carrillo for helping me to formulate my thoughts for this essay. The images included in this chapter were photographed by the author.

171

As evidence she cites the failure to wrestle with some of Western Christology's classical themes.

> In their emphasis on the concrete faith experiences of Latino/a communi-
> ties, Latino/a christologies have avoided some of the "classic" Christological
> themes such as atonement, the scandal of particularity, triumphalism, and
> the question of redemptive suffering. While some would argue that the lan-
> guage and discourse of these Christological themes are couched in a Western
> European theological construction (and thus inconsequential to a *Latino/a*
> theology), I disagree. Latino/a theologians are still theologians, ones that—
> for better or worse—are steeped in the Western European theological tradi-
> tion. To ignore central theological concepts that have shaped the discourse
> of systematics is to isolate the theological impact of Latino/a christologies.[3]

The essays in this book are a step in that direction. As a pastoral theologian, I am often fascinated by the way that people pray and the impact of that type of prayer on their lives. What settings do they seek, and what objects do they engage in their prayer? What inspires them or provides for them certain "doors to the sacred" that allow them to enter into the mystery which is God? What results as a fruit of this prayer and contemplation? Recent work in the exploration of mate-rial culture reminds us of the power of these tangible symbols, whether they be sacred objects, architecture, or the rituals that are performed in these settings.[4]

Three popular representations of Jesus in many Latino/a Catholic homes, mainly, *El Niño Dios* or *El Santo Niño* (the child Jesus), the various representations of the suffering or crucified Jesus, and that of the *Sagrado Corazón de Jesús* (the Sacred Heart of Jesus), not only evoke some aspects of Christ as experienced in these believing communities but also highlight three key characteristics related to him: his vulnerability, brokenness, and divine love. Two of these images, the child Jesus and the crucified Savior, are found in virtually all Iberian-inspired Catholic popular piety, capturing the vulnerability of a God who becomes human.[5] Both of these, in the form of el Santo Niño (Holy Child) de Atocha, and Nuestro Señor de Esquipulas (our Lord of Esquipulas), are found in el Santuario de Chimayó, what is today the most frequented pilgrimage site in the United States. Located outside of Santa Fe, New Mexico, this adobe shrine was built in the early 1800s, but the site, known for its healing qualities, was sacred to the indigenous peoples even before then. Tens of thousands of pilgrims, especially during Holy Week, come today, many on foot, to this small village in the Santa Cruz Valley to be renewed spiritually. As one pilgrim said, "We leave our daily lives behind to follow in the footsteps of Our Lord. This is the road of life which leads to our sanctuary. For us, walking to Chimayó is truly coming home."[6]

The Santo Niño de Atocha venerated in the shrine's side chapel is seen in the photo on page 173. He himself is a pilgrim, evidenced by his cloak with its shell, which pilgrims wore on their way to Santiago Compostela in Spain, as well as the staff and water gourd he holds in his hand. He is often seen holding a basket of bread or, in this case, flowers. A perennial traveler on his errands of mercy, his devotees are fond of leaving him little shoes, as he quickly wears them out. While the image is actually a composite of several devotions com-

ing from Mexico and Spain having to do with Jesus and his mother, Mary, the general story told around the image—retold here by Thomas Steele, who took it from E. Boyd's *Saints and Saint Makers of New Mexico* (Santa Fe: Laboratory of Anthropology, 1946)—is usually rendered as follows:

> In Atocha, a section of Madrid, the Moors imprisoned many Spanish Christians during the later years of the occupation. The conquerors forbade all persons except little children to enter the prison on errands of mercy, not even allowing priests to bring consolation to the dying. The prisoners' relatives, knowing that they lacked food and water and all spiritual con- solation, prayed that the Lord would bring the captives some comfort. So one day a child, dressed like the pilgrims of the time, came into the prison carrying a basket of bread and a staff with a gourd full of water tied to the top. To the astonishment of the Moors, the gourd and the basket were not empty after all the captives had been served, and each one, as he received nourishment, received also the child's blessing. In answer to his people's prayers, Christ had returned to earth to serve those who needed spiritual and tangible help.[7]

Today the many discarded crutches, *ex-votos*, or small metal objects which are related to a healing petition or a received miracle, together with pictures of loved ones—especially those in the armed services—symbolize God's continuing intervention in people's lives.

The main altar or *reredo* (altar screen) with a large wooden crucifix carved around 1818 by Antonio Molleno, a *santero* from the area, also serves as an icon for the pilgrims wishing to contemplate the mysteries of salvation (see page 175). While the corpus hangs on a green cross with seven branch stumps—echoes of both the Christian and indigenous tree of life, not to mention seven as the symbol of perfection—its large gaping shoulder wound is shaped more like a flower; from its side, as written in John's Gospel, flows blood and water (John 19:34), two elements associated with both physical and spiritual life. Despite its ghastly, bloody appearance, there is a serene, contemplative glow to the dying Christ who is surrendering his spirit to his heavenly Father. The brightly painted curtains behind him, a decoration together with that of simulated tiles, sometimes seen in older, poor missions, reminds us that a powerful scene is taking place, one that the faithful are invited to witness. Thomas Steele elaborates on the spirituality of these types of crucified images for the fraternity of the Penitentes, a lay religious group of men in New Mexico and southern Colorado, and the *santero* artists who created these images of devotion:

> The Brothers and the santeros who worked for them found this "terrible beauty" in a glorious suffering. In the Gospel of John, Christ's crucifixion is simultaneously his exaltation: "When I am lifted up, I will draw all things to myself." And before a later hand added the summary of Matthew's and Luke's Easter narratives, the Gospel of Mark ended with an empty tomb after the centurion stated, "Surely this man was a son of God." For the Brothers, specialists in "doing Lent," Easter is sheer anticlimax, for their spirituality dates from the later Middle Ages, when Bernard of Clairvaux and Francis of Assisi focused devotion on the mutable humanity of Jesus of Nazareth in his infancy and his passion and death. When they enact the Resurrection, it more often than not takes the form of opening the coffin, removing the figure of Christ in the Tomb, and returning it to the cross. From that ironic throne, still clothed only in the royal purple of his own blood, crowned only with thorns, and nailed hand and foot so as to be as helpless as an infant in swaddling clothes, Jesus rules New Mexico.[8]

These two devotions centering on Jesus as a child as well as that of the crucified Lord come together at Chimayó in the following contemporary prayer: "Our Father, Lord of Chimayó, Wind of the North; Our Father, Lord of Esquipulas, Wind of the South, we come with heart in hand, hear our prayers. Holy Child of Atocha, watch over us on our journey, may our innocence be born anew!"[9]

Finally, in our initial trilogy on images of Christ, the *Sagrado Corazón de Jesús*, a postresurrection symbol, speaks of God's love and mercy manifested through Jesus.[10] The photograph on page 176 is a detail of part of the main altar of the domestic chapel at the Sacred Heart Jesuit Center in Los Gatos, California. Painted in 1915 by the Mexican Jesuit artist Gonzalo Carrasco, it was done

in gratitude to the California Jesuit community for offering refuge to the exiled Mexican Jesuits who fled religious persecution in Mexico. Within its crowning half moon, the risen Christ, heart on fire with mercy and love, is depicted as standing on the earth amid the clouds. Despite the turmoil in Mexico during this revolutionary period and the church-state conflict that almost became another civil war, the love of Jesus holds prominence.

Furthermore, these three images of Christ are often associated with certain devotional practices, many of them enacted outside church doors (as in the home, such as those involving the Christmas crib) or in the streets (such as the *Via Crucis*, or the live reenactment of the passion of Christ).[11]

In the formation of the Christian tradition, artistic expression, or enactment, as in the case of the sacraments of baptism and Eucharist, has often come before doctrinal definition. Margaret Miles insists that at the time of the fourth-century Trinitarian and christological controversies, the appeal of the masses was not

linguistic but rather, for pagans becoming Christians, the Christian faith's visual splendor, for within its embrace, "They were instructed by its imagery, a visual program that deliberately and skillfully included and set in a new next context of meaning a broad spectrum of cultural inheritance."[12] If, in fact, before there were clearly defined christological definitions there already existed depictions of Jesus the Christ, a closer examination of these images in Latin American art may shed some light on the challenge which González poses above, particularly as visual texts, which served as key instruments in the evangelization of these peoples. While not directly responding to the challenges surrounding a Latino/a Christology posed by González, this essay introduces the crucial role of visual images for many Latino/a communities against a backdrop of a larger Christian tradition, especially as related to worship. This correlation between right worship and right belief is key since, according to Jaime Lara,[13] the early missionaries to Mesoamerica felt that true worship would eventually lead to true belief, as in the ancient dictum *Lex orandi, lex credendi,* which can be translated "as the church prays so she believes"; that is, theology follows worship, not the other way around.

ART, RELIGION, AND ICONOCLASM

Drawing on the work of several historians, besides that of his own expansive investigations both in the field and in texts, Jaime Lara demonstrates how for the

Aztec culture, materiality and performance were key in translating the Christian message to their neophytes.[14] While the words of the Friars were important, equally if not more important were their adaptations of Christian ritual, a phenomenon that was very familiar to these Mesoamericans, one they desperately longed for in the years following the conquest. Commenting upon the work of Mexican colonialist historian Serge Gruzinksi, Lara goes a step further in demonstrating the power of symbol, myth, and ritual:

> In a brilliant essay Serge Gruzinski has suggested that the real conquest of Mexico was one of the native imagination, and in doing so he has given a backhanded compliment to the missionary friars. Preaching, catechesis, moral instruction in confessional counseling—he says—conquered, colonized, formed, and re-formed the indigenous way of imaging the world and the Mesoamerican's place in it. But Gruzinski has underestimated the all-embracing aspect of the Church's public worship and liturgical devotions. All the verbal activities, such as preaching, moral exhortation, and catechesis, were aimed at bringing the Indians into liturgical action and the reception of the sacraments. The Nahua converts were desperate for cosmic order and for new rituals, and they had a passion to perform them. Social scientists have long recognized that metaphor, ritual, and the enactment of meta-stories are therapeutic as well as mechanisms for learning and modifying behavior—what Kavanagh calls "conversion therapy."[15]

As modern, post-Enlightenment people, we often look to the articulation of truth in verbal categories, yet for Mesoamericans and many Indigenous peoples, truth was best articulated through the visual, not only in its visual representations but also in its dramatic and musical forms, many of which engaged the senses of sight, hearing, taste, touch, and even smell (as in the use of copal, a type of incense used by the Aztecs that the missionaries incorporated in their liturgies).[16]

Even today one hears that the incorporation of sacred images in Catholic worship is equivalent to idolatry. One of the most famous Scripture passages cited to substantiate this claim is taken from Exodus 20:4: "You shall not make for yourself an idol, whether in the form of anything that is in heaven above, or that is on the earth beneath, or that is in the water under the earth. You shall not bow down to them or worship them; for I the LORD your God am a jealous God."[17] This ancient prohibition taken from the Ten Commandments appears elsewhere in sacred Scripture, particularly in the Old Testament, and has to be read in context, to the extent that "Imageless worship of the Lord made Israel's faith unique in the ancient world where natural powers were personified and statues of them (animal or human) were worshiped."[18] Yet cautions or prohibitions against the use of images by Jews and Christians also partly stemmed from a concern that the more prophetic aspects of religion would be ignored. Their concerns had to do with a fear that religion would become overly ritualistic at the expense of its ethical demands.

> The prophetic side of Christianity has from the beginning been suspicious of human imagination, voicing objection to the disassociation of the aesthetic from the ethical or the holy. The words of Amos echo in other

historical periods: "Take away from me the noise of your song; to the melody of your harps I will not listen. But let justice roll down like waters, and righteousness like an everflowing stream" (Amos 5:23–24). Furthermore, the iconoclastic impulse to resist the use of art emerges in the name of holiness to guard against idolatrous confusion of images with the divine reality they are to represent or express.[19]

Within Christianity, the iconoclast controversy came to a head in later centuries when various cultural views came to the surface as Christianity became more of a global player. By that time, art, as mentioned above, had already played a major role in its spread. According to Diane Apostolos-Cappadona,

> The iconoclastic controversies of the eighth and ninth centuries were the most critical period for art. At the heart of these tensions were the dialectical foundations of the Christian tradition: the Hebraic injunction against images and the Greco-Hellenistic appreciation of the beautiful. The added element in the discussion was the emerging influence of Islam, especially its ban against veneration of images. These controversies which disrupted the church eventually were resolved by the Second Council of Nicaea (787) and an Eastern Church Synod of 843 in which the distinction between idols and images made by John Damascene was accepted in conjunction with regulations as to the choice of subject and style of execution of visual images. As a result, the canonical role of the visual was clearly stated and restored within the daily life of the church. However, the "image destroying" tendency within Christianity would re-surface sporadically throughout the history of the church.[20]

Among its most famous reoccurrences was the Protestant Reformation in the sixteenth century. While all the Reformers were not of the same mind, during this period, many religious images were systematically destroyed as the Reformers sought to redirect a style of Christian worship that was excessively nonverbal, while restoring the central role of sacred Scripture.[21] As Don E. Saliers recounts,

> The 16th century simplifications were partly a result of a new stress on scripture as a primary source of liturgical norms arising in that period; but they also depended upon an opposition between reason and emotion, alongside a dualism of spirit and the physically sensate. Luther was not such a liturgical purist. In fact, as the liturgical iconoclasm of the Reformation grew more extreme, he spoke, even while defending simplification of the rites, of his eagerness to "see all the arts, especially music, in the service of him who gave and created them."[22]

One of the ways in which the arts took a different turn for Protestants during this time was to put more stress on the Word. What resulted was a greater recourse to poetry and music as had happened in the Hebraic tradition.[23] The response of the Catholic Reformation was to defend the use of images, especially for didactive purposes. Thus, "a new Christian iconography developed as a visual expression and defense of the teachings of the Church of Rome, most especially of those teachings criticized by the Reformers such as the seven corporal works of mercy, the sacrament of penance, and specific images of the Virgin Mary."[24]

In the hope of developing a more substantial Latino/a Christology, one which draws substantially from popular visual images of Christ, I have briefly mentioned up to this point the contribution that the arts have made to its formulation from the time of early Christianity. Similarly, I have hinted at some of the iconoclastic tendencies that have impeded a greater acceptance of these images by some Christians, particularly since the Reformation. Of course, part of the polemic here involved not only images of Christ but also those of Mary and the other saints. A more recent setback in understanding the power of these images has been the lack of dialogue between art historians and theologians regarding their aesthetic and theological value. Perhaps one of the more recent contributions of U.S. Latino/a theology to the larger theological world is to help foment this exchange. The work of Alejandro García-Rivera is already a milestone in this interdisciplinary dialogue.[25] Likewise, the writings of Roberto Goizueta, particularly in his *Caminemos con Jesús: Toward a Hispanic/Latino Theology of Accompaniment*,[26] reveal a profound spirituality of accompanying Jesus even to his death. It is noteworthy that other theologians of color also write about hope despite much human suffering.[27]

THE CROSS AND THE CRUCIFIX

The cross, although today predominantly a primary Christian symbol, also predates Christ and is found in other cultures and religions. In fact, it is one of the oldest symbols in the world and is found in its various manifestations in ancient Egypt, Phoenicia, Greece, and even in Buddhist and Hindu contexts, such as the Swastika cross of Sanskrit origin. Its meanings in these various contexts may or may not be known.[28] In the Christian context, however, the cross always points to Jesus. For these believers, "The cross signifies that Christians are called to participate spiritually and intentionally in both Jesus' death and in his resurrection."[29] That is, as Elisabeth Koenig states, "As the identifying symbol of the Christian movement, the cross has challenged followers of Jesus to find their own ways to express sacrificial love."[30] In fact, to accent this belief, many of the early baptismal fonts were built in the shape of a cross or a tomb so that the baptized would ritually die and rise to Christ in the same gesture.[31] T. Jerome Overbeck explains some of the meanings of the cross.

> True to the nature of symbol, the significance of the cross is multivalent in its meanings. Jesus' cross communicates a contradiction: how could an instrument of death be a sign of life? It is a paradox of Christian faith that such a sign of ignominious death (cf. Deut 21:23) could reveal the divinity of a human person. Jesus' cross reminds the believer that God *saves*

through the cross (1 Cor 1:17, Eph 2:16, Col 1:20, Gal 6:14). Belief in this fact allows a Christian to face the cross with a certain equanimity and trust in the power of God. Another significance of the cross is that it reveals the extent to which God has gone to manifest God's love for all people. The cross means freedom from slavery to selfishness (Rom 6:6). The cross means reconciling with God and neighbor, being willing and able to return to one another, face to face (Eph 2:16, Col 1:20, 2:14). The cross means renewing life in this world and finding life in the next (Gal 3:1, 6:14). The cross is the means of modeling Jesus (Gal 5:24). To be a true disciple and follower of Jesus, one must choose to take up the cross, even daily (Luke 9:23, 14:27, Mark 8:34, Mt. 16:24).[32]

But in and of itself, the cross has not been at the center of iconoclast controversies. A more controversial symbol, the crucifix, which is a cross with the tortured corpus of Jesus on it, today often marks the difference between Protestant and Catholic worship. A little bit of history here is also helpful in that it demonstrates that the crucifix has not always been part of Christian worship.

There is some evidence that the crucifix dates to the 5th century. The early church emphasized the risen Christ, so only a lamb or other biblical symbol or the risen body of Jesus would adorn the cross. In 692 the Council of Constantinople ordered the presence of Jesus' human body on the cross and not, e.g., a lamb. The Carolingian period encouraged a more realistic portrayal of the extent of Jesus' suffering. This increasing emphasis upon stark, graphic realism about Jesus' wounded and bloody body reached its apex between the 12th and 14th centuries. By this point the crucifix replaced the cross as an object of veneration.[33]

In many ways, this medieval type of representation is what came to the Americas. At the time of the early conquest and evangelization of Mexico in the sixteenth century, the cross becomes a major symbol, one that underwent a great deal of evolution in its artistic design and incorporation of Aztec symbology.[34]

After the medieval physical representations of Jesus in bodily fashion, both as a child and as a man, came also those of the Renaissance. In a fascinating study entitled *The Sexuality of Christ in Renaissance Art and in Modern Oblivion,*[35] Leo Steinberg demonstrates how artists used art to communicate theological beliefs concerning the nature of Christ. Whether in accenting the mystery of the incarnation, or the role of sexuality in the adult Christ or even the risen Lord, visual images often spoke much louder than words. Steinberg states his case succinctly in the opening parts of the book:

These, then, are my three initial considerations. The first reminds us that the humanation of God entails, along with mortality, his assumption of sexuality. Here, since the verity of the Incarnation is celebrated, the sex of the newborn is a demonstrative sign.

In the second consideration, touching Christ's adult ministry, sexuality matters in its abeyance. Jesus as exemplar and teacher prevails over concupiscence to consecrate the Christian ideal of chastity. We have no call to be thinking of private parts.

But we do again on the third turn. Delivered from sin and shame, the freedom of Christ's sexual member bespeaks that aboriginal innocence which in Adam was lost. We may say that Michelangelo's naked Christs—on the cross, dead, or risen—are, like the naked Christ Child, not shameful, but literally and profoundly "shame-less."[36]

In some ways, some of the Reformers found this very type of sensuality problematic. Apostolos-Cappadona explains,

> Among the causes of the Reformation was hostility to the Italian Renaissance and its arts. The celebration of beauty in nature and the human body which the Renaissance fostered and introduced into Christian worship was incompatible with the Reformers' emphasis on original sin and human finitude. The Reformers also sought a purification of the church, and the mediation of visual images in liturgical worship and devotional piety was seen as a hindrance to direct contact with God.[37]

Contemporary Methodist theologian Justo L. González has written a provocative essay in which he addresses "the empty cross" in Latino/a Protestantism, especially as it relates to identity. In this essay, he states,

> The empty cross stands for much of what has come to characterize Latino "mainline" Protestantism. Among such characteristics, the most obvious is that we have been taught to define ourselves—and many of us still do—in terms of opposition to Roman Catholicism. Roman Catholicism is the faith of the crucifix; therefore, we must reject the crucifix and cling to the empty cross. At an earlier time, Hispanic Protestantism, even in its "mainline" manifestations, was radically anti-Catholic. What characterized our churches, and an important point of pride, was precisely that we got rid of everything that was in the least suspect of "popery." We had no images, no candles, no vestments, and only vestiges of the liturgical year—usually no more than Christmas, Epiphany, and Holy Week. The empty cross, precisely because it was empty, reminded us of all that was no longer there, and thus became for us a powerful symbol of difference.
>
> Second, the empty cross became for us a symbol of victory over the powers of death that have so long prevailed in our communities and our histories. As the early Protestant missionaries and preachers constantly inculcated in us, the empty cross is a reminder of the resurrection, of life, of victory. In many ways, the empty cross symbolizes much of what Latinos and Latinas in the early days found attractive in Protestantism.[38]

González, referring in large part to the situation of the U.S. appropriation of the Southwest in the nineteenth century, notes how, at the symbolic level, for these Hispanic Protestants, "The crucifix, with its dead Christ, both symbolized and glorified the suffering of the masses . . . while the empty cross, on the other hand, spoke of victory even over death, of an order in which evil, injustice, and oppression do not have the last word."[39] Thus, the embrace of the empty cross and the rejection of the crucifix take on a symbolic dimension in that through this choice, "Those early Latino Protestants were also claiming all their freedoms, and even the iconoclast tendencies that are usually associated with American Protestantism and democracy."[40]

He goes on to elucidate, however, that this empty cross came with a high price:

> Much of what Protestant missionaries said in criticism of the crucifix was also derogatory toward our culture—we were a people fixed on gore and suffering; we did not know how to leave death behind, but must constantly meditate on it; we were much given to thinking in terms of images and examples, rather than in terms of ideas and principles. As a result, to reject the crucifix and to embrace the empty cross was also to reject and be rejected by much of one's own culture and even family.[41]

González appeals to Luis Pedraja's essay in the same collection to say that both the empty cross and the crucifix have a place in Hispanic piety:

> It is in the presence and from the experience of the crucifix that the empty cross comes as a word of assurance and liberation. Without the crucifix, the empty cross risks becoming a symbol of triumphalism for those who already stand atop the social pyramid, and a means of oppression, subjugation, and denial of identity for those who do not. Without the empty cross, the crucifix risks becoming a symbol of fatalism and a call to acquiescence in the face of suffering and injustice. As Hispanics, we are acutely aware of the manner in which this functions in the majority culture. The churches whose missionaries told us that our minds and emotions were too fixed on the suffering Christ of the crucifix have evolved along those lines to such a point that today many of them do not even gather for worship on Good Friday. They glide easily from Palm Sunday to Easter, as if the agony in Gethsemane, the betrayal, the trial, and the crucifixion were merely a series of unfortunate events on the way to the empty tomb. Little wonder, then, that so many preachers have little to say about Easter beyond the common springtime platitudes about nature being reborn and butterflies springing from cocoons! Little wonder that churchgoers find it so difficult to speak of their suffering and failures. And little wonder that there is such malaise in most of the mainline Protestant denominations. Without the correction of the crucifix, the empty cross has led many to an "all is O.K." sort of religion—and the irony is that such a religion is certainly not O.K.![42]

In the same essay, he posits that, in reality, the ongoing passion of Christ is very much present in Latino/a Protestant worship. As he remarks, "The words may be about the cross; the mental images are about the crucifixion."[43] As evidence of this reality, he describes the *testimonios* or oral testimonies in which the speaker narrates a passage from Palm Sunday (a time of high hopes), to that of Good Friday (a time filled with death and hopelessness), to that of Easter (which brings with it new life out of death).[44] In this oral way, the persons sharing these *testimonios* are relating their experience of the paschal mystery, the primordial root metaphor in Christianity.

After a final thought on the scandal of the cross, something which can often be overlooked in a society that focuses on earthly success, I provide some propositions to continue our quest for a Latino/a Christology, while bringing art and religion further into dialogue.

THE SCANDAL OF THE CROSS

For Jews demand signs and Greeks desire wisdom, but we proclaim Christ crucified, a stumbling block to Jews and foolishness to Gentiles, but to those who are the called, both Jews and Greeks, Christ the power of God and the wisdom of God. For God's foolishness is wiser than human wisdom, and God's weakness is stronger than human strength.

1 Corinthians 1:22–25

A scene from the video *Soul of the City/Alma del Pueblo*[45] which often grabs people's attention is that of a little boy, about six or so, who, witnessing the enactment of the crucifixion of Christ, covers his ears so as to shield himself from the horror of what he is witnessing. A woman, probably his mother, holds him gently so as to soothe his anxiety. In one of my recent showings of the film at a workshop for pastoral agents on sabbatical, a therapist asked the group if this kind of exposure was "too much, over the top" and thus if it might actually harm the child to see an enactment of this torture. Several persons responded by noting that suffering and death are part of life and that we cannot shield our children from them. Moreover, in the act of this child being held within this faith community, he was being accompanied amid the pain and sorrow. Another person gave the example of the Irish three-day wake of her brother, one that she feared would be traumatic for her little nieces and nephews. Yet, much to her amazement, they brought symbols of love such as teddy bears, and caressed his dead body lovingly.

Could it be that we have become so accustomed to the cross which today often appears as a fashion accessory that we have forgotten what a scandal it actually is? After all, Jesus was executed by the state as a common criminal. As one of my former teachers was fond of reminding us, if he had been executed today, we might be wearing little gold electric chairs around our necks. Moreover, as the corpus was removed from the cross, particularly in the post-Reformation period, might there have crept in a certain loss of the particularity of the Christ event, as in the incarnation, because the body on a cross will more likely depict certain racial and ethnic characteristics, to say nothing of invoking in the believer a certain sense of compassion, as opposed to simply an empty cross, often beautifully polished, which, as Justo González argues, rushes us to the resurrection?

CONCLUSION

I want to leave the reader with some propositions to further our exploration of Latino/a Christology, especially as it relates to visual images of Christ, particularly that of the Christ child, the suffering Jesus, and the risen Lord or the Sacred Heart of Jesus.

1. An openness to the divine mystery and a strong resistance to idolatry mean that God cannot be limited to words and that imagination is a God-given gift, not something to be discouraged. In fact, far more than teaching, imagination is evocative. Through the use of the senses, it calls something forth from the person. Because it is often ambiguous, it can be understood in many ways. Walter Burghardt, known for his effective preaching, makes this point as he narrates a story about Martha Graham, the famous dancer, who was asked what her dance meant, to which she replied, "Darlings, if I could tell you, I would not have danced it!" In his view, "Something is lost when we move from imagining to reasoning, from art to conceptual clarity."[46] If we are to develop an authentic Latino Christology, we will have to study all the nonconventional "texts" such as music, dance, drama, and material culture which is part of our religiosity.

2. Given the effects of the Enlightenment, the Reformation, Trent, and some aspects of Vatican II which at times placed reason over emotion, we have to make an attempt to recover religion as primarily a matter of the heart. This is an area where Latino/a popular piety, although not without its dark side, can continue to move us in that direction. The U.S. Bishops, in their 1986 pastoral letter titled *Art and Environment in Catholic Worship*, had this to say on the subject: "In view of our culture's emphasis on reason, it is critically important for the Church to reemphasize a more total approach to the human person by opening up and developing the non-rational elements of liturgical celebration: the concerns for feelings of conversion, support, joy, repentance, trust, love, memory, movement, gesture, wonder" (par. 35).[47]

3. It is not fair to say that images of the infant Jesus necessarily promote infantilism, dismissing human agency, or that those of the crucified Christ are fatalistic. In all fairness to those who use them to pray, whether individually or as a community, they speak of God's vulnerability and brokenness, a factor that makes them appealing to oppressed peoples—the previously discussed Santo Niño de Atocha and the Nuestro Señor de Esquipulas at Chimayó serving as examples. At the same time, they are only part of the story and serve as a window into the paschal mystery, one that includes not only the sufferings of Jesus but also his resurrection, a victory over sin and death as depicted in the image of the Sacred Heart.[48]

4. While it is often said that the corpus of Jesus was removed from the cross around the time of the Protestant Reformation—and to some degree, it was—in the primitive Christian community, the visual cross was not the focal point; even after it became the preeminent symbol of Christianity in later centuries, it was not necessarily the cross with the corpus. In other words, as this essay has sought to demonstrate, although visual images of Jesus play a key role in Roman Catholic devotion, they have not always done so, acknowledging that such symbols are not ends in themselves but rather point and help to embody the mysteries that they evoke. In a sense, even absence is evocative. Therefore, one way in the Christian tradition of looking at this dichotomy of crucifix versus the empty cross is to view the crucifix as being kataphatic, from the Greek *kata-*

phatikos, which means "affirmative"—in this case that which "stresses the idea that God manifests the divine Self in the world and can be known by means of created things." The empty cross represents the more apophatic, from the Greek *apophatikos* or negative—that is, reflective of a type of "mystical theology which emphasizes the difference between God as Creator and the human person as creature, yet encourages knowledge and experience of God by means of negation."[49] The contributions on the topic of the cross by such Protestant Latino/a theologians as Justo González and Luis Pedraja should not be overlooked.

5. While the danger of focusing excessively on particular visual images or rituals that do not necessarily lead to a more rigorous practice of the Christian ethic exists, a noted biblical concern since the time of the prophet Amos, over the course of centuries many saints and activists have been moved not only to charity but also to prophetic denunciation because of their contemplation of the broken, vulnerable Jesus. Even in modern times, Spanish Jesuit Ignacio Ellacuria, killed by the Salvadoran government for his role in the peace process in the late 1980s, wrote about the power of prayer before the crucifix to touch our conscience and work for justice.[50]

6. I end with a caution. It is curious to note that more Latino than Latina theologians have written about the spirituality of the cross. Why is that? Some recent theological writings are raising some concerns as to whether the cross empowers or disempowers the oppressed.[51] Similar to what has been done around the devotion to Our Lady of Guadalupe, research around people's feelings toward the vulnerability of God as manifested images of the child Jesus or the crucified Lord is desperately needed given the importance of those manifestations for Latinos/as in the Americas.

NOTES

1. As quoted in Jaime Lara, *Christian Texts for Aztecs: Art and Liturgy in Colonial Mexico* (Notre Dame, IN: University of Notre Dame Press, 2008), 260.
2. Michelle A. González, "Jesus," in *Handbook of Latina/o Theologies,* ed. Edwin David Aponte and Miguel De La Torre (St. Louis: Chalice Press, 2006), 22–23.
3. Ibid.
4. See Meredith B. McGuire, *Lived Religion: Faith and Practice in Everyday Life* (Oxford: Oxford University Press, 2008), and Robert Anthony Orsi, *The Madonna of 115th Street: Faith and Community in Italian Harlem,* 2nd ed. (New Haven, CT: Yale University Press, 2002). See also David Freedberg, *The Power of Images: Studies in the History and Theory of Response* (Chicago: University of Chicago Press, 1989). Freedberg reminds us of an image's ability to move us, a power often invoked by religious artists: "We may no longer have much leisure to contemplate the images before us, but people once did; and they turned contemplation into something useful, therapeutic, elevating, consoling, and terrifying. They did so in order to attain a state of empathy; and when we examine how they did so, a brilliant light is cast not only on the function of the images but on a potential that for many of us remains to be activated" (161).

5. Art historian and liturgist Jaime Lara reminds us of the long tradition behind these two manifestations of the God-made-human: "The best known and best-loved devotions of Christendom ever since medieval times have been concentrated on two paradigmatic moments in Christ's life: his Nativity and his redemptive Passion; and liturgical props were important features of both moments" (*Christian Texts for Aztecs*, 202).

6. As quoted in Sam Howarth and Enrique R. Lamadrid, *Pilgrimage to Chimayó: Contemporary Portrait of a Living Tradition* (Santa Fe: Museum of New Mexico Press, 1999), 9.

7. Thomas J. Steele, SJ, *Santos and Saints: The Religious Folk Art of Hispanic New Mexico* (Santa Fe, NM: Ancient City Press, 1994), 70.

8. Thomas J. Steele, SJ, "Foreword," in *New Kingdom of the Saints: Religious Art of New Mexico, 1780–1907* (Santa Fe, NM: Red Crane Books, 1992), xiv.

9. Howarth and Lamadrid, *Pilgrimage to Chimayó*, 22.

10. This devotional image, that of the Sacred Heart, was one of the defining symbols of Roman Catholicism from the late seventeenth to the mid-twentieth centuries. While its more modern form is closely associated with the visions of Margaret Mary Alacoque (1647–1690), a French Visitation nun from Paray-le-Monial, its roots go back to the patristic era, its allegorical use found in the writings of such persons as Augustine, Ambrose, Cyprian, and Jerome (see Wendy M. Wright, "Sacred Heart," in *The New Westminster Dictionary of Christian Spirituality*, ed. Philip Sheldrake [Louisville, KY: Westminster John Knox Press, 2005], 556–57). It is often said that its stress on the love and mercy of God counteracted Jansenist tendencies, a movement in the seventeenth century attributed to Bishop Cornelius Jansen that opted for a more rigorist position in regard to free will and grace than that of the Jesuits, who stressed the goodness of nature and its cooperation with grace.

11. I have described these practices elsewhere in more detail. See *Mexican American Catholics* (Mahwah, NJ: Paulist Press, 2007), particularly chapter 4, "Viva La Virgen! Mexican Feasts and Customs." For an example of the *Via Crucis* or Way of the Cross as it is ritualized in the Mexican neighborhood of Pilsen in Chicago, see Roberto Goizueta's essay, "The Symbolic World of Mexican American Religion," in *Horizons of the Sacred: Mexican Traditions in U.S. Catholicism*, ed. Timothy Matovina and Gary Riebe-Estrella, SVD (Ithaca, NY: Cornell University Press, 2002).

12. Margaret Miles, *Image as Insight: Visual Understanding in Western Christianity and Secular Culture* (Boston: Beacon Press, 1985), 57. In the same place, she elaborates, "The curling vine tendrils of Dionysis adorned chalices, where they symbolized the blood of Christ, the fruit of the vine. Christ rides a chariot across the sky as the sun god in one fourth-century mosaic. The ability of the new churches of the fourth century to provide a vivid new context for ancient symbols, a context that guaranteed their interpretation in ways compatible with Christianity, is probably the most striking aspect of fourth-century visual evidence."

13. See Lara, *Christian Texts for Aztecs*.

14. Curiously enough, according to Denise Kimber Buell, for the early Christians, "Race was often deemed to be produced and indicated by religious practices." See "Rethinking the Relevance of Race for Early Christian Self-Definition," *Harvard Theological Review* 94, no. 4 (2001): 449–76.

15. Lara, *Christian Texts for Aztecs*, 260.

16. Ibid., 206–7.

17. Exodus 20:4–5a.

18. See also "Idol," in *The Interpreter's Dictionary of the Bible*, vol. 2 (Nashville: Abingdon Press, 1962), 673–75.

19. Don E. Saliers, "Aesthetics, Liturgical," in *The New Dictionary of Sacramental Worship*, ed. Peter Fink, SJ (Collegeville, MN: Liturgical Press, 1990), 32.

20. Diane Apostolos-Cappadona, "Art," in *The New Dictionary of Theology*, ed. Joseph A. Komonchak et al. (Collegeville, MN: Liturgical Press, 1987), 60. Boniface Ramsey, OP, summarizes Damascene's *First Apology against Those Who Attack the Divine Images* 16, in which he makes the argument that "all matter—and hence images—had been ennobled by the Incarnation and was worthy of bearing representation of the holy and of the divine" (see Ramsey, "Iconoclasm," *New Dictionary of Theology*, 502).

21. See Mia M. Mochizuki, *The Netherlandish Image after Iconoclasm, 1566–1672: Material Religion in the Dutch Golden Age* (Burlington: Ashgate, 2008).

22. Saliers, "Aesthetics, Liturgical," 32.

23. Apostolos-Cappadona, "Art," 61.

24. Ibid., 62. It is not fair to say that Catholics throughout history have ignored the Bible. As Timothy A. Lenchak, SVD, demonstrates, Catholics have tended to have a greater interest in the biblical *story* rather than in the biblical *text*. "Bible stories have always played important roles in liturgical celebrations and catechesis. Catholics tend to have no trouble with non-literary forms of proclaiming the gospel: story-telling, art, drama, dance and music. Such means to present the gospel message have been especially successful in India and Africa. The Jesuits used paintings and drawings to illustrate gospel stories in seventeenth-century China, and the Capuchins promoted biblical plays in nineteenth-century India. Catholics have often been encouraged to develop non-literary means of expressing the Word of God for people of oral cultures who are unable to read the printed word" ("The Function of the Bible in Roman Catholic Mission," in *Scripture, Community, and Mission: Essays in Honor of D. Preman Niles,* ed. Philip L. Wickeri [Hong Kong: Christian Conference of Asia and the Council for World Mission, 2002], 3–19, quote on 11).

25. Alejandro García-Rivera, *The Community of the Beautiful: A Theological Aesthetics* (Collegeville, MN: Michael Glazier/Liturgical Press, 1999).

26. Maryknoll, NY: Orbis Books, 1995.

27. While Orlando Espín speaks about a "Hispanic epistemology of suffering," Dwight Hopkins refers to "years of cross bearing"; George Cummings, to "structures that sustain hope and resistance"; and Ada María Isasi-Díaz articulates a praxis theology constructed around *la lucha*. In various shapes and forms, all of these writers attest to the presence of an empowering grace that is revealed through a community's experience of the cross (*La Cosecha: Harvesting Contemporary United States Hispanic Theology [1972–1998]* [Collegeville: Michael Glazier/Liturgical Press, 2000], 174).

28. T. Jerome Overbeck, SJ, "Cross," in Fink, *New Dictionary of Sacramental Worship*, 304.

29. Elisabeth Koenig, "Cross and Spirituality," in Sheldrake, *New Westminster Dictionary of Christian Spirituality*, 220.

30. Ibid.

31. T. Jerome Overbeck, SJ, *Ancient Fonts, Modern Lessons*, Meeting House Essays 9 (Chicago: Liturgy Training Publications, 1998).

32. Overbeck, "Cross," 305.

33. Ibid., 305–6. See also Cyril E. Pocknee, *Cross and Crucifix in Christian Worship and Devotion* (London: A. R. Mowbray, 1962).

34. See Lara, *Christian Texts for Aztecs,* particularly chaps. 8 and 9.
35. Leo Steinberg, *The Sexuality of Christ in Renaissance Art and in Modern Oblivion,* 2nd ed., rev. and exp. (Chicago: University of Chicago Press, 1996).
36. Ibid., 24.
37. Apostolos-Cappadona, "Art," 61.
38. Justo L. González, "Hanging on an Empty Cross: The Hispanic Mainline Experience," in *Protestantes/Protestants: Hispanic Christianity within Mainline Traditions,* ed. David Maldonado Jr. (Nashville: Abingdon Press, 1999), 293–94.
39. Ibid., 295.
40. Ibid.
41. Ibid., 295–96.
42. Ibid., 298–99.
43. Ibid., 300.
44. Ibid., 300–301.
45. Houston: JM Communications, 1996.
46. Walter J. Burghardt, SJ, "Preaching as Art and Craft," in Fink, *New Dictionary of Sacramental Worship,* 970.
47. As quoted in Saliers, "Aesthetics, Liturgical," 37.
48. Having described many practices and sacred images that appear even today during Holy Week in Mesoamerica, Lara concludes, "Easter may have been delayed or postponed, but the resurrection was and is certainly celebrated in Latin America. Thus, contrary to the popular opinion of some modern historians, colonial Nahuas did not have a fatalistic Christology that terminated with Jesus' death and burial; they indeed celebrated the resurrection—beginning on the Sábado de Gloria and stretching all the way to the Fiesta de Cruz in May—in a way unique to Latin Americans who had been formed in the medieval and baroque Catholicism of those initial centuries of the evangelization" (*Christian Texts of Aztecs,* 227). As demonstrated above, Thomas Steele, in describing the spirituality of the Christ of the Penitentes, does not ignore the resurrection.
49. Both of these definitions are taken from Mary Ann Hinsdale's entry "apophatic theology" in *An Introductory Dictionary of Theology and Religious Studies,* ed. Orlando O. Espín and James B. Nickoloff (Collegeville, MN: Liturgical Press, 2007), 69. I am indebted to Philip Wickeri, my colleague at the Graduate Theological Union, for this observation.
50. Describing Ellacuria's meditation on the "crucified peoples," Kevin Burke recounts its origin: "He arrived at this image through the colloquy at the foot of the cross from the First Week of the *Exercises,* where one kneels before the crucified and asks, 'What have I done for Christ? What am I doing for Christ? What ought I to do for Christ?' In Ellacuría's adaptation of this exercise, believers are urged to place their 'eyes and hearts upon these peoples who are suffering so much, some from misery and hunger, others from oppression and repression, and then, before this people thus crucified, to make the colloquy . . . by asking, what have I done to crucify them? What am I doing in order to uncrucify them? What ought I to do so that this people will be raised?'" (quoted in Kevin F. Burke, *The Ground beneath the Cross: The Theology of Ignacio Ellacuría* [Washington, DC: Georgetown University Press, 2000], 26).
51. As Elisabeth Koenig reports, "Some contemporary liberation theologians, feminists and womanists find themselves repelled by the cross because they believe that it has perpetuated the suffering of oppressed groups, especially

women, people of color and inhabitants of the third world. They point out that an ascetic and moralizing focus on the cross, or a 'spiritual' one, can render meaningless the importance of the cross in history, specifically in personal stories of people struggling against tyranny. Others point out that the symbol of the cross continues to raise stress levels in Jewish-Christian relations. And psychologists warn against masochistic identification with Jesus in his suffering" (from "Cross and "Spirituality," in Sheldrake, *New Westminster Dictionary of Christian Spirituality*, 222).

Chapter 12

La Capilla de Nuestro Señor de los Milagros

Encountering Christ at a Texas Shrine

TIMOTHY MATOVINA

The Marian devotion and sanctuaries of Mexican-descent and other Latina and Latino Catholics are more widely known than their christological piety. Yet in colonial Mexico more than 40 percent of the shrines dedicated to miraculous images focused on an image of Christ. In various locales these shrines have been continuous centers of faith since the Spanish colonial era, sometimes under clerical supervision, but in other instances founded and developed through lay initiative.[1]

Representations of Christ have long been the primary sacred images at the most famous shrine in the Southwest United States, El Santuario de Chimayó, located on the western side of New Mexico's Sangre de Cristo Mountains. Tewa Indians acclaimed the healing properties of Chimayó's sacred earth centuries before Catholic settlers arrived. Under the patronage of prominent lay resident Bernardo Abeyta, Spanish subjects completed the first chapel at the site in 1816 and dedicated the Santuario de Chimayó to Nuestro Señor de Esquipulas (Our Lord of Esquipulas), a Guatemalan representation of the crucifixion associated with a Mayan sacred place of healing earth. During the 1850s, however, devotees of the Santuario de Chimayó added a statue of the Santo Niño de Atocha (Holy Child of Atocha) in response to a new local shrine dedicated to the Santo

Niño. Subsequently the Santo Niño and the miraculous dirt became the primary focal points for Santuario devotees. They remain so today for the thousands of pilgrims who continue to visit Chimayó.[2]

Another shrine renowned among devotees on both sides of the U.S.-Mexican border is San Antonio's Capilla de Nuestro Señor de los Milagros (Chapel of Our Lord of Miracles), a place Chicana novelist Sandra Cisneros describes as "no bigger than a garden shed" but where visitors encounter "a hundred flickering candles, a hundred needs."[3] Theological reflection on this private chapel, its sacred imagery, and the worshipers who visit it illuminates understandings of Christ in the faith and piety of Mexicans, Mexican Americans, and other Latinos/as, as well as the pastoral and theological significance of their relations with Jesus at his most vulnerable moments: in his childhood and in the crucifixion. This reflection also exemplifies a means to engage the lived experience of Latinos/as in the development of christological insights and formulations.

LA CAPILLA DE LOS MILAGROS

No exact date is known for the founding of la Capilla de Nuestro Señor de los Milagros, or la Capilla de los Milagros, as it is sometimes called. Most sources agree that around 1813 local residents rescued a crucifix from a fire or other disaster at San Antonio's San Fernando parish and subsequently enshrined it in a private chapel. Members of two families named Ximénez and Rodríguez, who were joined by marriage, served as caretakers of the site and its sacred image. Though in its foundation and throughout its history local clergy have reportedly responded to this private chapel with lackluster support or even outright hostility, by the end of the nineteenth century it had become a popular pilgrimage site that reportedly attracted worshipers from far and near and "always [had] devotees within it whenever it [wa]s open." Numerous visitors to the shrine and its central Christ image offered both their orations and material expressions of their prayer, such as lighted candles, flowers, or *milagritos*—miniature hands, arms, or other limbs presented in thanksgiving or intercession for the healing of particular body parts or illnesses. According to an early-twentieth-century source, one such supplicant was a wealthy widow who came on pilgrimage from Mexico to offer a golden crown of thorns and petition divine relief from a painful head malady. The crutches of the lame left behind at the chapel provided silent testimony to the numerous cures that devotees attributed to prayers offered there.[4]

Mexican émigrés dramatically increased San Antonio's Mexican-descent population during the first decades of the twentieth century, further enhancing the chapel's popularity. Assisted with the freewill offerings this growing number of devotees left in gratitude before the Lord of Miracles image, the chapel's caretakers embellished the sacred space in their charge with various statues of Jesus, Mary, and the saints. A photograph and the field notes of a researcher from

Exterior view of la Capilla de Nuestro Señor de los Milagros, 1942. Courtesy University of Texas Institute of Texan Cultures, San Antonio.

Manuel Gamio's landmark 1926–27 study of Mexican immigrants reveal that statues of St. Helen, Nuestra Señora de Dolores (Our Lady of Sorrows), Our Lady of Perpetual Help, Our Lady of Guadalupe, and the Sacred Heart of Jesus, among others, now accompanied the chapel's primary image of Nuestro Señor de los Milagros. *Milagritos* engulfed the loincloth of the Señor de los Milagros crucifix. The chapel walls were covered with letters, crutches, locks of hair, and photographs of those who received divine assistance from prayers offered at the chapel, as well as *retablos,* paintings that offered testimonials and expressions of gratitude for favors rendered. For example, one *retablo* contained a few sentences and a painted sketch of a man covered with bales of hay that had fallen from a truck: this gift was an offering of thanks from a farm laborer who had been saved from deadly harm when he called out to Nuestro Señor de los Milagros. Other *retablos* gave thanks for soldiers sheltered from injury during World War I, celestial protection for families who traveled north as migrant workers, and, as always, miraculous cures and other favors. Similarly, a 1928 newspaper report deemed the shrine a "beloved rival of the ancient pool called Bethesda" and described the large numbers and wide variety in the ages and backgrounds of devotees who lined up to visit the chapel and its Christ image. The report also recounted testimonials dating as far back as 1860 and ranging from a miraculous cure from smallpox to the return home of a wayward son to the escape from Native American captors of one María Espinosa de Alvarez.[5]

Devotees at la Capilla, 1942. Courtesy University of Texas Institute of Texan Cultures, San Antonio.

Though the offering of candles, other remembrances, and personal prayers in intercession or gratitude has always been the primary form of worship at the chapel, another significant tradition practiced during the early twentieth century was the *pastorela,* a dramatic proclamation of the shepherds who worshiped the child Jesus. One observer noted in the late 1920s that on Christmas Eve a pathway of lanterns led the way to the chapel for the *pastorela* celebration, which included scenes such as Mary's espousal to Joseph, the Visitation, the journey to Bethlehem, Mary and Joseph with the newborn Christ child, and the visit of the Magi. According to the account, in the central acts of the live *pastorela* nativity narrative the angels Gabriel and Michael announce the holy birth to twelve shepherds, whose pilgrimage to visit the child Jesus is imperiled by the manipulations and comical antics of a demonic cohort. The shepherds' journey through trial and tribulation to finally reach Bethlehem parallels the disciple's call to struggle against temptation and render God true adoration. Once they arrive at the crib the baby Jesus is unveiled, and the shepherds lead the assembled worshipers in approaching one by one to offer him homage. Even the clay forms of animals molded for the scene—sheep, cows, burros, and birds—are depicted as kneeling before the Christ child, symbolically revealing that at Christmas all living beings are in Christ's presence, seek his blessing, and "rejoice in newborn hope." Commenting on embodied religious traditions such as these, in 1929 San Antonio's

Participants in the *pastorela* enactment of the shepherds who worshiped the infant Jesus, San Antonio, 1893. Courtesy University of Texas Institute of Texan Cultures, San Antonio.

first archbishop, Arthur J. Drossaerts, wrote of Mexican-descent Catholics in his see: "They bring the great events of Christ's life and of His saints to the very doors of their hearts. In their vivid imagination Christ, lying in the cold manger of Bethlehem, or Christ hanging bruised and bleeding on the cross, is present before them: they see Him; they hear Him; they touch Him; they speak with Him."[6]

The chapel's ongoing popularity as a place of prayer was evident during the difficult days of World War II, a conflict in which numerous Mexican-descent residents enlisted in the U.S. military. At the announcement that the war had ended, devotees gathered at the chapel, many to thank God that their sons and other relatives who were soldiers had survived the ordeal of armed conflict. But after the war, San Antonio's increasing urbanization encroached on the chapel and threatened its very existence. Originally located among the family homes in a Mexican barrio, the chapel is now virtually in the shadow of Interstates 10 and 35, surrounded by a large warehouse and an apartment building. Successful community efforts to save the chapel from destruction or relocation culminated during the early 1980s in the site's entry in the National Register of Historic Places. Meanwhile, personal and family pilgrimages to the chapel continued unabated. A 1950s visitor noted the chapel is especially appealing

> on some clear Sunday morning when the altar is sweet with jasmine and roses, when points of candles gleam, and still figures kneel at prayer . . . A soldier brings a rude cross in gratitude for some mercy granted. A

country-looking boy and girl enter shyly to lay a wedding bouquet on the altar. . . . An old man kneels with head upraised and arms outstretched, himself a cross.[7]

Over time the chapel caretakers enshrined a wide array of sacred imagery, displacing many of the *retablos* that had previously lined the chapel walls. Reflecting the preferences of chapel caretakers and visitors who donated representations of their favorite patrons and spiritual guides, this iconography encompasses canonized saints and celestial beings like San Martín de Porres, St. Theresa of Lisieux, St. Anthony, the infant of Prague, el Santo Niño de Atocha, and various Marian images, as well as other images such as Don Pedro Jaramillo, a popular nineteenth-century *curandero* (faith healer) in South Texas.

Devotees I've met at the chapel during my periodic visits over the past three decades express their faith in ways similar to those described in extant historical documentation. As has been the case since the chapel's foundation, people of varied races and backgrounds visit, but the overwhelming majority are Mexican-descent devotees—men, women, and children. They are there to light candles and present flowers, to fulfill a promise or a vow, to plead and to thank, to adore and to converse with God and the saints. Their prayers of intercession and thanksgiving offered at the chapel flow in a continuous cycle, their trust and confidence in divine providence seemingly unshakeable. If doubts ever do creep into their hearts and minds, they are loath to mention them. The comment of one elderly man I met sums up the views of numerous devotees. As he left the chapel after lighting a candle and spending some time there in silence, he responded succinctly to my inquiry about his reasons for visiting that day: "Nunca me falla" (the Lord of Miracles never fails me).

ENCOUNTERING CHRIST AT LA CAPILLA

I first visited la Capilla de los Milagros in 1982 when I was a student at the Mexican American Cultural Center (MACC, now the Mexican American Catholic College), San Antonio's renowned institute for language studies and Hispanic and multicultural ministries. Subsequently, as a MACC faculty member I accompanied program participants and my colleague Roberto Piña on site visits to the chapel. During the 1990s, the dozen or so MACC participant groups with whom I visited the chapel included Mexican American parish leaders from San Antonio and the environs, along with women religious, lay leaders, and clergy from varied racial, ethnic, denominational, and geographic backgrounds across the United States. In facilitating these groups, we invited them to be "observing participants" at the chapel: to immerse themselves in the prayer offered there, to converse with other worshipers about their experience and motivations for coming to this place of prayer, and to notice the gestures, images, sights, sounds, smells, and general ambience that surrounded them. We then returned to MACC for a brief overview of the chapel's history and a theological reflection session on our encounter with the chapel, its devotees, and Our Lord of Miracles.

The fundamental question for this session is based on the claim of MACC's founding president, Virgilio Elizondo, that the most important faith expressions for pastoral and theological analysis are those "celebrated voluntarily by the majority of the people, transmitted from generation to generation by the people themselves and which go on with the church, without it or even in spite of it."[8] As applied to la Capilla de los Milagros, Elizondo's premise is that this long-standing sacred site and its enduring religious traditions are a *locus theologicus*, a window into the soul of Hispanic devotees that reveals significant insights about the horizon of their faith. The analysis that follows is based on my own observations and experiences and on notes from the MACC theological reflection sessions in which I worked with others to probe the understanding of Christ developed, mediated, and celebrated at this Texas shrine.

A Relational Christology

Confirming an observation of various Latino/a and other theologians, the most recurrent insight among participants in theological reflection on la Capilla de los Milagros is that the starting point for the Christology embodied there is the extended family of Jesus.[9] While formal courses on Christology often begin with the Gospels or the christological formulations of the early church councils, this Hispanic Christology begins with seeing Jesus in relationship to Mary, the saints, and the wider household of God. As one woman from a San Antonio parish put it: "For the Hispanic, we cannot know someone without knowing their family. The first question we ask when we meet someone is, 'Where are you from? Who is your family?' It is within the family that we begin to relate to Jesus and come to know him." The response of many first-time visitors to the chapel was delight at finding their favorite sacred figures represented: locating Jesus among familiar images and saints enhances the sense that a devotee knows him and is known by him. My MACC colleague Roberto Piña summed up this spontaneous response at one reflection session: "We [Hispanics] walk into the Chapel of Miracles and begin to identify and salute our family members." Another group participant echoed his sentiments, pointing out that the chapel reflects the multiplication of images in numerous Hispanic *altarcitos* (home altars) and that "it's just like the Gospels, where Jesus is almost never seen alone."

Numerous *dichos* (sayings or proverbs) avow that a person is profoundly shaped and known by their relationships, such as the popular *dicho* "dime con quién andas y te diré quién eres" ("tell me with whom you walk and I will tell you who you are"). Knowing Jesus necessarily entails knowing him in the relationships that formed him, especially his relationship with his mother. As a Hispanic deacon noted in one of our reflection groups, "We learn of Mary from the behavior of Jesus, because the son learns from the mother. . . . The Gospels tell us Jesus was always surrounded by women. He was comfortable with them because of his good relations with his own mother. These and other aspects of Mary's life are apparent in the behavior of her son." Thus, as Roberto Goizueta succinctly states, "From a Mexican American perspective, love of Jesus and love of Mary do not compete for primacy; rather, they necessarily imply each other."[10]

Latina theologians have noted the deep resonance between the communal emphasis in Jesus' life and mission and that of Hispanic women. Ada María Isasi-Díaz identifies three core elements from the daily lives of Latinas as resources for Christology: their hunger for relationships that enact the "kin-dom of God" Jesus proclaimed, their embrace of Jesus as a faithful companion in their struggles, and their conviction that "only in so far as we become part of God's family" through an ethic of mutual responsibility for one another's well-being "can we really say that we believe in *Jesucristo,*" whose solidarity with the marginal was one of his most striking features. In an essay that treats the transfiguration, Isasi-Díaz observes passages in Mark, Matthew, and Luke just before this occurrence that relate Jesus' attempt to discuss with his disciples the danger he faced from some Jewish authorities who opposed him. But his followers ignored or even resisted his efforts to converse with them, as they failed to recognize "the urgency Jesus had to speak about the events that he saw coming." Isasi-Díaz highlights the unique Lukan text that mentions what the transfigured Jesus discussed with Moses and Elijah on the mountaintop: "his departure, which he was about to accomplish at Jerusalem" (9:31). An important element of her reading of this text is that, since the disciples will not provide the communal support and discernment partners that Jesus needs, Moses and Elijah are enlisted for the task. In this and various other writings her presumption is that Jesus is not an isolated "individualistic" savior, but a deeply communal person whose profound hunger for relationship and solidarity we are all called to follow.[11]

Jesus' circle of relationships is not just Mary, the disciples, and the saints. (Note Isasi-Díaz's link between Jesus and Hispanic women's solidarity and Piña's comment that Hispanic visitors to the chapel encounter "*our* family members.") It also encompasses the devotees still on earth who in faith and prayerful accompaniment become part of their sacred household. As the U.S. Catholic Bishops said in their 1987 *National Pastoral Plan for Hispanic Ministry:* "The Hispanic people find God in the arms of the Virgin Mary. . . . The saints, our brothers and sisters who have already fulfilled their lives in the following of Jesus, are examples and instruments of the revelation of God's goodness through their intercession and help. All this makes Hispanic spirituality a home of living relationships, a family, a community."[12] The frequent claims of divine assistance attributed to Our Lord of Miracles reveal devotees' conviction that belonging to this household of faith bridges the chasm between this world and the next, connecting careworn human beings to the power and passion of Jesus as well as our other celestial relatives. All this culminates in what Goizueta deems an embodied "theology of accompaniment": Latino/a devotees accompany Jesus in prayer, particularly in Jesus' hour of greatest need on Good Friday, with the full confidence that Jesus and his heavenly companions will also accompany them in their joys and struggles.[13]

Yet this relational view of Jesus encompasses a fundamental pastoral and theological concern. Seeing Jesus in his relationships provides an intimate way of knowing him, loving him, and following him, but it also presents a challenge for theological reflection and pastoral ministry. Does such a starting point for Christology reduce Jesus to just another saint, one heavenly relative among many to whom the faithful can turn for help and consolation? Is Jesus the Savior, *the* mediator between earth and heaven, between sinful humanity and God, or is he merely another patron saint whose specific functions of healing and rendering aid complement those of others in the heavenly realm? Though perhaps more powerful, is Jesus merely another intercessor like Mary and the saints, just another member in what one MACC participant called the Chapel of Miracles' "hall of fame" for saints? Is he Jesus the Christ, or merely "Saint Jesus"?

Various members of MACC reflection groups have raised such critical questions and observed that the multiplication of sacred images at la Capilla de los Milagros can diminish the chapel's original focus on Jesus crucified. Several participants have pointed out that today at the chapel there are more images of Mary than Jesus. Some participants from local parishes have even stated that these diverse Marian images reflect what they perceive are theologically debatable convictions such as "it is easier to go to Mary because she is a woman," and Mexican Americans and other Hispanics "always pray to Mary, because we go to the mother to get what we want from the father."

Orlando Espín contends that such statements have a long historical trajectory, dating back to the initial stages of evangelization in Mexico and elsewhere, when the context of Spanish conquest and domination severely distorted the transmission and the native people's reception of Christian faith in Trinitarian monotheism. According to Espín, in this context,

> it was only a matter of time before the vanquished projected their family and social experiences onto God, and there being no trinitarian inculturated catechesis to critique these projections, the people's God all too often resembled their earthly fathers and lords. In this context the mother of Jesus became a necessary religious symbol of compassion and care in an otherwise cruel system.[14]

Espín further contends that an adequate pastoral response to the Christology embodied in places like la Capilla de los Milagros necessarily entails both inculturated catechesis and a vigorous effort to confront the situations of suffering and oppression that continue to shape Hispanic understandings of Christ and the Trinity. Worship leaders and other pastoral ministers who accompany Latino/a faith communities continue to face the challenge of enabling believers to transcend notions of "Saint Jesus" and embrace Jesus Christ as our Savior who is both compassionately human and benevolently divine.

God Becomes One of Us

Such pastoral challenges illuminate two vividly juxtaposed elements of the Christology embodied at the Chapel of Miracles: the focus on Jesus' humanity and on his power to help and heal. As the U.S. Catholic Bishops stated in their 1983 pastoral, *The Hispanic Presence: Challenge and Commitment,* "Hispanic spirituality places strong emphasis on the humanity of Jesus, especially when he appears weak and suffering, as in the crib and in his passion and death." Their observation is consistent with the premier image of the crucified One enshrined at the chapel, auxiliary images of the Christ child that devotees subsequently added, and the past practice at the chapel of worshiping Christ in the *pastorela,* a joyous enactment that Elizondo deems "a celebration of the rejection that became election in the birth of Christ."[15]

The core significance of Latino/a devotion to the child Jesus became clearer to me when a visitor to the shrine and fellow parishioner at San Fernando Cathedral invited me to her home for her family's annual *levantada del niño* celebration. Literally this means "taking up the child." It entails a solemn removal of the child Jesus from the nativity scene, marking the end of the Christmas season. Family and friends gather at home for this ritual to venerate the infant Jesus with songs, prayers, an embrace or kiss to symbolically conclude the forty days of Christmas, and a meal or other festive gathering. The family *levantada* ritual in which I took part revealed that the piety expressed at the Chapel of Miracles and in the homes of its visitors mutually reinforce and enhance one another.

When I arrived at my hosts' home I joined other guests in their living room to offer a silent prayer at a *nacimiento* (nativity scene) decorated with colorful serapes, poinsettias, other flowers, and Christmas lights. This *nacimiento* extended along three walls of the living room and was like none I had ever seen. The usual cast of characters was there, of course: the magi with their camels and gifts, the shepherds and their flocks, the angels announcing the good news, Mary and Joseph, and the infant Jesus. What most caught my attention, however, were other characters, persons I recognized but had never seen depicted in nativity scenes. Elizabeth reached out with open arms to embrace her kinswoman Mary. Simeon looked with wonder at the child in his arms while the prophetess Anna raised her eyes and voiced her thanks to God. Jesus' *abuelos* (grandparents), Joachim and Ann, were also there, visible reminders that he had loved ones who rejoiced at his birth and concerned themselves with his well-being.

Other figures recalled the harsh events connected to the story of Jesus' coming among us. A Roman official held an opened scroll and barked out Caesar Augustus's command that all residents return to their place of origin and register for the census. One of Herod's soldiers stood with a bloody sword over an anguished mother who embraced the murdered body of her son. Mary and Joseph hastened on the flight to Egypt, Joseph looking back over his shoulder for signs of unwanted pursuers.

This was not the sanitized version of the Christmas narrative to which I was accustomed, but the scandalous, unedited, full biblical account of the Savior's birth. In retrospect I imagine through these images the arrogance of Caesar Augustus, the jealous rage of Herod, the blind and brutal obedience of his soldiers, the uncontrollable tears of the mothers of the Hebrew innocents, the fear of the refugees Mary and Joseph, the sisterhood of Elizabeth and Mary, the wisdom of Anna and Simeon, the pride and concern of Ann and Joachim at their grandson's birth.

Theologically, this *levantada* celebration impressed on me the shocking scandal that is the incarnation, the outrageous belief that the creator of the universe became a child completely vulnerable to the actions of fellow humans. On a personal level, it offered me a sensual encounter with an approachable God who takes on the vulnerability of a child and expresses God's love in the tenderness of a newborn babe. These reflections are consistent with the insight that Latinos/as engage Jesus in the moments when he appears most human, vulnerable, and approachable. Similarly, a priest from Minnesota who participated in a MACC reflection session noted simply that people visit the Lord of Miracles chapel because "it is a way of connecting with a Jesus who listens." He also observed that such "images make Jesus real, concrete" and afford devotees the opportunity to touch him and converse personally with him. Another participant commented that the chapel's representations of Jesus' childhood, such as the infant of Prague and el Santo Niño de Atocha, helped visitors "relate to Jesus' innocence and his acceptance of each person."

The Lord of Hope in Suffering

Yet this human and vulnerable Jesus is also a powerful Jesus. He is seen as a child and in agony and dying on the cross, but at the same time is alive and remains the Lord of Miracles. Indeed, the fundamental christological affirmation at la Capilla de los Milagros is that the innocent, suffering Jesus and the powerful Christ is one and the same person. Commenting on this juxtaposition of human vulnerability and divine power, one participant in a reflection session stated that visitors to the Chapel of Miracles encounter a human Jesus who knows their pain and receives them as an intimate friend, but is also risen, alive, and present to all who need and call upon him. As Espín puts it, devotions like those to el Señor de los Milagros are "not a direct or indirect denial of the Resurrection" since "the crucified and dying Jesus [is] always addressed as eternally living." Goizueta concurs that, in a Hispanic understanding of Christ, "The supremely human crucified Jesus *is* the resurrected Jesus."[16]

The healing and saving power of the suffering Jesus that devotees encounter at la Capilla reflects the widespread Latino/a devotion to Christ crucified, particularly on Good Friday, the Latino/a "celebration *par excellence*."[17] In many Hispanic faith communities, the Good Friday ritual entails a public reenactment of Jesus' trial, Way of the Cross, and crucifixion, or an outdoor Way of the Cross

Contemporary photograph of El Señor de los Milagros image at the chapel.
Courtesy University of Texas Institute of Texan Cultures, San Antonio.

procession. Karen Mary Davalos's study of the Way of the Cross in Chicago's
Pilsen neighborhood encompassed conversations with leaders in the Good Friday ritual like Patricia, who summed up the power of the event: "Christ suffered
way back two thousand years ago, but he's still suffering now. His people are
suffering. We're lamenting and wailing. And also we are a joyful people at the
same time. . . . So this is not a story, this is not a fairy tale. It happened, and
it's happening now." For such participants the power of the ritual is its capacity to mediate an encounter with God that transcends limiting distinctions like
those between Pilsen and Calvary Hill, Chicago and Jerusalem, our "secular"
age and the "sacred" time of Jesus. They engage religious traditions not merely

as pious reenactments but as sacred events integrated with the everyday world that animates devotees to struggle for the transformation of their personal and collective lives and enables them to confront present trials and hardships with the power of faith. One of the first coordinators for the Pilsen Way of the Cross, Claudia, deemed this public ritual "the real way of praying" because it is "the opportunity to reflect and analyze how we are living and the things we have to [do] in order to have a better life." In the Latino/a world, Good Friday is the radical confrontation of life as it is, but with the firm conviction that suffering and death cannot destroy us. Confessing the seemingly defenseless and crucified Lord's power and solidarity with us is the ultimate expression of this core christological belief mediated in Good Friday rituals and in shrines like la Capilla de los Milagros.[18]

Though a number of participants in the MACC reflection sessions offered insights such as these, some were still concerned that la Capilla visitors and other Hispanic faithful tend to focus more on Christ's passion than on the centrality of the resurrection for Christian faith. Several participants commented on the relatively small attendance among Hispanics at the Holy Saturday Vigil as compared to their massive processions and rituals on Good Friday. But others noted the pastoral hypocrisy of taking away the people's symbols of suffering without struggling to eliminate the root causes of personal and collective tribulations that make those symbols so meaningful. Still others stated that Easter celebrations among European-descent Christians in the United States tend to exhibit the crown without the cross, the triumphalistic distortion of celebrating victory and salvation without confronting suffering and the need for continuous conversion. Such comments reveal the ongoing challenge to foster a balanced and active christological faith. The prayer and worship of devotees at la Capilla de Nuestro Señor de los Milagros illuminate this crucial need to proclaim a Christ who shares in our humanity, struggles, and suffering, but also engenders hope and transformation through the power of his resurrection and presence among us. Elizondo has forcefully articulated this pastoral and theological challenge: "The cross without the resurrection would be without value and only a curse, but the resurrection without the way of the cross would be a pure utopian dream or illusion. It is only in the whole mystery of Jesus Christ that the mystery of humanity is truly revealed."[19]

FINDING CHRIST ON THE ROAD TO EMMAUS

The account of the disciples on the road to Emmaus (Luke 24:13–35) parallels the encounters devotees have with Jesus at la Capilla de los Milagros. Like numerous faithful who visit the chapel, these two disciples met Jesus in an intimate way. They came to know him even more deeply as they poured out to him their hopes and disappointment, their wonder and disillusionment, their loss and their sorrow. The fact that there are *two* disciples and that Jesus draws on examples from "Moses and all the prophets" (v. 27) indicates how these disciples' approach to Jesus is mediated through community, the network of relationships among themselves, Jesus, and their ancestors in the faith. Yet, for all their knowledge and intimacy with Jesus, they are so focused on the scourge of the cross that they are slow to recognize the risen Christ who accompanies them. Their pitfall was their failure to understand that "the Messiah [had to] suffer these things and then enter into his glory" (v. 26). Above all, however, they were disciples who found hope in Christ even in the midst of tragedy and suffering. They recognize him "in the breaking of the bread" (v. 35). Significantly, like Our Lord of Miracles devotees, they also recognize him as crucified yet risen when he later invites them, the eleven, and other disciples in Jerusalem to "look at my [wounded] hands and my feet" and to "touch me and see" (v. 39).

Theologians, Latino/a faithful, and pastoral ministers who accompany Hispanics and other believers can gain at least three important christological insights from theological reflection on the Chapel of the Lord of Miracles and on the Emmaus account. First, one obvious concern is the need to witness and celebrate—both in the worship of the churches and in our daily lives—that the pilgrim of Emmaus is indeed risen and with us. This concern is prevalent in Latino/a Christologies as it is in any other. At the same time, however, the gift and challenge of the chapel's devotees is that, as compared to the disciples of Emmaus, they more readily understand a messiah who suffers. These devotees remind us that, though it is only when we experience the risen Christ that the cross has ultimate meaning for us, it is also true that we cannot arrive at authentic Easter faith without entering into the prayer and imagery of Good Friday and the wisdom and struggles for justice of today's crucified peoples. Their relations with Jesus contest all forms of triumphalistic Christology, especially those that emphasize the power and victory of Christ while ignoring the solidarity with the crucified that Christ's paschal mystery demands. Third, Christian believers can gain much from the insight that we are called to know Jesus not just as an individual person, but also within the network of relationships that further illuminate his core identity and message. This does not necessarily confine him to being merely "Saint Jesus"—one heavenly companion among others—since his relationships encompass those of the Trinity. Our faith is not centered on Christ as an isolated individual, but on Christ as the model of solidarity that mirrors Jesus of Nazareth's communal relations as well as the communal relations in the triune God.

One element of the Christology enacted at the shrine that could be further accentuated is the connection between the way Jesus chose to live and the way he died. The devotions and images prevalent at la Capilla de los Milagros rarely entail explicit attention to Jesus' preaching and Galilean ministry, much less the links between his attempts to transform oppressive realities, his confrontations with religious authorities, and his subsequent crucifixion. Michelle González has observed that "the Jesus of Good Friday" so central to Latino/a faith "stems from a theological worldview that strongly emphasizes Jesus' humble origins, his prophetic message, and his active presence in the present-day lives of Christians, in particular his solidarity with the oppressed and the marginalized."[20] But the essential connections between Jesus' suffering and death and his life commitments and message—and the implication that these connections demand that contemporary believers integrate their christological devotions with struggles for justice in everyday life—are not central in the Christology mediated at the Chapel of Miracles.

The analyses of MACC participants who visited the Capilla underscore the significance of theological reflection on a faith community's sacred imagery and pious traditions. Theologians and pastoral leaders can engage in a similar collective reflection within their own contexts and enhance understanding, appreciation, and pastoral responses to the horizons of faith and Christology mediated in Latino/a communities. The approach for examining Christology developed at MACC and outlined in this chapter can be adapted and expanded for faith communities of various ethnic backgrounds and denominations, as is evident in theological investigations like Edwin Aponte's studies of *coritos* among Latino/a Protestants,[21] and the chapter by Eduardo Fernández in this volume. Hispanic faith expressions such as music, testimonies, Jesus imagery, rituals, and devotions are a potent starting point for engaged christological analysis. My experiences at MACC and in other places convince me that field work is an integral component for the study of Christology from a Hispanic perspective.

For pastoral agents in Hispanic faith communities, conducting such field work is also crucial, preferably in collaboration with local leaders who are essential partners in discerning the operative Christologies in their community, recognizing their valuable insights about Jesus and ways they might be developed further, and enacting pastoral initiatives to deepen the community's relationship with Christ. Of course, this is not a singular process, but one that can and must be repeated again and again. In particular, the one-on-one and small-group conversations that are at the core of such a study make up not only a fascinating collective theological project but also a superb means to generate faith sharing rooted in Christ. Like the disciples of Emmaus, such conversations about what Latino/a communities hear, see, and speak of Jesus will illuminate the treasure of their faith expressions, mutually engage those expressions with the Scriptures and the christological formulations of the Christian churches, and further open hearts, eyes, and minds to the presence of Christ suffering and risen in our midst.

NOTES

1. William B. Taylor, review of D. A. Brading, *Mexican Phoenix: Our Lady of Guadalupe: Image and Tradition across Five Centuries*, *Hispanic American Historical Review* 82 (2002): 359–60. See also William B. Taylor, "Two Shrines of the Cristo Renovado: Religion and Peasant Politics in Late Colonial Mexico," *American Historical Review* 110 (October 2005): 945–74.

2. Ramón A. Gutiérrez, "El Santuario de Chimayó: A Syncretic Shrine in New Mexico," in *Feasts and Celebrations in North American Ethnic Communities*, ed. Ramón A. Gutiérrez and Genevieve Fabre (Albuquerque: University of New Mexico Press, 1995), 71–86.

3. Sandra Cisneros, "The Tejano Soul of San Antonio," *New York Times Magazine* (17 May 1992), 25, 36.

4. Charles Merritt Barnes, "Chapel of the Miracles," *San Antonio Express*, 28 April 1907.

5. Manuel Gamio, *Mexican Immigration to the United States: A Study of Human Migration and Adjustment* (Chicago: University of Chicago Press, 1930), 122–24; photo of interior of la Capilla de Nuestro Señor de los Milagros, c. 1920s, Ellen Quillan Collection, no. 74–72, University of Texas Institute of Texan Cultures, San Antonio; "Templo del Señor de los Milagros" (typescript of field notes), 2 Marzo 1927, Gamio Papers, box 3, folder 12, the Bancroft Library, University of California, Berkeley; "Observaciones. Capilla del Sr de los Milagros" (typescript of field notes), n.d., Gamio Papers, box 3, folder 15, Bancroft Library; Bess Carroll, "Pilgrims Trek to Miracle Chapel," *San Antonio Light*, 27 January 1926; Vivian Richardson, "Texas Has Strangest Miracle Shrine," *Dallas Morning News*, 22 July 1928 (quotation).

6. Charles A. Arnold, "Folklore, Manners, and Customs of the Mexicans in San Antonio, Texas" (MA thesis, University of Texas, Austin, 1928), 22–24; Arthur J. Drossaerts, American Board of Catholic Missions report, 1929, Catholic Archives at San Antonio, Chancery Office, Archdiocese of San Antonio.

7. Lillie May Hagner, *Alluring San Antonio through the Eyes of an Artist* (San Antonio: Naylor, 1940), 106–7; Sam and Bess Woolford, *The San Antonio Story* (Austin: Steck, 1950), 130; Steve Schlather, "Chapel Offers Pilgrims Hope of Health, History," *San Antonio Light*, 25 September 1983; Julia Nott Naugh, *The Silver Cradle* (Austin: University of Texas Press, 1955), 159–60 (quotation).

8. Virgilio Elizondo, "Popular Religion as Support of Identity: A Pastoral-Psychological Case-Study Based on the Mexican American Experience in the USA," in *Popular Religion*, ed. Norbert Greinacher and Norbert Mette (Edinburgh: T&T Clark, 1986), 37.

9. For an overview of the communal dimension of Hispanic theological anthropologies intrinsically related to this starting point for understanding Christ, see Miguel H. Díaz, *On Being Human: U.S. Hispanic and Rahnerian Perspectives* (Maryknoll, NY: Orbis Books, 2001), esp. chap. 2, "On Being Human from U.S. Hispanic Perspectives."

10. Roberto Goizueta, "The Symbolic World of Mexican American Religion," in *Horizons of the Sacred: Mexican Traditions in U.S. Catholicism*, ed. Timothy Matovina and Gary Riebe-Estrella (Ithaca, NY: Cornell University Press, 2002), 134. See also Miguel H. Díaz, "*Dime con quién andas y te diré quién eres*: We Walk with Our Lady of Charity," in *From the Heart of Our People: Latino/a Explorations in Catholic Systematic Theology*, ed. Orlando O. Espín and Miguel H. Díaz (Maryknoll, NY: Orbis Books, 1999), 153–71.

11. Ada María Isasi-Díaz, "Christ in *Mujerista* Theology," in *Thinking of Christ: Proclamation, Explanation, Meaning*, ed. Tatha Wiley (New York: Continuum, 2003), 157–76, at 159–60; Isasi-Díaz, "La palabra: Comunicación como comunión," in *Camino a Emaús: Compartiendo el ministerio de Jesús*, ed. Ada María Isasi-Díaz, Timoteo Matovina, and Nina M. Torres-Vidal (Minneapolis: Augsburg Fortress, 2002), 73–81, at 77.

12. National Conference of Catholic Bishops, *National Pastoral Plan for Hispanic Ministry* (Washington, DC: United States Catholic Conference, 1988), no. 94.
13. Roberto Goizueta, *Caminemos con Jesús: Toward a Hispanic/Latino Theology of Accompaniment* (Maryknoll, NY: Orbis Books, 1995).
14. Orlando O. Espín, *The Faith of the People: Theological Reflections on Popular Catholicism* (Maryknoll, NY: Orbis Books, 1997), 59.
15. National Conference of Catholic Bishops, *The Hispanic Presence: Challenge and Commitment* (Washington, DC: United States Catholic Conference, 1984), no. 12; Virgilio Elizondo, *Galilean Journey: The Mexican-American Promise* (1983; rev. ed. Maryknoll, NY: Orbis Books, 2000), 39.
16. Espín, *Faith of the People,* 49; Goizueta, *Caminemos con Jesús,* 68 (emphasis in original).
17. Elizondo, *Galilean Journey,* 41.
18. Karen Mary Davalos, "'The Real Way of Praying': The Via Crucis, *Mexicano* Sacred Space, and the Architecture of Domination," in Matovina and Riebe-Estrella, *Horizons of the Sacred,* 60–61.
19. Elizondo, *Galilean Journey,* 81.
20. Michelle A. González, "Jesus," in *Handbook of Latina/o Theologies,* ed. Edwin David Aponte and Miguel A. De La Torre (St. Louis: Chalice, 2006), 17.
21. Edwin David Aponte, "*Coritos* as Active Symbol in Latino Protestant Popular Religion," *Journal of Hispanic/Latino Theology* 2 (February 1995): 57–66.

Suggested Readings

Abalos, David T. *Latinos in the United States: The Sacred and the Political.* 2nd ed. Notre Dame, Ind.: University of Notre Dame, 2007.

Alvarez, Alma Rosa. *Liberation Theology in Chicana/o Literature: Manifestations of Feminist and Gay Identities.* New York: Routledge, 2007.

Anzaldúa, Gloria. *Borderlands/La Frontera: The New Mestiza.* 2nd ed. San Francisco: Aunt Lute Press, 1999.

Aponte, Edwin David. "Hispanics." In *Handbook of U.S. Theologies of Liberation,* edited by Miguel A. De La Torre, 162–72. St. Louis: Chalice Press, 2004.

Aquino, Maria Pilar. "Theological Method in U.S. Latina Theology: Toward an Intercultural Theology for the Third Millennium." In *From the Heart of Our People: Explorations in Catholic Systematic Theology,* edited by Orlando O. Espín and Miguel H. Díaz, 6–48. Maryknoll, N.Y: Orbis Books, 1999.

———, Daisy Machado, and Jeannette Rodriquez, eds. *A Reader in Latina Feminist Theology: Religion and Justice.* Austin: University of Texas Press, 2002.

Badillo, David A. *Latinos and the New Immigrant Church.* Baltimore: Johns Hopkins University Press, 2006.

Bañuelas, Arturo J., ed. *Mestizo Christianity: Theology from the Latino Perspective.* Maryknoll, N.Y.: Orbis Books, 1995.

Cardoza-Orlandi, Carlos. "Drum Beats of Resistance and Liberation: Afro-Caribbean Religions, the Struggle for Life, and the Christian Theologian." *Journal of Hispanic/Latino Theology* 3, no. 1 (1995): 50–61.

Chavez, Leo R. *The Latino Threat Narrative: Constructing Immigrants, Citizens, and the Nation.* Stanford, CA: Stanford University Press, 2008.

Conde-Frazier, Elizabeth. "Latina Women and Immigration." *Journal of Latin American Theology: Christian Reflections from the Latino South* 3, no. 2 (2008): 54–75.

———, and Loida I. Martell-Otero. "U.S. Latina Evangélicas." In *Encyclopedia of Women and Religion in North America,* edited by Rosemary Radford Ruether and Rosemary Skinner Keller, 477–83. Bloomington: Indiana University Press, 2006.

Costas, Orlando E. *Christ outside the Gate: Mission beyond Christendom.* Maryknoll, N.Y.: Orbis Books, 1982.

———. *Liberating News: A Theology of Contextual Evangelization.* Grand Rapids: William B. Eerdmans Publishing Company, 1989.

Delgado, Richard, and Jean Stefancic, eds. *The Latino/a Condition: A Critical Reader.* New York: New York University Press, 1998.

Elizondo, Virgilio. *Galilean Journey: Mexican-American Promise.* Rev. ed. Maryknoll, N.Y.: Orbis Books, 2000.

Espín, Orlando O. *The Faith of the People: Theological Reflections on Popular Catholicism.* Maryknoll, N.Y.: Orbis Books, 1997.

————. *Grace and Humanness: Theological Reflections Because of Culture.* Maryknoll, N.Y.: Orbis Books, 2007.

Espinosa, Gastón, Virgilio P. Elizondo, and Jesse Miranda, eds. *Latino Religions and Civic Activism in the United States.* Oxford and New York: Oxford University Press, 2005.

Espinosa, Gastón, and Marlo T. Garcia. *Mexican American Religions: Spirituality, Activism, and Culture.* Durham, N.C.: Duke University Press, 2008.

Fernández, Eduardo C., S.J. *La Cosecha: Harvesting Contemporary United States Hispanic Theology (1972–1998).* Collegeville, Minn.: Liturgical Press, 2000.

García, Alberto L. *Cristología-Cristo Jesús: Centro y Praxis del Pueblo de Dios.* St. Louis: Editorial Concordia, 2006.

Garcia, John A. *Latino Politics in America: Community, Culture, and Interests.* Lanham, Md.: Rowman & Littlefield Publishers, 2003.

Goizueta, Roberto S. *Caminemos con Jesús: Toward a Hispanic/Latino Theology of Accompaniment.* Maryknoll, N.Y.: Orbis Books, 1995.

González, Juan. *Harvest of Empire: A History of Latinos in America.* New York: Penguin Books, 2000.

González, Michelle A. "Jesus." In *Handbook of Latina/o Theologies,* edited by Edwin Aponte and Miguel De La Torre, 17–24. St. Louis: Chalice Press, 2006.

Groody, Daniel, and Gioacchino Campese, eds. *A Promised Land, A Perilous Journey: Theological Perspectives on Migration.* Notre Dame, Ind.: University of Notre Dame Press, 2007.

Guardiola-Saenz, Leticia A. "Border-Crossing and Its Redemptive Power in John 7:53–8:11: A Cultural Reading of Jesus and the Accused." In *John and Postcolonialism,* edited by Musa W. Dube and Jeffrey L Staley, 129–52. London: Sheffield Press, 2002.

Haight, Roger. *The Future of Christology.* New York: Continuum, 2007.

Herrera, Marina. "Who Do You Say Jesus Is? Christological Reflections from a Hispanic Woman's Perspective." In *Reconstructing the Christ Symbol: Essays in Feminist Christology,* edited by Maryanne Stevens. New York: Paulist Press, 1993. Reprint, 72–94. Eugene, Ore.: Wipf & Stock Publishers, 2004.

Isasi-Díaz, Ada María. *Mujerista Theology: A Theology for the Twentieth-First Century.* Maryknoll, N.Y.: Orbis Books, 1996.

————, and Fernando F. Segovia, eds. *Hispanic/Latino Theology: Challenge and Promise.* Minneapolis: Fortress Press, 1996.

Leon, Luis D. *La Llorana's Children: Religion, Life, and Death in the U.S.-Mexican Borderlands.* Berkeley: University of California Press, 2004.

Machado, Daisy L. "Promoting Solidarity with Migrants." In *Justice in a Global Economy: Strategies for Home, Community, and World,* edited by Pamela K. Brubaker, Rebecca Todd Peters, and Laura A. Stivers, 115–26. Louisville, Ky.: Westminster John Knox Press, 2006.

Mahler, Sarah J. *American Dreaming: Immigrant Life on the Margins.* Princeton, N.J.: Princeton University Press, 1995.

Maldonado, David, Jr., ed. *Protestantes/Protestants: Hispanic Christianity within Mainline Traditions.* Nashville: Abingdon Press, 1999.

Martell-Otero, Loida I. "Liberating News: Towards a U.S. Hispanic/Latina Soteriology of the Crossroads." PhD diss., Fordham University, 2004.

————. "Lo Cotidiano: God in the Spaces of the Everyday." *Witness* 83, no. 12 (December 2000): 21–22.

————. "Of Satos and Saints: Salvation from the Periphery." *Perspectivas* 4 (Summer 2001): 7–33.

Matovina, Timothy, and Gary Riebe-Estrella. *Horizons of the Sacred: Mexican Traditions in U.S. Catholicism.* Ithaca, N.Y.: Cornell University Press, 2002.

Pedraja, Luís. *Jesus Is My Uncle: Christology from a Hispanic Perspective.* Nashville: Abingdon Press, 1999.

Pinn, Anthony B., and Benjamin Valentin, eds. *The Ties That Bind: African American and Hispanic American/Latino/a Theology in Dialogue.* New York: Continuum, 2001.

Recinos, Harold. *Good News from the Barrio: Prophetic Witness for the Church.* Louisville, Ky.: Westminster John Knox Press, 2006.

———. *Jesus Weeps: Global Encounters on Our Doorstep.* Nashville: Abingdon Press, 1992.

———. *Who Do You Say That I Am? Jesus at the Margins.* Nashville: Abingdon Press, 1997.

Rodriguez, Jeanette. *Our Lady of Guadalupe: Faith and Empowerment among Mexican-American Women.* Austin: University of Texas Press, 1994.

Rodriguez, José David, and Loida I. Martell-Otero. *Teología en Conjunto: A Collaborative Hispanic Protestant Theology.* Louisville, Ky.: Westminster John Knox Press, 1997.

Rodriquez, Havidan, Rogelio Saenz, and Cecilia Menjivar, eds. *Latinos/as in the United States: Changing the Face of America.* Newark: University of Delaware, 2008.

Sánchez, David A. *From Patmos to the Barrio: Subverting Imperial Myths.* Minneapolis: Fortress Press, 2008.

Sanchez-Walsh, Arlene M. *Latino Pentecostal Identity: Evangelical Faith, Self, and Society.* New York: Columbia University Press, 2003.

Segovia, Fernando F. "Hispanic American Theology and the Bible: Effective Weapon and Faithful Ally." In *We Are a People! Initiatives in Hispanic American Theologies.* Edited by Roberto S. Goizueta, 21–49. Minneapolis: Fortress Press, 1992.

Solivan, Samuel. *The Spirit, Pathos, and Liberation: Toward an Hispanic Pentecostal Theology.* Journal of Pentecostal Theology Supplement Series 14. Sheffield: Sheffield Academic, 1998.

Suro, Roberto. *Strangers among Us: How Latino Immigration Is Transforming America.* New York: Alfred A. Knopf, 1998.

Sylvest, Edwin E., Jr. "Religion in Hispanic America since the Era of Independence." In *The Encyclopedia of the American Religious Experience: Studies of Traditions and Movements.* Edited by Charles H. Lippy and Peter W. Williams. 3 vols., 201–22. New York: Scribner's, 1988.

Urrea, Luis Alberto. *The Devil's Highway: A True Story.* New York: Back Bay Books, 2004.

Valentin, Benjamin. *Mapping Public Theology: Beyond Culture, Identity, and Difference.* Harrisburg, Pa.: Trinity Press International, 2002.

Contributors

Carlos F. Cardoza-Orlandi is an ordained minister of the Christian Church (Disciples of Christ) in Puerto Rico, the United States, and Canada, and Professor of World Christianity at Columbia Theological Seminary, in Decatur, Georgia. A Puerto Rican, he holds a PhD from Princeton Theological Seminary in the fields of Mission, Ecumenics, and the History of Religions. Cardoza-Orlandi actively participates in intercultural and interreligious activities in the Atlanta area, the Caribbean, and Latin America. He also is very active among Christian communities, teaching and lecturing on Christian mission and intercultural studies. He also contributes to Hispanic/Latino/a theological endeavors as a faculty member and chair of the board of the Hispanic Summer Program, and a mentor in the mentors' program of the Hispanic Theological Initiative. His most recent work includes *A todas las naciones: Una historia del movimiento misionero cristiano*, coauthored with Justo L. González and forthcoming in English and Portuguese; "Christian Mission in an Age of World Christianity," a chapter in *Chalice Introduction to Theology*, edited by Peter Goodwin Heltzel; and "Vodou, Santería, and Spiritism," a chapter in the *Encyclopedia of Women and Religion in North America*, edited by Rosemary Skinner Keller and Rosemary Radford Ruether.

Miguel A. De La Torre teaches Christian Social Ethics at the Iliff School of Theology in Denver, Colorado. A native of La Habana, Cuba, he is an ordained Southern Baptist minister and earned a doctorate from Temple University in 1999. Since obtaining his doctorate, Dr. De La Torre has authored numerous articles and over fourteen books, including the award-winning *Reading the Bible from the Margins* (Maryknoll, NY: Orbis Books, 2002); *Santería: The Beliefs and Rituals of a Growing Religion in America* (Grand Rapids: Wm. B. Eerdmans, 2004); and *Doing Christian Ethics from the Margins* (Maryknoll, NY: Orbis Books, 2004). He has just completed the *Encyclopedia on Hispanic American Religious Culture*, a two-volume set (ABC-CLIO Publishers, 2009). Within the academy he serves on the Board of Directors of the American Academy of Religion and the Society of Christian Ethics. A scholar-activist, Dr. De La Torre has written numerous articles in popular media and has served with several civic organizations.

Virgilio Elizondo is Notre Dame Professor of Pastoral and Hispanic Theology. A receipient of numerous honorary degrees, Elizondo received his PhD at Institut Catholique de Paris, 1978; the MA degree in Pastoral Studies from the Ateneo University, Manila, 1969; and a Diploma in Pastoral Catechetics from the East Asian Pastoral Institute, 1969. In 1997, he received the Laetare Medal, the highest honor of the University of Notre Dame. The Catholic Theological Society of America named Elizondo its 2007 John Courtney Murray Award Winner for his distinguished work in theology. His writings include *The Treasure of Guadalupe* (2006); *A God of Incredible Surprises* (2004); *Way of the Cross* (2002); *The Future Is Mestizo* (1988); *Guadalupe, Mother of the New Creation* (1997); and *Galilean Journey: The Mexican American Promise* (8th ed., 2000).

Eduardo C. Fernández, S.J., teaches pastoral theology and missiology at the Jesuit School of Theology in Berkeley and the Graduate Theological Union. A native of El Paso, Texas, he earned a doctorate in theology at the Pontifical Gregorian University in Rome in 1995. He is past president of the Academy of Catholic Hispanic Theologians of the United States (ACHTUS). His ministerial experience includes high school and university teaching, parish and campus ministry, and retreat work. Along with his many articles, he has also authored *La Cosecha: Harvesting Contemporary United States Hispanic Theology (1972– 1998)* (Collegeville, MN: Liturgical Press, 2000), and also coauthored, with James Empereur, S.J., *La Vida Sacra: Contemporary Hispanic Sacramental Theology* (Lanham, MD: Rowman and Littlefield, 2006). His latest book is *Mexican American Catholics* (Mahwah, NJ: Paulist Press, 2007).

Ada María Isasi-Díaz has been professor of Christian Social Ethics and Theology since 1991 at the Theological School of Drew University, Madison, New Jersey. She was born and raised in La Habana, Cuba, and came to the United States in 1960. After being a missionary in Lima, Peru, for three years and living in Spain, she settled in Rochester, New York, in 1975 and worked as a minister in inner-city Catholic parishes for four years and then became the Regional Developer for Women's Ordination Conference. She moved to New York City in 1983 and pursued studies at Union Theological Seminary, receiving her PhD in 1990. Since the late 1980s Isasi-Díaz has worked in the elaboration of *mujerista* theology based on the religious understandings and practices of Latinas living in the United States. She has lectured throughout the United States on issues of justice, women's liberation, and Latina/o theology. She has been visiting professor in Cuba, Korea, and the Philippines, and has lectured in these countries and in Germany and Zimbabwe. She coauthored, with Yolanda Tarango, *Hispanic Women: Prophetic Voice in the Church,* the first Latina theology book published in the United States. Her other three books are *En La Lucha—In the Struggle, Mujerista Theology,* and *La Lucha Continues.* She has coedited several other books, and her articles are part of countless other books and journals. At present she is working on *JUSTICIA: A Reconciliatory Praxis of Care and Tenderness*, to be published by Fortress Press in 2010.

Michael E. Lee is Assistant Professor of Systematic Theology at Fordham University in New York City. He is also affiliated with its Institute for Latin American and Latino Studies. The son of Puerto Rican parents, Dr. Lee was born in Miami, Florida, and earned a PhD in Systematic Theology from the University of Notre Dame. He serves on the governing board of the Academy of Catholic Hispanic Theologians of the United States (ACHTUS) and the administrative team of the Christology topic session area for the Catholic Theological Society of America (CTSA). Along with articles in the *Journal of Religion* and *Theological Studies*, he has published *Bearing the Weight of Salvation: The Soteriology of Ignacio Ellacuría* (New York: Crossroad, 2009).

Hugo Magallanes teaches at Perkins School of Theology at Southern Methodist University as an Associate Professor of Christianity and Cultures. He is the author of *Introducción a la Vida y Pensamiento de Juan Wesley* (Nashville: Abingdon, 2005). Professor Magallenes was born in Mexico and has served Methodist churches in Mexico and in the United States, including a migrant-worker church in South Georgia.

Zaida Maldonado Pérez is Professor of Church History and Theology at Asbury Theological Seminary, Dunnam Campus, Florida. A native of Puerto Rico, Pérez earned an MDiv from Eden Theological Seminary and a PhD in historical theology from St. Louis University. Prior to joining the Asbury Theological Seminary faculty, she was Director of the Hispanic Theological Initiative, a program of the Pew Charitable Trusts, housed at Princeton Theological Seminary. She is coauthor with Justo L. González of *An Introduction to Christian Theology* and has written on subjects including the Trinity as *familia*, the legacy of the early church for *evangélicas/os*, the subversive role of martyrs in early Christianity, and the recruiting and retaining of Latino/a seminarians. Her ministry experience includes conferencing, preaching, and teaching in Spanish- and English-speaking church and seminary communities. She is a member of the United Church of Christ.

Loida I. Martell-Otero is Associate Professor of Constructive Theology at Palmer Theological Seminary, in Wynnewood, Pennsylvania. She received her doctoral degree in Constructive Theology from Fordham University in 2005. She is an ordained minister in the American Baptist Churches/USA and a doctor of veterinary medicine. After leaving her private practice, she pastored in New York City. She has taught at various institutions, including the University of Puerto Rico and the Center for Urban Ministerial Education. Her writings include "Of Satos and Saints: Salvation from the Periphery" (2001); *Teología en*

Conjunto: A Collaborative Hispanic Protestant Theology, coedited with José D. Rodríguez (Louisville, KY: Westminster John Knox Press, 1997); and "Women Doing Theology: Una Perspectiva Evangélica" (1994). She was a founding member of the Association for Hispanic Theological Education (AETH) and is a past president of American Baptist Churches/NYC.

Timothy Matovina is Professor of Theology and the William and Anna Jean Cushwa Director of the Cushwa Center for the Study of American Catholicism at the University of Notre Dame. He works in the area of Theology and Culture, with specialization in U.S. Latino/a theology and religion. His most recent book is *Guadalupe and Her Faithful: Latino Catholics in San Antonio, from Colonial Origins to the Present* (Baltimore, MD: Johns Hopkins University Press, 2005). In addition to his scholarly work, Matovina offers presentations and workshops on Latino/a theology and ministry throughout the United States.

Harold J. Recinos is Professor of Church and Society at the Perkins School of Theology at Southern Methodist University. Professor Recinos received his master's in divinity in 1982 from Union Theological Seminary, a doctor of ministry in parish ministry in 1986 from New York Theological Seminary, and a PhD with honors in cultural anthropology in 1993 from the American University in Washington, DC. In addition to numerous articles in scholarly publications and journals, Recinos has written four books: *Hear the Cry! A Latino Pastor Challenges the Church* (Louisville, KY: Westminster John Knox Press, 1989), *Jesus Weeps: Global Encounters on Our Doorstep* (Nashville: Abingdon Press, 1992), *Who Comes in the Name of the Lord? Jesus at the Margins* (Nashville: Abingdon Press, 1997), and *Good News from the Barrio: Prophetic Witness for the Church* (Louisville, KY: Westminster John Knox Press, 2006). Recinos is an ordained elder and member of the Baltimore-Washington Annual Conference of the United Methodist Church.

Luis R. Rivera is Dean of the Faculty, Vice President of Academic Affairs, and James G. K. McClure Professor of Theological Education at McCormick Theological Seminary (PC(USA)) in Chicago. A native of Puerto Rico and member of the United Methodist Church, Dr. Rivera received his BA from the University of Puerto Rico, the MDiv from the Evangelical Seminary of Puerto Rico, and the ThM and ThD from the Divinity School at Harvard University. His recent research and teaching focus on the theological and hermeneutical challenges posed by the experiences of global migrations and the formation of diaspora communities and congregations amid multicultural societies in a globalized world. He has published several essays, book chapters, and reviews on ethics, theology, and diaspora hermeneutics. He is coeditor of *Diccionario de Intérpretes de la Fe* (Spanish [2004]; Portuguese [2005]; English [2006]), and contributor to the *Encyclopedia of Religion and Violence* (New York: Routledge, 2004).

Arlene M. Sánchez-Walsh is an Associate Professor of Church History and Latino Church Studies at C. P. Haggard Graduate School of Theology at Azusa Pacific University. She received her PhD from Claremont Graduate University, 2001. She is the author of *Latino Pentecostal Identity: Evangelical Faith, Society, and Self* (2003).

Index

217